PROGRAMMED COLLEGE VOCABULARY

SEVENTH EDITION

George W. Feinstein Pasadena City College

PEARSON

Prentice Hall

Upper Saddle River, New Jersey 07458

Library of Congress Cataloging-in-Publication Data

Feinstein, George W.
    Programmed college vocabulary / George W. Feinstein.–7th ed.
      p. cm.
    ISBN 0-13-148766-3
    1. Vocabulary–Programmed instruction. I. Title.
    PE1449 .F38 2006
    428.1'07'7–dc22

                               2004053510

Editorial Director: Leah Jewell
Senior Acquisitions Editor: Craig Campanella
Assistant Editor: Jennifer Conklin
Editorial Assistant: Joan Polk
Marketing Manager: Kate Stewart
Marketing Assistant: Mariel DeKranis
VP/Director Production & Manufacturing: Barbara Kittle
Production Editor: Maureen Benicasa
Manufacturing Manager: Nick Sklitsis
Manufacturing Buyer: Ben Smith
Creative Design Director: Leslie Osher
Art Director: Nancy Wells
Interior Design: Seven Worldwide
Cover Art Director: Jayne Conte
Cover Art Design: Bruce Kenselaar
Cover Illustration/Photo: Bruce Kenselaar/Prentice Hall, Inc.

This book was set in 11/12 Times Roman by Seven Worldwide Publishing Solutions and was printed by Edwards Brothers, Inc. The cover was printed by Phoenix Color Corp.

Pearson Education LTD.
Pearson Education Singapore, Pte. Ltd
Pearson Education, Canada, Ltd
Pearson Education–Japan

Pearson Education Australia PTY, Limited
Pearson Education North Asia Ltd
Pearson Educación de Mexico, S.A. de C.V.
Pearson Education Malaysia, Pte. Ltd
Pearson Education, Upper Saddle River, New Jersey

10 9 8 7 6 5
ISBN 0-13-148766-3

Contents

To the Instructor

A rose," said Juliet, "by any other name would smell as sweet." This manual has changed its name, and we believe it smells as sweet as ever. Our title has sprouted an extra *m*. *Programed* will henceforth be replaced in the title by the variant *Programmed,* in keeping with popular computer usage.

The reader will smell other sweet changes. For one thing, this seventh edition is published now not only as a comprehensive volume (304 pages) but also as a convenient compact volume (197 pages). A revised *Instructor's Manual* will provide chapter tests and teaching aids for each book.

Programmed College Vocabulary has been designed to supplement freshman English. This manual differs from most vocabulary textbooks in that (1) it focuses on literary and academic terms, and (2) it is autoinstructional. It stresses words that are particularly useful to English students, and—in easy, repetitive steps—elicits responses from each student with immediate verification, a process that psychologists call reinforcement. Students enjoy this painless programmed technique, a system that has been used very successfully at three hundred colleges in the past thirty-six years.

Added materials in the full seventh edition include "Business and Law," "Natural Science," and "Rhetoric." The five chapters involving Latin and Greek derivatives have been tailored and improved. Quizzes and chapter tests have been revised throughout the manual.

The compact volume offers two new condensed chapters of Latin and Greek derivatives, and it highlights important areas such as "Words Often Confused," "Figures of Speech," "Social Science," and "Computer Words," plus barrels of descriptive and action words.

Class procedures are flexible. The teacher can leave vocabulary instruction entirely to the programmed text itself and simply give chapter tests to the class at convenient intervals. But the *Instructor's Manual* includes review suggestions as well as tests, and the teacher may be tempted in class to discuss provocative terms such as *malapropism, psychosomatic, Gresham's law,* and *carcinogen.* Thus, the freshman English course can take on brave new dimensions.

Acknowledgments

I give warmest thanks to a battalion of sharp professors for their valuable suggestions: Patrick Haas, Glendale Community College; Tim Florschuetz, Mesa Community College; Helen Carr, San Antonio College; Susan C. Bazylak, Reading Area Community College; Mike Sullivan, Mt. San Antonio College; Evelyn Koperman, Broward Community College; Rebecca Suarez, University of Texas–El Paso; Robert A. Mathews, Miami-Dade College.

Also, I am deeply grateful for the help of Karen S. Alderfer, Ellen Bourland, Vivian R. Brown, Wolfson Campus, Jessica I. Carroll, Peter Connolly, Barbara Dicey, Patricia B. Gates, Delmar D. Gott, Patricia R. Grega, Mary Alice Hawkins, Charlene Hawks, James F. Jester, Patricia A. McDermott, Maggi Miller, Elizabeth Wahlquist, and the English staff of Pasadena City College.

Let me add one more admirable word to this word book: Edith.

GEORGE W. FEINSTEIN
Pasadena, California

How to Use This Manual

COVER THIS STRIP ▼

1. Cover the answers at the left side of each page (in the grey area) with a strip of cardboard.
2. Study carefully the definitions and examples at the beginning of each "frame," or word group.
3. Complete each statement—and immediately verify your answer—throughout the rest of the frame. Fill blanks with word choices, letter choices, or completions as indicated, without looking back to the definitions.
4. After completing each statement, uncover enough of the key at the left to check your answer.
5. If your answer is correct, go on to the next statement.
6. If you have made an error, study the explanations again at the top of the frame, or consult a dictionary, before you go on.
7. Take the quizzes and the review tests when you reach them, but wait until you have completed each quiz or review test before checking or grading your answers to it.
8. Throughout this manual, fill in the blanks completely and with correct spelling. The act of writing, as well as the repetition, will help the learning process.

Pronunciation Key			
a cat	i hit	oo took	ü *as in French* vue
ā hate	ī kite	oi coil	zh *for* si *in* vision
â rare	o hot	ou out	ə *for* a *in* alone
ä far	ō note	u up	ṅ *nasal, as in French*
e men	ô corn	ū amuse	bon
ē evil	o͞o fool	û burn	

PART ONE

Words Often Confused I

To use a medicine because it looks "something like" the one you need can lead to trouble. To use a word because it sounds "something like" the one you need also leads to trouble.

Some common words, with their frame numbers, are listed above. These words look as harmless as old luggage, yet each should be handled as if it held a little bomb. "A sandy *desert*" is hardly the same as "a sandy *dessert*," and "*marital* music" is hardly the same as "*martial* music"; so be sure you know your homonyms.

Most of the word pairs in this chapter sound alike or are very similar in sound. You should train both your ear and your eye to notice the slight difference in sound or spelling in each pair, so that you will choose the correct word.

Study carefully the words at the top of each frame. Then fill each blank with the correct word. As always, keep a dictionary near you. A dictionary is bound to be useful, and that's not just a pun.

Enough *foreword*—now go *forward*!

EXERCISES

1. **accept** (ak-sept′): to take or receive. "*Accept* the lemons of life, and make lemonade."
2. **except** (ik-sept′): all but; excluding. "This singer has everything *except* talent." *Except* has to do with an *exception*.

accept
except

■ The church will ac *cept* all your paintings ex *cept* the nude.

except, accept

■ Every teacher *except* Smedley will *accept* the two percent raise.

accept
except

■ The opera singer was glad to *accept* the gift package, which was quite ordinary *except* for its ticking sound.

except
accept, except

■ Flem had no coins *except* a wooden nickel, yet he would never *accept* a free drink— *except* when he was awake.

3. **adapt:** to fit for a new use; to adjust to a new situation. "Can man *adapt* to life on the moon?" "This play is an *adaptation* of a novel."
4. **adopt:** to take into one's family; to pick up and use as one's own. "They found me in a trash barrel and *adopted* me."

adapt

■ I could ad *apt* to army life if they'd let me sleep till noon.

adopt
adapt

■ If we *adopt* a bright chimpanzee, it would probably *adapt* quickly to California life.

adapt
adopt

■ Hollywood wants to *adapt* your life story to film. Better *adopt* a pseudonym because this movie may be X-rated.

adopt

■ Who deserves little Ignatz—his natural mother or the couple who happened to *adopt* and raise him?

5. **advice** (ad-vīs′): *Noun*—counsel. "Dad gives me *advice*, not money."
6. **advise** (ad-vīz′): *Verb*—to counsel; to recommend. "Please *advise* me."

advice advise	■ As a young singer I asked a vocal critic for ad _vice_____. He said: "I __advise_____ you to sell fish."
advice	■ Joe's ___advice_____ costs nothing, and it's worth it.
advise, advice	■ I __advise_____ you to take your teacher's __advice_____.
advise advise, advice	■ My friends __advise_____ me to forget my lost sweetheart. Believe me, it's easier to __advise_____ than to take __advice_____.
Advice, advise	■ __Advice_____ rhymes with "ice"; __advise_____ rhymes with "eyes."

7. **affect** (ə-fect′): *Verb*—to produce a change; to influence. "The damp air may *affect* Joe's lungs."
8. **effect** (i-fect′): *Noun*—result. "Physicists study cause and *effect.*" *Verb*—to cause or bring about. "Dad tried to *effect* a change in my study habits."

affect	■ Marriage will __affect_____ Tony's career. [Verb: means "to influence."]
effect	■ Marriage will have an excellent __effect_____ on Tony. [Noun: means "result."]
effect	■ Marriage will __effect_____ an improvement in Tony's habits. [Verb: means "to bring about."]
affect effect	■ The concussion did not __affect_____ my academic grades, which were low anyhow, and seemed to have no lasting __effect_____.
effect effect	■ Baseball representatives can probably __affect_____ a compromise, but they must consider the __effect_____ on the box office.
effect affect	■ Drugs had a tragic __effect_____; his hallucinations still __affect_____ him day and night.

QUIZ

Write the letter that indicates the best definition.

1. (c)
2. (e)
3. (d)
4. (a)
5. (b)
6. (g)
7. (h)
8. (f)

(**c**) 1. advise   a. to receive something offered
(e) 2. except   b. a result
(d) 3. adopt   c. to recommend; to give opinion
(a) 4. accept   d. to take into one's family
(b) 5. effect (*n.*)   e. all but
(g) 6. advice   f. to produce a change; influence
(h) 7. adapt   g. an opinion or recommendation
(f) 8. affect   h. to adjust to a new use

9. **allusion:** a casual reference. "Flaky resented my *allusion* to his driving record."
10. **illusion:** a misleading image; a misconception; delusion. "The hundred-dollar bill was an optical *illusion*."

■ I crawled across the hot sand, and horrors! The lake was an _illusion_.

illusion

■ When I made an _allusion_ to a ghost I had seen, Tom turned pale. "I've seen it, too," he said. "Then it's not an _illusion_. That's the spirit!"

allusion

illusion

■ Louie had the _illusion_ that he'd get better grades if he dropped a casual _allusion_ now and then to Bill Shakespeare or Hank Longfellow.

illusion
allusion

■ The bully made a nasty _allusion_ to my maternal ancestry, and I, unfortunately, was under the _illusion_ that I could knock him down.

allusion
illusion

11. **amount:** quantity; mass.
12. **number:** refers to countable objects. "Joe ate a huge *amount* of ice cream and a small *number* [not *amount*] of doughnuts."

number

■ Sheila collected an unusual _number_ of mosquito bites.

number

amount

■ The mugger separated me from a large _number_ of credit cards and a small _amount_ of cash.

number

■ The sink had no drainpipe, so I washed a great _number_ of dishes and my feet at the same time.

number
amount

■ St. Patrick chased a vast _number_ of snakes out of Ireland, but they return to those who drink a certain _amount_ of whiskey.

13. **brake:** a device for stopping a vehicle. "Step on the _brake_."
14. **break:** to shatter. "_Break_ the glass."

brake

■ All my car needs is br_ake_ pads and a new motor.

brake, break

■ Hit the _brake_, or we'll _break_ our necks!

break

■ "Waiter," I asked, "did this chicken _break_ its leg?" "You wanna eat it, mister, or dance with it?"

brake
break

■ The emergency _brake_ stopped us in time. Now let's drive so that we don't _break_ the law.

break

■ The drug addict couldn't _break_ his dangerous habit.

▐ QUIZ

Write the letter that indicates the best definition.

1. (d)	(_d_) 1. illusion	a. countable objects (ex., eggs)
2. (a)	(_a_) 2. number	b. to crack into pieces
3. (e)	(_e_) 3. brake	c. a reference to something
4. (f)	(_f_) 4. amount	d. a mistaken impression
5. (c)	(_c_) 5. allusion	e. a car-stopper
6. (b)	(_b_) 6. break	f. quantity (ex., dirt)

15. **capital:** _Adjective_—excellent; written with large letters; involving execution. "She is against _capital_ punishment." _Noun_— accumulated assets; a city which is the seat of government. "The _capital_ of Alabama is Montgomery."
16. **capitol:** the statehouse; the building where legislators meet. "The governor stood on the steps of the _capitol_."

capital
capital

■ A backer of cap_ital_ punishment says he has a _capital_ idea: "Suspend the criminal instead of the sentence."

capitol

- Rain leaked through the roof of the _capitol_ and soaked a senator making a dry speech.

capitol
capital

- "We can repair the dome of this _capitol_," said the senator, "but that will take _capital_."

capital
capitol

- Printed in _capital_ letters above the main entrance to the _capitol_ was the word LEGISLATURE.

17. **complement:** _Noun_—that which completes a thing; the counterpart. "Her white shoes serve as a _complement_ to her black dress." _Verb_—to complete. "Her shoes _complement_ her dress."
18. **compliment:** _Noun_—words of praise. "Thanks for the _compliment._" _Verb_—to praise. "Such a dessert! Let me _compliment_ the chef."

complement

- Gardens _complement_ the tidy English cottages.

compliment
complement

- "You have brains, Gwendolyn, and that's not an idle _compliment_," said Mother. "You'll be the perfect _complement_ to Sir Percy, who is a shmoe."

complement
compliment
complement

- "Here's a rosy apple, Teacher, to _complement_ your cheeks."— "What a sweet _compliment_, Archy! I hope you can earn an _A_ today to _complement_ that _F_ you got yesterday."

compliment

- Like perfume, a _compliment_ should be inhaled, not swallowed.

19. **continually:** often repeated; again and again. "Football players are _continually_ breaking arms and legs."
20. **continuously:** without stopping. "The chairman spoke _continuously_ for ninety minutes and never grazed a fresh idea."

continually

- George Bernard Shaw quoted himself _con tinually_, claiming, "It adds spice to my conversation."

continually
continuously

- Blizzards strike Montana _con tinually_, and one storm raged _con tinuously_ for three days.

continuously
continually

- A mountain road winds _continuously_ from Crestville to Helengone, and accidents occur on it _continually_.

continually
continuously

- Louie the Loafer is _continually_ fired from his jobs, and he has never held one job _continuously_ for six months.

21. **decent:** proper and fitting. "Joe had a *decent* burial."
22. **descent:** a coming down; ancestry. "A man of Irish *descent* made a *descent* into the cellar."

descent

- The elevator's rapid de _scent_ made my stomach hit my tonsils.

decent

- Mary thinks I'm not making a _decent_ salary as a custodian, but I'm cleaning up.

descent
decent

- The parachute slowed Edna's _descent_, and she made a fairly _decent_ landing in an elm tree.

descent
decent

- Hugo is of Austrian _descent_, and he bakes a very _decent_ apple strudel.

QUIZ

Write the letter that indicates the best definition.

1. (h)
2. (f)
3. (g)
4. (b)
5. (d)
6. (a)
7. (c)
8. (e)

(h) 1. continually
(f) 2. descent
(g) 3. complement
(b) 4. capital
(d) 5. continuously
(a) 6. decent
(c) 7. compliment
(e) 8. capitol

a. in good taste; respectable
b. assets; involving execution
c. words of praise
d. without stopping
e. the statehouse
f. a going down; ancestry
g. the counterpart; that which completes
h. repeatedly; again and again

---

23. **desert:** *Noun* (dez'ərt)—a dry wasteland. *Verb* (di-zûrt)—to abandon one's post or duty. "She's rich. He won't *desert* her."
24. **dessert:** a delicacy served at the end of a meal.

desert
dessert

- "Only a rat would des _ert_," said our sergeant, as he cut a slab of apple pie for _dessert_. "Pass me the cheese."

desert
dessert

- Crossing the sandy _desert_, we had dates for _dessert_.

desert

- I'll never _desert_ my ship," said the brave captain, "glub ... glub ...."

dessert

- What has a double portion of *s*'s and calories? _dessert_.

25. **disinterested:** impartial; not biased. "A jury should be made up of *disinterested* citizens."
26. **uninterested:** not interested. "Grandma was *uninterested* in the soccer game."

- I tried to explain calculus to the baby, but she seemed *uninterested*.

uninterested

- We prefer an honest referee if such exists—a truly *disinterested* fellow.

disinterested

- I don't blame you if you're *uninterested*, but please don't yawn in my face.

uninterested

- A disinterested judge is *fair-minded* [excitable / fair-minded]; an uninterested judge is probably *bored* [bored / alert].

fair-minded
bored

27. **dual:** *Adjective*—double; twofold.
28. **duel:** *Noun*—a combat between two antagonists.

- Macbeth and Macduff have a *duel* to the death.

duel

- In a warplane with *dual* wings, the Red Baron won many a fiery *duel*.

dual
duel

- Dmitri has a *dual* personality. You never know whether he's going to embrace you or *duel* with you.

dual
duel

- When challenged to a *duel*, Mark Twain told the gunslinger, "How about a *duel* with water pistols at sixty paces?"

duel
duel

- With *dual* exhaust pipes you can pollute the air twice as fast.

dual

QUIZ

Write the letter that indicates the best definition.

1. (e)	(e)	1. uninterested	a.	not prejudiced
2. (c)	(c)	2. duel	b.	pie, ice cream, etc.
3. (d)	(d)	3. desert (n.)	c.	a fight between two rivals
4. (f)	(f)	4. dual	d.	a dry, sandy region
5. (a)	(a)	5. disinterested	e.	bored
6. (b)	(b)	6. dessert	f.	double

29. **every body:** each separate body. "*Every body* had bruises on it."
30. **everybody:** every person. "*Everybody* is welcome."

every body

- The surgeon examined *every body* as it was carried in.

Everybody

- *Everybody* who is a nonreader is a threat to civilization.

everybody
every body

- At ballet school *every body* exercises daily, and *every body* is attractive in its proportions.

everybody
every body

- The butchers killed the pigs, and then *everybody* got busy cutting *every body* into ham, bacon, and knuckles.

(b)

- *Everybody, anybody,* and *somebody* refer to (a) bodies, (b) persons. (*b*)

(a)

- *Every body, any body,* and *some body* refer to (a) bodies, (b) persons. (*a*)

31. **foreword:** a preface; introductory note.
32. **forward:** onward; toward what lies ahead.

forward
foreword

- Our nation will go *forward*, according to the author in his *foreword*.

forward

- Volunteers, please step *forward*.

foreword
forward

- Read the *foreword* of a technical book before plunging *forward* into the chapters ahead.

forward

- My mule is backward about going *forward*.

forward

- Percival says he's looking *forward* to his thirtieth birthday. He's looking from the wrong direction.

foreword

- The introduction or "before" word of a book is known as the *foreword*.

33. **imply** (im-plī′): to hint at; to suggest without stating; to signify.
34. **infer** (in-fûr′): to draw a conclusion.

imply
infer

- These bloodstains *imply* that the victim may have been knifed. What do you *infer*?

imply

- Her high grades *imply* unusual intelligence.

infer

imply

imply

infer

inferred

- From various evidence I *infer*_____ that the baseball fans no longer admire Lefty Smeeby. Their jeers *imply*_____ that they have lost confidence in him.

- Melvin's smiles *imply*_____ success. We can *infer*_____ that Betty has accepted his marriage proposal.

- Hot tar was spilled at the intersection, from which the police _____*inferr*ed that there was dirty work at the crossroads.

35. **instance:** an example. "She recalled an *instance* of wifebeating in the bridal suite."
36. **instants:** moments. "Tragedy struck within *instants*."

instance

- The playboy cited an *instance*_____ of a New Year's party that broke up in March.

instants

- The three sprinters hit the tape within *instants*_____ of each other.

instance

instants

- I was worried, for *instance*_____, when the old plane shook for several *instants*_____ and a voice said: "This is your pilot, Orville Wright."

instance

- Using my toothbrush to clean his typewriter keys was another *instance*_____ of poor manners.

instants

- The lights turned green, and *instants*_____ later the horns were honking up a storm.

QUIZ

Write the letter that indicates the best definition.

1. (e)
2. (g)
3. (h)
4. (c)
5. (f)
6. (a)
7. (d)
8. (b)

(e)	1. instance	a.	moments
(g)	2. forward	b.	each person
(h)	3. imply	c.	a preface to a book
(c)	4. foreword	d.	to judge from evidence; conclude
(f)	5. every body	e.	an example; case
(a)	6. instants	f.	each of the bodies
(d)	7. infer	g.	toward what is ahead
(b)	8. everybody	h.	to hint or suggest

37. **its** (possessive): "The basset hound stepped on *its* ear."
38. **it's** (contraction): it is. "Frankly, *it's* a hot dog."

- Surely *it's* _____ no fun for a rabbit to be held by *its* _____ ears. (Hint: Write *it's* only if "it is" can be substituted for it.)

  it's / its

- As for this camel, *it's* _____ a poor specimen; it has bumps on *its* _____ back.

  it's / its

- I wanted to be a lion tamer, but when the circus lion bared *its* _____ fangs and *its* _____ claws, I decided to become a clown.

  its, its

- This lake is perfect, except that *its* _____ fish are tiny and *its* _____ mosquitoes are big as eagles.

  its / its

- Truly *it's* _____ lucky to own a shiny penny—if *it's* _____ wrapped in fifty-dollar bills.

  it's / it's

- "If *it's* _____ true that the cow jumped over the moon," Junior asked his teacher, "how did it get *its* _____ thrust?"

  it's / its

39. **ladder:** a device with steps for climbing. "Climb a *ladder* and get up in the world."
40. **later:** afterward; more late. "He returned *later*."
41. **latter:** the last mentioned. "Stephen Douglas or Abe Lincoln? Mary Todd married the *latter*."

- It's *later* _____ than you think.

  later

- Moe held the *ladder* _____ for Curly and Jack, and the *latter* _____ fell off the *ladder* _____ a minute *later* _____.

  ladder / latter, ladder / later

- On his deathbed my grandfather bargained with Sid and Max and sold his old *ladder* _____ to the *latter* _____.

  ladder, latter

- We're out of dates and figs, but we'll have the *latter* _____ a little *later* _____.

  latter / later

- An hour *later* _____ I knocked the paint bucket off my *ladder* _____ onto the new Persian rug. Mr. and Mrs. Schultz seemed quite unhappy, especially the *latter* _____.

  later / ladder / latter

42. **leave:** to depart. "We will *leave* at dawn."
43. **let:** to allow. "Please *let* us help."

let

- Society must le*t*_____ women develop to their full potential.

leave, let

- Before we le*ave*_____, le*t*_____ us come to an understanding.

let
leave

- The hostess will _____*let*_____ you kiss her when you _____*leave*_____.

let, leave

- The pacifist would not _____*let*_____ his son _____*leave*_____ for the front.

QUIZ

Write the letter that indicates the best definition.

1. (e)
2. (f)
3. (g)
4. (d)
5. (c)
6. (a)
7. (b)

(*e*) 1. let
(*f*) 2. later
(*g*) 3. leave
(*d*) 4. its
(*c*) 5. ladder
(*a*) 6. latter
(*b*) 7. it's

a. the last one mentioned
b. it is
c. a climbing device
d. belonging to it
e. to permit; allow
f. afterward
g. to go away

Write in full the word that is indicated in brackets.

instance

1. Slavery was an [instan-] of low minimum wages.

allusion

2. Felicia made an [-lusion] to her Mayflower ancestor.

continuously

3. He warned me [contin-ly] not to play Ping-Pong with my mouth open.

affect

4. Drugs have a bad [-fect] on brains, if you have any.

advise

5. I [adv-e] against selling jewelry on credit to hoboes.

break

6. "Pay up," snarled Flem to the pianist, "or we [br-k] your fingers."

descent

7. The yodeler was of Swiss [d-c-nt].

duel

8. Two little scholars fought a [du-l] with spitballs.

foreword

9. I read the book from [for-rd] to index.

compliment

10. A [compl-m-nt] a day keeps divorce away.

capital

11. Spend the interest, but don't touch the [cap-t-l].

adopt

12. The orphanage was sure nobody would [ad-pt] me.

uninterested

13. Ben wanted to play chess, but Fifi was [-interested].

its

14. Life is an elevator. It has [it-] ups and downs.

affect

15. Would sudden wealth [-fect] me? I'll never find out.

accept

16. The grateful native offered me his pet boa constrictor, but I didn't [-cept] it.

advice

17. Free [advi-e] is often worth what you pay for it.

capitol

18. Presidents have walked the floors of our [cap-t-l].

desert

19. Having crossed the [des-t] twice without bathing, John was called "a dirty double-crosser."

every body

20. Buffalo Bill killed the herd and let [ev-body] rot.

Write the correct word in full.

let

imply

_it's_

illusion

number

21. Don't [leave / let] Junior play with those razors.

22. Medical tests [imply / infer] that I may last until Sunday.

23. Fay got rid of 279 ugly pounds—[its / it's] her husband.

24. Our hen had an optical [illusion / allusion] and sat on a snowball.

25. I ate a large [amount / number] of watermelon slices and my ears got washed.

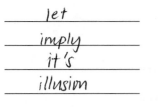 **KEY TO REVIEW TEST**

Check your test answers with the following key. Deduct 4% per error from a possible 100%.

1. instance	10. compliment	19. desert
2. allusion	11. capital	20. every body
3. continually	12. adopt	21. let
4. effect	13. uninterested	22. imply
5. advise	14. its	23. it's
6. break	15. affect	24. illusion
7. descent	16. accept	25. number
8. duel	17. advice	
9. foreword	18. capitol	

Score: _____ %

loose, **1**	past, **16**	than, **31**
lose, **2**	personal, **17**	their, **33**
marital, **3**	personnel, **18**	then, **32**
martial, **4**	plain, **19**	there, **34**
medal, **5**	plane, **20**	they're, **35**
metal, **6**	principal, **21**	weak, **36**
miner, **7**	principle, **22**	weather, **38**
minor, **8**	quiet, **23**	week, **37**
moral, **9**	quite, **24**	whether, **39**
morale, **10**	shone, **25**	who's, **40**
nauseated, **11**	shown, **26**	whose, **41**
nauseous, **12**	stake, **27**	your, **42**
naval, **13**	stationary, **29**	you're, **43**
navel, **14**	stationery, **30**	
passed, **15**	steak, **28**	

Continue as in the previous chapter. Study the homonyms at the top of each frame. *They're there* **to be studied, not admired, so notice** *their* **differences.**

As always, be sure to cover the answers in the left-hand column until you have completed the frame. (If you *peek* before you write, you won't reach the *peak* of your potential.)

✚ EXERCISES

1. **loose** (rhymes with *goose*): not tight; unfastened.
2. **lose:** to suffer a loss.

loose, lose

■ The goose is lo *ose*_____! We must not lo *se*_____ it.

loose
lose

■ In time of war a lo *ose*_____ tongue can cause us to lo *se*_____ a troopship.

lose, loose

■ When I _*lose*_____ weight, my pants hang _*loose*_____.

lose
lose, loose

■ Not only did I _*lose*_____ the fight, but I may also _*lose*_____ this _*loose*_____ tooth.

loose

■ The word *goose* rhymes with the word l *oose*_____.

3. **marital:** pertaining to marriage.
4. **martial:** pertaining to war.

marital

■ "Thanks to my husband for three years of mar *ital*_____ bliss," said Mrs. Roe on her golden anniversary.

martial
martial

■ Will nations abolish mar *tial*_____ conflict or will mar *tial*_____ conflict abolish nations?

marital

■ Love one another, if you want _*marital*_____ happiness.

marital
martial

■ Wagner's "Wedding March" is _*marital*_____ music; "Marine's Hymn" is _*martial*_____ music.

5. **medal:** a decorative award for a distinguished act.
6. **metal:** a substance such as silver, tin, or steel.

medal

■ Goering wore many a me *dal*_____ on his uniform and probably on his pajamas.

metal
medal
medal

■ Gold is a precious me *tal*_____, and Olympic winners are awarded a gold me *dal*_____. Those in second place are awarded a silver me *dal*_____.

metal

■ Ben's mouth, with its _*metal*_____ fillings, looks like mother lode country.

medal
metal

■ I was to receive a _*medal*_____ for being Most Careful Driver, but on the way I hit a _*metal*_____ post.

7. **miner:** somebody who works in a mine.

8. **minor:** somebody who is below legal age; of lesser importance.

miner

- "Gold! I found gold!" whispered the dying *miner*_____.

miner, minor

- The old *miner*_____ sang in a *minor*_____ key about a goat.

minor
minor

- A young draftee complains, "As a *minor*_____ I can die for my country, yet as a *minor*_____ I cannot vote."

miner
minor

- At the end of a hard day a coal *miner*_____ does not look like Snow White. However, that to him is of *minor*_____ importance.

QUIZ

Write the letter that indicates the best definition.

1. (c)	(c)	1. minor	a.	iron, tin, etc.
2. (f)	(f)	2. medal	b.	untied; not bound together
3. (e)	(e)	3. martial	c.	a youth; less important
4. (g)	(g)	4. miner	d.	to suffer a loss
5. (b)	(b)	5. loose	e.	concerning war
6. (h)	(h)	6. marital	f.	a decoration, as for heroism
7. (a)	(a)	7. metal	g.	a mine worker
8. (d)	(d)	8. lose	h.	concerning marriage

9. **moral** (mor′əl): *Adjective*—virtuous; of good character, as in "a *moral,* law-abiding family"; virtual—"a *moral* victory." *Noun*—the lesson in a story.

10. **morale** (mər-al′): *Noun*—state of mind as to confidence and enthusiasm.

morale
moral

- After ten losses our team was low in *morale*_____, and this tie was like a *moral*_____ victory.

moral

- Some people are *moral*_____ only because they've never been tempted.

moral

- A pox on any film of violence whose only *moral*_____ is "Shoot first!"

morale

- Malaria can damage one's *morale*_____.

morale
moral

- High _____morale_____ is desirable, but to succeed you also need talent, skills, and _____moral_____ character.

11. **nauseated:** sickened; disgusted; ill at the stomach. "Those unhappy people at the ship rail are *nauseated*."
12. **nauseous:** sickening; disgusting; causing to vomit. "The overripe fruit was rotting and *nauseous*."

nauseous
nauseated

- Disgusting things are *nauseous_____*. People sickened by such things are *nauseated_____*.

nauseated
nauseous

- Several strikers were *nauseated_____* when struck by a stinkbomb with an extremely *nauseous_____* odor.

nauseous
nauseated

- The contaminated salmon at "Hepatitis Hotel" was _____nauseous_____, and several members of the wedding party were _____nauseated_____.

nauseated
nauseous

- Norma was *nauseated_____* to see the baby seals clubbed to death. "What a _____nauseous_____ sight!" she moaned.

13. **naval:** pertaining to a navy.
14. **navel:** umbilicus; "belly button."

naval

- In 1588 England won a great *naval_____* victory.

naval
navel

- One sailor on the *naval_____* vessel was stripped to the waist and scratching his *navel_____*.

navel
navel

- An orange that has a scar on it like a human *navel_____* is called a _____navel_____ orange.

naval
navel

- After a lengthy parade honoring our _____naval_____ fleet, one flagbearer complained of an enlarged *navel_____*.

15. **passed:** went by (verb, past tense of *pass*). "The gassy truck *passed* the joggers."
16. **past:** beyond; earlier; an earlier period. (*Past* is not a verb.) "During the *past* minute, six gassy trucks have gone *past* the joggers."

passed

- Tony *passed_____* the tavern. (Here Tony is the subject of a missing verb, and the verb ends in *ed*.)

past

- Tony walked *past_____* the tavern. (Here Tony is the subject of the verb *walked,* and the missing word is not a verb.)

past
passed

- Some years in the *past* _____ Tom wanted to be a barber. He took a licensing test and *passed* _____ by a hair.

past
passed
passed

- The bullet screamed _*past*_ _____ my ear, and I heard it twice: first, when it _*passed*_ _____ me, and then when I _*passed*_ _____ it.

past
passed

- At half- _*past*_ _____ ten Mary bid six spades, and I _*passed*_ _____.

QUIZ

Circle the choice that results in the more acceptable sentence.

navel
past
morale
moral
nauseated

1. At the deli a caraway seed got lodged in Art's [naval / (navel)].
2. Every boy [(past) / passed] five is told he'll be president, and the threat is bad for his [moral / morale].
3. Except for the orgies, they were [(moral) / morale] citizens.
4. Sue ate too much health food and became [nauseous / (nauseated)].

---

17. **personal:** *Adjective*—private. "It's a *personal* problem."
18. **personnel** (accent on *nel*): the people employed in a business. "Miss Boe is in charge of *personnel*."

personnel
personal

- Any business can succeed if the *per* _*sonnel*_ _____ take a *per* _*personal*_ _____ interest in their work.

personal
personnel

- I made a *personal* _____ application for a job at the mortuary, but the *personnel* _____ manager said business was dead.

personal
personnel, personal

- My _*personal*_ _____ opinion is that when the head of _*personnel*_ _____ calls me a nerd, he's getting too _*personal*_ _____.

personnel

- Our office _*personnel*_ _____ have gear trouble: They talk in high and think in low.

19. **plain:** *Adjective*—clear; common looking. *Noun*—a prairie.
20. **plane:** *Noun*—an airplane; a flat, two-dimensional surface.

plain
plane

- We need *plain* _____ talk between nations, not a *plane* _____ loaded with bombs.

plain

- The rain in Spain fell on the grassy *plain* _____.

plane plain	■ Our baby, Wayne, born on a speeding __plane__, looks rather __plain__, but we can't complain.
plane, plain	■ Gus studied __plane__ geometry, and the __plain__ fact is that he didn't like it.
plain plain	■ Abraham Lincoln was a __plain__ man and he used __plain__ words.

21. **principal:** main; head of a school; chief actor or doer; a capital sum. " 'Spend the interest and save the *principal*'—that was the *principal* lesson that the school *principal* taught us."
22. **principle:** a rule of action or conduct. (Note that *principle* and *rule* both end in *le*.) "Isaac Newton worked out the *principle* of gravitation."

principle	■ The professor explained a basic *prin__ciple__* of thermodynamics. (Refers to a *rule*.)
principal	■ The *prin__cipal__* cause of divorce is marriage.
principal, principal	■ The high school *pr__incipal__* played the *pr__incipal__* role in the faculty comedy.
principle principal	■ Jane Pittman was a woman of lofty __principle__, and that is a __Principal__ reason we honor her.
principal principle	■ My __principal__ objection is to speech courses that stress the questionable __principle__, "Say it with sincerity, whether you believe it or not."

23. **quiet** (kwī'-ət): silent; silence.
24. **quite** (kwīt): really; entirely.

quiet, quite	■ To be *qui__et__* is often *qu__ite__* as important as to talk.
quite quiet	■ Since Albert broke his stereo, our house is *q__uite__* __quiet__.
quiet	■ The baby is __quiet__. Go see what's the matter.
quite quiet	■ Slim told __quite__ a few jokes, but we stifled our laughs and remained __quiet__.

Write the letter that indicates the best definition.

1. (f)
2. (g)
3. (e)
4. (a)
5. (c)
6. (d)
7. (b)
8. (h)

(f) 1. principal   a. silent
(g) 2. plane   b. private
(e) 3. personnel   c. a prairie; ordinary looking
(a) 4. quiet   d. a rule of conduct
(c) 5. plain   e. a staff of employees
(d) 6. principle   f. the head of a high school
(b) 7. personal   g. an aircraft
(h) 8. quite   h. really; entirely

---

25. **shone** (past tense of *shine*): "The sun *shone*."
26. **shown** is related to *show*. "I was *shown* the fish."

shone

■ The moon *shone* _____ at night, according to Abner, when we needed it most.

shown

■ She smoked too much. I was *shown* _____ her newborn baby, and it had yellow fingernails.

shone
shown

■ The pirate's eyes *shone* _____ when he was *shown* _____ the treasure chest.

shown

■ Such a doctor! Break an ankle and you'll be _shown_ _____ how to limp.

shown
shone, shown

■ The customer was _shown_ _____ twelve pairs of shoes, but suddenly his face _shone_ _____ when he was _shown_ _____ the yellow oxfords.

shone

■ The candle _shone_ _____ like a good deed in a naughty world.

27. **stake:** a stick or post; something wagered or risked.
28. **steak:** a slice of meat or fish.

stake

■ Joan of Arc was burned at the *stake* _____.

stake

■ We have a *stake* _____ in the future of our nation.

steak

■ Grandpa ate a fat, oily *steak* _____, and he doesn't squeak any more.

stake stake	■ The prospector drove a *stake* into the ground to *stake* his claim.
steak steak	■ I used to order a *steak* rare. Now I order a *steak* rarely.
stake steak	■ "I'll *stake* a dollar," muttered the waitress, "that this health nut orders the halibut *steak*."

29. **stationary:** not moving.
30. **stationery:** writing paper.

stationery	■ At Christmas I got six boxes of sta*tionery*.
stationery, stationary	■ Stanley buys st*ationery*; then he sits st*ationary* in front of his typewriter.
stationery	■ The word "paper" has an *er* in it, and so does the word *stationery*.
stationary	■ Is that hydrant really *stationary*, or did it move out and hit my fender?
stationery stationary	■ On official *stationery* Clarence confessed: "If an irresistible force hits a *stationary* object, I'm probably the driver."

31. **than** (used in comparisons). "Fido bites harder *than* Rover."
32. **then:** at that time. "We were younger and thinner *then*."

then	■ Now and th*en* Junior loses a tooth.
than	■ The wrestler's nose was flatter th*an* a bicycle seat.
then than	■ Our government operated on a smaller budget *then* *than* now.
then than	■ The shepherd saw her sweater and *then* realized that the wool looked better on the girl *than* on the sheep.
than *then*	■ The word *than* suggests a comparison; the word *then* suggests time.

Write the letter that indicates the best definition.

1. (d)
2. (c)
3. (e)
4. (g)
5. (b)
6. (h)
7. (a)
8. (f)

(d) 1. stationery   a̸. at that time
(c) 2. shown   b̸. compared with
(e) 3. steak   c̸. displayed; exhibited
(g) 4. shone   d. writing paper
(b) 5. than   e̸. a slice of meat
(h) 6. stake   f̸. not moving
(a) 7. then   g̸. was shining
(f) 8. stationary   h̸. a post; something wagered

---

33. **their** (possessive). "*Their* dog has fleas."
34. **there:** in that place. "Sit *there* and wait."
35. **they're:** they are. "*They're* sleeping."

their
they're
- The dentist will have to straighten *th*ei̱r̲_____ teeth, because *th*ey'ṟe_____ not going to straighten themselves.

there
their
- Soon the three wise men arrived *th*eṟe̲_____ on *th*ei̱r̲_____ camels.

they're, their
- The old folks say ___they're___ happy in ___their___ merry Oldsmobile.

there
they're
their
- The salespeople over ___thi̱re̲___ are live wires. A widow wants a burial suit for her husband, and ___they're___ selling her ___thei̱r___ best silk suit with two pairs of pants.

36. **weak:** lacking in strength; feeble.
37. **week:** a seven-day period.

week,
weak
- After a *we*ek̲_____ of fasting, I was as *we*ak̲_____ as a baby.

week
- "God created man at the end of the *we*ek̲_____," says Mark Twain, "when God was tired."

weak
week
- The strong have oppressed the ___weak___, not just for a day or a ___week___ but for centuries.

weak
- "Don't sneer at our coffee," said the waiter. "You, too, will be old and ___weak___ some day."

38. **weather:** *Noun*—atmospheric conditions. "Stormy *weather!*"
    Verb—to wear away; to survive.
39. **whether:** if. "He'll decide *whether* to operate."

weather, whether
- We predict the w _eather_ , but I doubt w _hether_ we can control it.

weather
- Fred has a thirty percent chance of becoming a w _eather_ forecaster.

whether
- Worries, worries! Rich people must decide _whether_ to drive the Rolls or the Cadillac.

weather, whether
- You'll love Dakota's winter _weather_ , _whether_ you prefer twenty below or forty below.

whether, weather
weather
- I doubt _whether_ we could _weather_ the rigors of Klondike _weather_ .

40. **who's:** who is. "*Who's* calling, please?"
41. **whose** (possessive). "*Whose* shoes are these?"

whose
who's
- Find out wh _ose_ car was smashed and wh _o's_ to blame. (Hint: Write *who's* only if "who is" would be correct in the blank.)

whose
who's
- The aged alumni, wh _ose_ class reunion this is, are getting together to see wh _o's_ falling apart.

who's
whose
- Mr. Bigmouth wants to know _who's_ marrying _whose_ daughter.

who's
- A girl _who's_ fit as a fiddle should have a beau.

who's
whose
- "I'd like to catch the actor _who's_ careless," said Hamlet, "and _whose_ spear keeps jabbing me in the third act."

whose
who's
- The word _whose_ is possessive; the word _who's_ means "who is."

42. **your** (possessive). "Put on *your* gas mask."
43. **you're:** you are. "*You're* beautiful."

you're, your
your
- Jason, if _you're_ serious about _your_ garlic diet, you'll lose two pounds and all _your_ friends.

you're

your
you're, your

you're
your

you're, your
your

you're
your
your

- Until April 15 yo _u're_ deep in the heart of taxes.
- Wilhelm, _your_ poems are so sweet that
  you're making _your_ readers throw up.
- When _you're_ famous, the public takes an interest in
  your sins.
- If y_ou're_ going to break y_our_ leg on
  y_our_ motorcycle, don't come running to me.
- "Listen," said Barnum to Tom Thumb, "_you're_ so little
  that you have to stand on _your_ chair to brush
  your teeth."

➕ QUIZ

Circle the choice that results in the more acceptable sentence.

1. who's
2. you're
3. there
4. weak
5. weather

1. Sam sang, "I wonder [whose / (who's)] kissing her now."
2. Read constantly, or [(you're) / your] wasting time in college.
3. All my friends were [(there) / their / they're]—both of them.
4. After seven days without water, I was [(weak) / week].
5. Twenty below zero—that was our warmest [(weather) / whether].

Write in full the word that is indicated in brackets.

whose   1. Find out [who-] toupee fell from the balcony.

steak   2. Now that I can afford a T-bone [st-], I have no teeth.

principle   3. To buy on credit is a dangerous [princ-p-].

week   4. After a [we-k] my sweatsuit stood up by itself.

morale   5. Getting fired didn't help my [mo-r-l-].

nauseated   6. At a gory movie, I feel [nause-].

than   7. Sheila is prettier [th-n] a tax refund.

stationery   8. The homesick soldier sniffed the perfumed [stat-n-ry].

passed   9. Ulysses came back when twenty years had [pas-].

whether   10. Hamlet debated [w-th-r] to be or not to be alive.

naval   11. John Paul Jones won a [na-l] victory.

past   12. An arrow whistled [past / passed] General Custer.

minor   13. Luke sang in [min-r] key of his untrue lover.

there   14. Art started at the bottom and stayed [th-r-].

quiet.   15. The baby is [qui-]. Go see if he is sick.

navel   16. A gangster's bullet hit Nick in the [nav-l].

loose   17. A [l-se] tooth is driving me to extraction.

personal   18. To ask your hostess her age is a bit [pers-n-l].

Write the correct word in full.

marital   19. Their [marital / martial] life was happy until they left the altar.

shone   20. The solar-powered cars moved when the sun [shone / shown].

their   21. The Martians landed and [there / their / they're] leader saluted a gas pump.

minor   22. The tavern won't sell liquor to a [miner / minor].

your   23. If the chute won't open, say [your / you're] prayers.

medal   24. In a laziness contest, Ken wins the gold [medal / metal].

plain   25. Jim's books come in a [plain / plane] wrapper.

KEY TO REVIEW TEST

Check your test answers with the following key. Deduct 4% per error from a possible 100%.

1. whose	10. whether	19. marital
2. steak	11. naval	20. shone
3. principle	12. past	21. their
4. week	13. minor	22. minor
5. morale	14. there	23. your
6. nauseated	15. quiet	24. medal
7. than	16. navel	25. plain
8. stationery	17. loose	
9. passed	18. personal	

Score: _____ %

SUPPLEMENTARY LIST

Class Exercise: Divide into panel groups. Each group will be responsible for discussing and clarifying a segment of the following list for the benefit of the rest of the class.

1. addition, edition	21. council, counsel	41. holey, holy
2. aisle, isle	22. costume, custom	42. incidence, incidents
3. alley, ally	23. dairy, diary	43. knew, new
4. allowed, aloud	24. dammed, damned	44. lessen, lesson
5. altar, alter	25. dear, deer	45. liable, libel
6. anecdote, antidote	26. deceased, diseased	46. mantel, mantle
7. angel, angle	27. device, devise	47. meat, meet
8. ascent, assent	28. disinterested, uninterested	48. pail, pale
9. bare, bear	29. dyeing, dying	49. peace, piece
10. base, bass	30. emigrate, immigrate	50. picture, pitcher
11. beach, beech	31. envelop, envelope	51. pole, poll
12. beat, beet	32. fair, fare	52. pore, pour
13. berth, birth	33. flea, flee	53. profit, prophet
14. board, bored	34. flour, flower	54. prophecy, prophesy
15. boarder, border	35. forth, fourth	55. respectfully, respectively
16. bridal, bridle	36. foul, fowl	56. ring, wring
17. censor, censure	37. heal, heel	57. sail, sale
18. cereal, serial	38. hear, here	58. steal, steel
19. chord, cord	39. hoarse, horse	59. summary, summery
20. coarse, course	40. hole, whole	60. threw, through

Latin Derivatives I

CHAPTER 3

Roots

am, amat, **1**	dic, dict, **8**	loqu, locut, **15**
ann, enn, **2**	duc, duct, **9**	mal, **16**
aqu, **3**	fid, **10**	mor, mort, **17**
aud, audit, **4**	frater, **11**	nov, **18**
capit, **5**	greg, **12**	omni, **19**
cent, **6**	litera, **13**	ped, **20**
cred, credit, **7**	loc, **14**	

Latin derivatives make up at least half of our language. A student without this half of English vocabulary would be like a sprinter with one leg. Luckily you are already familiar with hordes of useful Latin derivatives, and by one technique or another you can learn hundreds more. Taking six years of classical Latin is an excellent method, but if that route is inconvenient, you can study common Latin roots and prefixes that have enriched our English language.

Chapters 3 and 4 focus on Latin roots and their clusters of derivatives. Chapter 5 reviews Latin prefixes.

First, memorize the Latin term and its definition, given at the beginning of each frame. Next, note carefully the example derivatives that follow in italics. Try to understand the connection between each of these derivatives and its Latin root. Then fill in the blanks.

EXERCISES

Roots

1. **am, amat:** love.

   Derivatives: *amateur, amative, amatory, amiable, amity, amorist, amours.*

loving
   - Since *amat* means *love,* an *amative* young man is ___loving___ [hostile / loving].

love
   - An *amateur* golfer plays for ___love___ [love / the fat fees] of the game.

am
   - The two letters in the words *amorist* and *amatory* that suggest *love* are ___am___.

amorist
amatory
   - The Casanova devoted to *love*-making is an ___amorist___ [atheist / amorist], and he has ___amatory___ [amatory / mandatory] adventures.

amours
   - Cleopatra's *love* affairs are her ___amo___rs.

amity
   - Warm friendship between nations is international ___amity___ [animosity / amity].

amiable
   - Friendly people are ___amiable___ [amiable / alienated].

2. **ann, enn:** year.

   Derivatives: *annals, anniversary, annual, annuity, biennial, centennial, millennium, perennial, superannuated.*

ann
   - The three letters in the words *annals* and *annual* that suggest *year* are ___ann___.

year
   - *Per annum* means per ___year___ [month / year].

annuity
   - *Yearly* income from a fund is called an ___annuity___ [excise / annuity].

superannuated
   - A man who has lived many *years* is said to be ___superannuated___ [superannuated / supercilious].

enn

- In some words, like *biennial, centennial,* and *perennial,* the Latin root for *year* is ___*enn*___ [ial / enn].

  3. **aqu:** water.

     Derivatives: *aquacade, aqualung, aquamarine, aquaplane, aqua regia, aquarium, aquatint, aqua vitae, aqueduct, aqueous humor, aquiculture, subaqueous.*

- To make an *aqueous* solution you dissolve something in ___*water*___ [alcohol / water].

water

- The three letters in *aqualung* and *aquiculture* that suggest *water* are ___*aqu*___.

aqu

water

- An *aquaplane* is towed on ___*water*___ [snow / water / rocks].

- A *water* festival which involves swimming and diving is sometimes called an ___*aqua*___cade.

aquacade

- Small fish may be kept in an ___*aquar*___ium.

aquarium

- The sign of the zodiac that represents a *water* bearer is ___*Aquarius*___ [Aquarius / Taurus].

Aquarius

  4. **aud, audit:** hear.

     Derivatives: *audible, audience, audile, audio-frequency, audiophile, audiovisual, audiphone, audit, audition, auditor, auditorium, auditory.*

hear

- You can assume that *auditory* nerves help you to ___*hear*___ [hear / see], since the five-letter Latin root for *hear* is ___*audit*___ [ditor / audit].

audit

audition
audience
auditorium

- After a successful critical *hearing,* or ___*audit*___ion, a singer might entertain an ___*audien*___ce in an ___*audrtoriu*___ium.

hearing

- An *audiometer* is an instrument which measures sensitivity of ___*hearing*___ [hearing / sight].

hi-fi

- An *audiophile* is enthusiastic about ___*hi-fi*___ [stamps / hi-fi].

- Which word has no business being in the following list? *audible, audiphone, audio-frequency, adenoids, auditor* ___*adenoids*___.

adenoids

5. **capit:** head.

Derivatives: *cap, capital, capitalism, capitate, capitol, caption, decapitate, per capita, recapitulate.*

head
caption

- *Capit* is a root that means h*ead*_____; so the *heading* of a chapter or an article is called a __*caption*____ [decoction / caption].

head

- A per *capita* tax is assessed as so much per h*ead*_____.

capit

- The Latin root for *head* is __*capit*____.

capital
decapitated

- In Paris, the _____*capit*___al of France, King Louis XVI got a sovereign cure for headaches—he was *de* *capitated*____.

recapitulate

- Newscasters sometimes *re* *capitulate*___ the day's news; such a *recapitulation* literally restates the news (a) in full, (b) by

(b)

headings. (*b*)

QUIZ

Write the meaning of each boldface Latin root.

year
hear
love
head
water

1. **ann**ual — y*ear*_____
2. in**aud**ible — h*ear*_____
3. en**am**ored — l*ove*_____
4. re**capit**ulate — h*ead*_____
5. **aqu**iculture — w*ater*_____

6. **cent:** hundred.

Derivatives: *cent, centavo, centenarian, centenary, centennial, centigrade, centigram, centiliter, centime, centimeter, centipede, centuple, centurion, century, tercentennial.*

cent
hundred
century

- The Latin root for *hundred* is c*ent*_____; thus, a *centenarian* has lived a __*hundred*___ years, in other words, an entire ___*cent*___ury.

centigrade

- There are one *hundred* degrees between the freezing and boiling points of water on the __*centigrade*__ [Fahrenheit / centigrade] thermometer.

centimeter	■ One *hundredth* of a meter is a __centimeter__ [centimeter / kilometer].
centigram	■ One *hundredth* of a gram is a __centigram__.
centennial hundred	■ A *centenary*, or __centennial__ ~~ial~~, is celebrated after one __hundred__ years.
2076	■ Since **tri** means *three,* the **tri**centennial of the Declaration of Independence should occur in the year __2076__ [(2076) / 2776]. You are all invited.

7. **cred, credit:** believe; trust.

Derivatives: *accredit, credence, credentials, credible, credit, creditable, creditor, credo, credulity, credulous, creed, discredit.*

cred believable	■ Since the Latin root for *believe* is __cred__ [cred / crud], a *credible* story is __believable__ [believable / absurd].
(b)	■ Your *creed,* or *credo,* is what you (a) fight, (b) believe in. (*b*)
believe	■ To give *credence* to a rumor is to __believe__ [deny / believe] it.
accredited credentials	■ An *ac*__credited__ college hires only those teachers who have proper __credent__ials.
believe	■ Your *credulity* is your readiness to __believe__ [love / believe].
incredulous	■ Sometimes news is so amazing that you are __incredulous__ [cretinous / incredulous].

8. **dic, dict:** say.

Derivatives: *addict, benediction, contradict, dictaphone, dictate, diction, dictograph, dictum, edict, indicative, indict, interdict, jurisdiction, malediction, predicate, predict, valedictorian, verdict.*

dict say	■ The four-letter Latin root of *dictate* and *dictum* is __dict__, and it means s__ay__.
predict	■ To *say* what will happen, or foretell, is to *pre*__dict__.

edict

■ An order issued by an absolute ruler is an _edict_ [edict/audit].

verdict

■ The judgment of a jury is a v _erdict_ .

predicate

■ The part of a sentence which *says* something about the subject is the *pre* _dicate_ .

indicative

■ The mood of a verb that merely states a fact is _indicative_ [subjunctive / indicative].

duck

■ *Dictaphone, contradict, indicate, duck, addict*—which word floated in by mistake? _duck_

9. **duc, duct:** lead.

Derivatives: *abduct, aqueduct, conducive, conduct, deduce, duchess, duct, ductility, duke, educate, educe, Il Duce, induce, introduce, produce, reduce, reproduce, seduction, traduce.*

duc, lead

■ To *educate* is literally to "lead out." The three-letter root of *education* is *d* _uc_ , and it means *l* _ead_ .

Leader

■ Mussolini was called *Il Duce,* which means "The ___ _Lead_ _er._"

dukes

■ Europe has had many princely *leaders* known as _dukes_ [schlemiels / dukes], but America's democratic climate is hardly *con* _ducive_ to the growth of a crop of *dukes* and their wives, _duchess_ _es._

conducive
duchesses

aqueduct

■ Water is sometimes *led* into a city through an *aq* _ueduct_ .

seducer

■ An innocent girl may be *led* astray by a _seducer_ [seducer / centuple].

ductility

■ The ability of a metal to be *led* into various shapes is called ___ _ductility_ [motility / ductility].

10. **fid:** faith; trust.

Derivatives: *affidavit, confidant, confide, confidence, confidential, diffident, fidelity, fiduciary, infidel, perfidious, perfidy.*

faith

■ To *confide* in a stranger is an act of _faith_ [leading / faith].

fid	■ The Latin root for *faith* is *fi**d**_____.
unfaithfulness	■ *Infidelity* means **unfaithfulness** [unfaithfulness / inability to provide].
perfidious	■ In betraying his *trust,* Benedict Arnold did a **perfidious** [perfervid / perfidious] thing; in other words, he committed an act
perfidy	of **perfidy** [perfidy / persiflage].
confident	■ A prizefighter who has *faith* in himself is said to be con **fident**_____.
diffident	■ A lad who is shy and lacks *faith* in himself is said to be **diffident** [amative / diffident].

◼ QUIZ

Write the meaning of each boldface Latin root.

1. say	1. bene**dic**tion	s **ay**
2. hundred	2. **cen**tury	h **undred**
3. faith	3. af**fid**avit	f **aith**
4. lead	4. de**duc**tion	l **ead**
5. believe	5. **cred**ential	b **elieve**

11. **frater:** brother.

Derivatives: *confraternity, frater, fraternal, fraternity, fraternize, fratricide.*

brother	■ *Frater* means b**rother**_____.
brotherly	■ *Fraternal* obligations are **brotherly** [fatherly / brotherly].
fraternize	■ To mingle with conquered people in a social or *brotherly* way is to **frater**_____nize with them.
fratricide	■ Killing one's own *brother* is called **fratri**_____cide.
brother	■ A girls' club should not be called a *fraternity* because *frater* means **brother**_____.
confraternity	■ A *brotherly* group devoted to charitable work is sometimes called a **confraternity** [fiduciary / confraternity].

12. **greg:** flock.

Derivatives: *aggregation, congregate, egregious, gregarious, segregate.*

greg
- The Latin root for *flock* is g **reg**_____.

congregation
- A minister's *flock* is called a con**gregation**_____.

segregation
- Separation from the main group or *flock* is se**gregation**_____.

flock
- Since *greg* means f **lock**_____, we may assume that
society
gregarious people like ____**society**____ [solitude / society].

egregious
- Insulting your teacher during examination week might stand out from your *flock* of lesser mistakes as an **egregious**_____ [egregious / diffident] blunder.

aggregation
- Bismuth is ineligible to play with the football ____**aggregation**____ [aggravation / aggregation].

13. **litera:** letter.

Derivatives: *alliteration, literacy, literal, literalism, literally, literary, literate, literati, literature, transliteration.*

litera
letter
- The Latin root of the word *literary* is l**itera**_____, and it means l**etter**_____.

literal
- Translating *letter* for *letter* results in a ____**liter**____al translation.

illiterate
- A person who can't read or write is *unlettered*, or **illiterate**_____ [illegitimate / illiterate].

literate
literature
- The person who reads and writes is **literate**_____ [literate / libelous] and possibly enjoys **literat**_____ure.

realistically
- *Literalism* in art means drawing things to the *letter,* that is, ____**realistically**____ [realistically / imaginatively].

14. **loc:** place.

Derivatives: *allocate, dislocate, locale, localism, locality, localize, location,* loco citato, *locus, relocate.*

loc
- A three-letter Latin root that means *place* is l**oc**_____.

place	■ The *locale* of a train wreck refers to the __place__ [place / cause].
locality, localism	■ An expression that is used only in a certain *place*, or __locali__ty, is called a __localism__ [barbarism / localism].
locus loci	■ In mathematics the set of points or *places* which satisfy a given condition is called the __loc__us. The plural of *locus* is __loci__ [locusts / loci].
place	■ In footnotes *loco citato* is abbreviated as *loc. cit.* and means "in the p__lace__ cited."

15. **loqu, locut:** talk.

Derivatives: *allocution, circumlocution, colloquial, colloquium, colloquy, elocution, eloquent, grandiloquent, interlocutor, loquacious, prolocutor, soliloquy.*

talkative	■ A *loquacious* child is __talkative__ [sulky / talkative].
colloquial	■ Most people talk informally, that is, in __colloquial__ [literary / colloquial] English.
locut	■ In *interlocutor* and *locution* the five-letter root that suggests *talk* is __locut__.
eloquent	■ Webster was an inspired *talker;* in fact, he was often el__oquent__.
grandiloquent	■ A windy orator who uses grand, phony expressions is __grandiloquent__ [magnanimous / grandiloquent].
circumlocution	■ Saying a thing in a roundabout way is known as __circumlocution__ [circumspection / circumlocution].

QUIZ

Write the meaning of each boldface Latin root.

1. talk	1. **eloqu**ent	talk
2. brother	2. **fratern**al	brother
3. flock	3. con**greg**ation	flock
4. letter	4. al**liter**ation	letter
5. place	5. dis**locate**	place

16. **mal:** bad.

Derivatives: *maladjusted, maladminister, maladroit, malaise, malapropos, malaria, malcontent,* mal de mer, *malediction, malefactor, malevolent, malfeasance, malformed, malice, malign, malignant, malinger, malnutrition, malocclusion, malodorous, malpractice.*

bad

■ *Malfeasance* in office refers to ___*bad*___ [bad / admirable] conduct.

bad

■ *Mal* means *bad*___.

malignant

■ The truly *bad* tumors are the ___*malignant*___ [benign / malignant] ones.

(b)

■ To hurl *maledictions* is to fling (a) small rocks, (b) evil words or curses. (*b*)

malevolent

■ Evil wishers are ___*malevolent*___ [benevolent / malevolent].

bad

■ *Malaise* is physical discomfort that hints of ___*bad*___ [good / bad] health.

maladroit

■ A clumsy child is said to be ___*maladroit*___ [maladroit / adroit].

malnutrition

■ A badly nourished child suffers from ___*malnutri*___tion.

malodorous

■ Goats don't smell good; they are ___*mal*___odorous.

17. **mor, mort:** death.

Derivatives: *immortal, moribund, mortal, mortality, mortgage, mortician, mortify, mortuary, postmortem,* rigor mortis.

death

■ The root *mort* suggests that a *mortician* is concerned with ___*death*___ [birth / death].

mortuary
mortis

■ The *mortician* operates a funeral home, which is known as a ___*mortua*___ry, and he is, no doubt, acquainted with the *stiffness of death* known as *rigor mortis*___.

dying
immortal

■ Greeting card sellers complain that the custom of sending valentines is *moribund*—that is, ___*dying*___ [too lively / dying]. If the custom never died, it would be ___*immortal*___ [immortal / immoral].

(a)

■ If you develop gangrene, your flesh *mortifies;* this means that it (a) decays and dies, (b) glows with health. (*a*)

18. **nov:** new.

Derivatives: *innovation, nova, Nova Scotia, novel, novelette, novella, novelty, novice, novitiate, novocain, renovate.*

new
■ The letters *nov* in *novelty* mean n *ew* _____.

new
■ An *innovation* is a _____ *new* _____ [crazy / new] idea or custom.

novice
novitiate
■ In a religious order a *new* member is called a _____ *nov* __ice and the probationary period is a _____ *noviti*ate.

(b)
■ A *nova* star is (a) a faithful old planet, (b) a brilliant new exploding star. (*b*)

renovate
new
■ When our landlord promises to _____ *renov*ate our apartment, we hope he knows that the word-root *nov* means *new* _____ [air / new].

19. **omni:** all.

Derivatives: *omniactive, omnibenevolent, omnibus, omnificent, omnipotent, omnipresent, omniprevalent, omniscient, omnium-gatherum, omnivorous.*

omni
■ In the words *omniscient* (all-knowing) and *omnipotent* (all-powerful) the four-letter root that means *all* is *omni* _____.

many
■ An *omnium-gatherum* is a collection of _____ *many* _____ [many / one or two] different things.

omnivorous
■ The cannibals ate anything—grass, bugs, missionaries. They were absolutely *omnivorous* [dyspeptic / omnivorous].

all
■ Because *omni* means _____ *all* _____ [all / small], we can assume that an *omnivorous* reader reads (a) only the funnies, (b) practically everything. (*b*)

(b)

omnibuses
■ To transport loads of students, a school usually buys *omnibuses* _____ [compacts / omnibuses].

20. **ped:** foot.

Derivatives: *biped, centipede, expedient, expedite, expedition, impediment, pedal, pedestal, pedestrian, pedometer, quadruped, sesquipedalian.*

foot

■ A *pedestrian* travels by ___*foot*___ [foot / jet plane].

ped

■ The three-letter word-root meaning *foot* is p _ed_____.

walked

■ A *pedometer* measures the distance ___*walked*___ [driven / walked].

biped

■ A man has two *feet* and so according to Aristotle man is a featherless ___*biped*___ [biped / slob].

feet

■ An *impediment* is literally something that obstructs or hinders the ___*feet*___ [feet / meals].

(a)

■ To *expedite* means, in a sense, to free the *feet,* hence, (a) to speed up the action, (b) to snarl things up. (*a*)

QUIZ

Write the meaning of each boldface Latin root.

1. death	1. **mort**uary	d _ea th_
2. all	2. **omni**potent	a _ll_
3. foot	3. quadru**ped**	f _eet_
4. new	4. in**nov**ation	n _ew_
5. bad	5. **mal**icious	b _ad_

Write True or False.

True	1. A *pedestrian* is one who walks.
True	2. An *innovation* is something newly introduced.
False	3. A *localism* is a universally popular pet phrase.
True	4. A *literal* translation follows the original very closely.
False	5. A *dictum* is someone injured in an accident.
True	6. *Loquacity* refers to talkativeness.
False	7. The name *Il Duce* means the "deuce" or "two-spot."

Write the meaning of each boldface Latin root. The first letter of each answer is given.

8. an **egregi**ous idiot   f_lock_

9. an in**cred**ible plot   b_elieve_

10. a Robert Frost **cent**ennial   h_undred_

11. an **am**orous sonnet   l_ove_

12. the im**mort**al Chaucer   d_eath_

13. a **frater**nity of poets   b_rother_

14. guilty of **mal**practice   b_ad_

15. **aqu**atic sports   w_ater_

Write the letter that indicates the best completion.

(_d_) 16. An *infidel* is one who has no (a) married parents, (b) schooling, (c) musical ability, (d) religious faith.

(_c_) 17. An *audible* kiss is one that (a) lasts a long time, (b) can be seen, (c) can be heard, (d) gives off steam.

(_b_) 18. That which is *omnipresent* is (a) nowhere, (b) everywhere, (c) a welcome gift, (d) invisible.

(_b_) 19. The Latin root for *head* is used in which word?—(a) aquatint, (b) caption, (c) deception, (d) amour.

(_a_) 20. The Latin root for *year* is used in which word?—(a) perennial, (b) banana, (c) birthday, (d) decade.

Check your test answers with the following key. Deduct 5% per error from a possible 100%.

1. True
2. True
3. False
4. True
5. False
6. True
7. False

8. flock
9. believe
10. hundred
11. love
12. death
13. brother
14. bad

15. water
16. (d)
17. (c)
18. (b)
19. (b)
20. (a)

Score: _____ %

Latin Derivatives II

CHAPTER 4

Roots

port, portat, **1**	sequ, secut, **8**	terra, **15**
prim, **2**	sign, **9**	tort, **16**
reg, **3**	sol, **10**	urb, **17**
rupt, **4**	son, **11**	vac, **18**
sanct, **5**	spec, spect, **12**	vit, viv, **19**
scrib, script, **6**	spir, spirat, **13**	voc, vocat, **20**
seg, sect, **7**	tempor, **14**	

This chapter continues our study of Latin roots and their derivatives. Follow the same procedure as in the previous chapter.

EXERCISES

Roots

1. **port, portat:** carry.

   Derivatives: *comport, deport, disport, export, import, portable, portage, portfolio, porter, portmanteau, purport, rapport, report, support, transport.*

   ■ The words *porter, export,* and *purport* all have the root
   port _____ *carry* _____, which means c~~arry~~ _____.

port, carry

   ■ One can easily *trans*~~port~~ _____ a ~~portable~~ _~~able~~
   typewriter, a ~~portfolio~~ _~~io~~ (briefcase), or a
   ~~portman~~ _____*teau* (leather suitcase that opens into two
   compartments like a book).

transport, portable
portfolio,
portmanteau

   ■ To make a *portage* between lakes means (a) to carry gear, (b) to
   stop for lunch. (a)

(a)

   ■ Your ~~deportment~~ _*ment* is your behavior or way of *carrying*
   yourself.

deportment

2. **prim:** first.

   Derivatives: *prima donna, primal, primarily, primary, primate, prime, prime minister, primer, primeval, primitive, primitivism, primogeniture, primordial, primrose, primula.*

prime

   ■ The *first* or top statesperson in England is the ~~prime~~ _____
   minister.

prima

   ■ The first female singer in opera is the ~~prima~~ _____*a* donna.

primula, primrose
prim

   ■ We can assume that the *first* flowers of spring include the
   ~~prim~~ _____*ula*—also called ~~prim~~ _____*rose*—because
   the Latin root ~~prim~~ _____ means "first."

primary
primer

   ■ We *first* went to a ~~primary~~ _~~ry~~ school, and our *first* book
   was a ~~primer~~ _~~er~~.

first

   ■ The system of *primogeniture* provided that one's estate and title
   went to the son who was born ~~first~~ _____ [first / last].

primarily

■ Breathing through your nose is wise, _____*primari*_ ly (mainly) because it keeps your mouth shut.

3. **reg:** rule.

Derivatives: *interregnum, irregular, regal, regalia, regency, regent, regicide, regime, regiment, Regina, region, regular, regulate, regulation.*

regulation
(a)

■ A soldier must obey an army _____*regula*_____ tion because the *reg* in *regulation* means (a) "rule," (b) "fool around." (*a*)

regiment
regalia

■ If you join our _____*regi*_ ment, you must wear our _____*regal*_ ia (official decorations).

Regina
region, regal

■ Elizabeth _____*Regina*_ na (Queen) *ruled* the entire _____*regi*_ on in a _____*reg*_ al (royal) manner.

■ In 1649 King Charles I was beheaded, an act of

regicide, irregular

_____*regic*_ ide as ir*regular*_____ as it was barbaric.

regimen

■ My doctor ordered me to follow a _____*regimen*_ men (health system) of tasteless food and hard exercise.

■ The *regents* evidently run a university, because the three-letter

reg

Latin root _____*reg*_____ means "rule."

4. **rupt:** break.

Derivatives: *corrupt, disrupt, erupt, interrupt, rupture.*

■ You're breaking into our conversation. Please don't

interrupt

in *terrupt*_____ us.

corrupt

■ Bribed? Then "Honest Abe" Jones is co*rrupt*_____ !

rupt

■ The Latin root for *break* is _*rupt*_____ .

erupt

■ Soon this rumbling volcano will e*rupt*_____ (break out).

rupture

■ Uncle Rudy dug deep and managed to _____*rupt* re (break) a gas main. For good measure, the heavy lifting gave Rudy an

rupture

abdominal _____*rupt* re.

disrupt

■ Hecklers may dis*rupt*_____ the political rally.

5. **sanct:** holy.

Derivatives: *sanctified, sanctify, sanctimonious, sanctimony, sanction, sanctitude, sanctity, sanctuary, sanctum, sanctorum.*

sanctified
- The Normandy beach is *holy* ground, __satisfied__ *ied* by the blood of American soldiers.

holy

sanctum, sanctorum
- Since *sanct* means __holy__ [drowned / holy], we refer to the *holy* of *holies* as the __sanctum__ *um* __sanctorum__ *um.*

sanctuary
- A church is a true __sanctua__ *ry* (holy refuge).

sanction
- Slavery? How can any nation __sanctio__ *n* (approve) it?

sanctimonious
- Tartuffe speaks __sanctimoni__ *ous* (pretending to be holy) words, but what a difference between the hypocrite's

sanctimony, sanctity
__sanctimo__ *ny* and genuine __sanctity__ *ty!*

QUIZ

Write the meaning of each boldface Latin root.

1. carry
2. holy
3. rule
4. break
5. first

1. **por**table — ~~carry~~ carry
2. **sanct**uary — ~~holy~~ holy
3. **reg**ulation — r ule
4. **erupt**ion — b reak
5. **prim**itive — f irst

6. **scrib, script:** write.

Derivatives: *ascribe, circumscribe, conscription, describe, inscribe, manuscript, nondescript, postscript, prescribe, proscribe, scribble, scribe, scripture, subscribe, transcribe, typescript.*

scrib, write
- The five-letter root of *subscribe, proscribe,* and *inscribe* is __scrib__, and it means w rite __.

postscript
- An afterthought *written* at the end of a letter is a p ostscript __.

conscription
- The army draft, or enrollment, is known as con scription __.

written	■ The Scriptures were so named because they were _written_ [sung / (written)], possibly _transcribed_ [transfused / (transcribed)] into beautiful *manuscripts* by industrious _scribes_ [porters / scribes].
transcribed	
manuscripts	
scribes	
prescription	■ My doctor peered at my tongue, then hastily wrote a *prescription* .
(b)	■ A *nondescript* dog is (a) a very individual type, (b) hardly individual enough to be written about. (*b*)

7. **seg, sect:** cut.

Derivatives: *antivivisection, bisect, dissect, intersect, sect, sectarian, section, sector, segment, trisect, vivisection.*

intersect	■ Our streets *cut* across one another, so let's meet where they *intersect* .
bisect,	■ *Cut* angle A into two equal parts and angle B into three equal parts; in other words, *bisect* angle A and *trisect* angle B.
trisect	
sect	■ Members of a strange religious _sect_ (cult) live in my _sect_ on (part) of town.
section	
sectarian	■ Splitting away from the main church are several small _sectar_ian groups.
vivisection	■ *Cutting* into a live animal for medical research is known as *vivisection* ; opposition to such experiments is *antivivisection* .
antivivisection	

8. **sequ, secut:** follow.

Derivatives: *consecutive, consequently, execution, executive, obsequies, obsequious, persecute, prosecute, sequel, sequence, subsequently.*

subsequently	■ *Tom Sawyer* was a success, and *subsequently* (at a following time) Mark Twain wrote a *sequel*el (followup) about Huck Finn.
sequel	
consecutive	■ If this baseball team loses eleven *consecutive* (in a row) games, these fans will hang the coach and won't even attend the *obsequies* (funeral rites).
obsequies	

(a)	■ The roots *sequ, secut* mean (a) follow, (b) sexy. (a)
obsequious	■ Lord Bigmouth had a *following* of *obsequious* (submissive) servants.
sequence	■ Shakespeare describes the seven ages of man in *se quence* (order), from infancy to feeble old age.
Consequently	■ Gravitation works day and night. *Consequently* (as a result), my lawn is covered with oak leaves.
prosecute persecute	■ In America we may *prosecute* (put on trial) a person in court; but we do not *per secute* (cruelly harass) our citizens.

9. **sign:** sign.

Derivatives: *assign, consign, countersign, design, designate, ensign, insignia, resign, signal, signalize, signatory, signature, signet, significant, signify.*

sign, sign	■ In the words *signalize, countersign,* and *designate* the root is ___sign___, and—who'd guess it?—means ___sign___.
signature	■ *Sign* the check with your own ___signa___ture.
signet	■ An initial or other special *sign* is carried on a ___signet___ [signet / garnet] ring.
an ensign	■ A military banner or other *sign* of authority is known as ___an ensign___ [lasagne / an ensign].
signatory	■ Countries that have *signed* a treaty are ___signatory___ [secessionist / signatory] nations.
sign assignment	■ Remember that the Latin root *sign* means ___sign___. If necessary, repeat it ten times—what an ___assign___ment!

10. **sol:** alone.

Derivatives: *desolation, isolate, sole, soliloquy, solitaire, solitary, solitude, solo.*

solitaire	■ Boomer sat *alone,* playing ___solitaire___ re.
solitary	■ The vicious prisoner was put in ___solitary___ y confinement.

solo, solitude

- I warbled my _____ _sol_ o, "In my _____ _solitu_ de I
  dream of you"—and my canary threw seeds at me.

isolate

- Smallpox? Then we must is_olate_ _____ you!

sole
soliloquy

- Macbeth was now the _____ _sole_ _____ character on stage. As
  though thinking aloud, he began his _____ _soliloquy_.

QUIZ

Write the meaning of each boldface Latin root.

1. cut
2. sign
3. alone
4. follow
5. write

1. bi**sect**   c _ut_
2. in**sign**ia   s _ign_
3. **isol**ation   a _lone_
4. con**secu**tive   f _ollow_
5. in**scribe**   w _rite_

---

11. **son:** sound.

   Derivatives: *assonance, consonance, resonance, sonar, sonata,
   sonatina, sonic, sonics, sonnet, sonorous, supersonic.*

sonic, supersonic

- The plane burst through the *sound* barrier, letting out a
  _____ _sonic_ _____ boom, and accelerated to *super_sonic_* _____
  (faster than sound) speeds.

dissonance

- Such discordant *sounds!* Such dis_sonance_ _____!

sonata
sonatina
resonance

- Yasha pounded out a four-movement Mozart _____ _sona_ ta
  and a short _____ _sonati_ na, then told us our piano had fine
  re_sonance_ _____ (vibrant sound).

sound

- The Latin root *son* means _____ _sound_ [boy / s⟨ound⟩].

sonar

- We located the sunken ship by means of *sound*-wave apparatus
  called _____ _sonar_.

sonnet, sonorous

- The poet read his _____ _sonne_ t in a rich _____ _sonor_ ous
  (deep and vibrant) voice.

12. **spec, spect:** look.

Derivatives: *aspect, circumspect, inspect, introspection, perspective, prospect, respect, retrospect, spectacle, specter, spectroscope, spectrum.*

spect
look

- The root in *inspect, aspect,* and *prospect* is ___*spect*___ , and it means *l*_____.

circumspect

- To be cautious and *look* around before acting is to be ___*circumspect*___ [circumspect / circumscript].

introspection

- Marcel Proust had a habit of *looking* into his mind and memories—he was given to ___*introspection*___ [introspection / interdiction].

retrospect

- *Looking* back he saw things in *ret*___*rospect*___ .

perspective

- Another viewpoint would have given him a different *per*___*spective*___ .

(d)

- One word that did *not* develop from the root for *look* is (a) specter, (b) spectrum, (c) spectacles, (d) spaghetti. (*d*)

13. **spir, spirat:** breathe.

Derivatives: *aspirate, aspire, conspire, expire, inspire, perspire, respiration, spiracle, spirit, spirometer.*

breathe

- *Spirat* means ___*breathe*___ [spin / breathe].

respiration
perspiration

- To *breathe* through the lungs is called *res*___*piration*___ ; to *breathe*—or seep—through the skin is *per*___*spiration*___ .

spiracle

- The zoological term for a whale's breathing hole is ___*spiracle*___ [spiracle / oracle].

spirit
expired

- In the sea battle Captain Ahab yielded up his ___*spirit*___ and *ex*___*pired*___ .

spirometer

- A machine which measures one's lung capacity, or *breath,* is called a ___*spirometer*___ [spectroscope / spirometer].

(a)

- Poetic *inspiration* was originally thought to be (a) a breathing in of a divine influence, (b) the product of indigestion. (*a*)

14. **tempor:** time.

Derivatives: *contemporary, extemporaneous, extempore, extemporize, pro tem, tempo, temporal, temporary, temporize.*

contemporary

- Emerson and Thoreau lived at the same *time*—they were **_contemporary_** [congruent / contemporary] writers.

tempor

- The root **_tempor_** means *time*.

time
temporarily

- To be chairperson *pro tem* means "for the **_time_** being," or **_temporar_** ily.

extemporaneous

- Talks or remarks made at the *time* without preparation are said to be **_extemporaneous_** [extenuating / extemporaneous].

temporize

- To delay, or consume *time,* by needless discussions is to **_temporize_** [temporize / expedite].

tempo

- Parade music has a brisk **_tempo_**.

15. **terra:** earth.

Derivatives: *disinter, inter, terrace, terra cotta, terra firma, terramycin, terraqueous, terrazzo, terrestrial, terrier, territory.*

earth

- *Terra firma* refers to firm **_earth_** [water / earth].

terra

- Unglazed, brown-red *earthenware* is known as t**_erra_** cotta.

(a)

- *Terrain* has to do with (a) land surfaces, (b) ammunition. (**a**)

terrestrial

- The *earth's land* as distinct from water is **_terrestrial_** [global / terrestrial].

terrier

- A small hunting dog which burrowed into the *earth* for small game was called a **_terrier_**.

(b)

- A body that is *interred* has been (a) cremated, (b) buried. (**b**)

Write the meaning of each boldface Latin root.

1. sound
2. breathe
3. look
4. time
5. earth

1. super**son**ic — s _ound_
2. in**spir**e — b _reathe_
3. per**spect**ive — l _ook_
4. con**tempor**ary — t _ime_
5. **terr**itory — e _arth_

16. **tort:** twist.

   Derivatives: *contortion, distort, retort, tort, tortoise, tortuous, torture.*

distort
- Scowls will *di_ctort_* _____ your face, so smile.

contortion
- The acrobat *twisted* into an odd con _tortion_ _____.

retort
- Groucho was quick with a *re _tort_* _____ (witty reply).

torture
- *Twisting* the limbs to encourage confessions or religious conversion was a type of medieval _____ _tortu_ re.

tort
- The Latin root *t_ort_* _____ means "twist."

twist
- Tabloids are guilty of *distortions.* This means that they __ _twist_ __ [verify / (twist)] the facts.

tort
- In law, an injury for which you can sue is a __ _tort_ __ [(tort)/ sanct].

tortuous
tortoise
- The road was so steep and _____ _tortu_ ous (twisted) that a __ _tortoi_ _se passed us twice.

17. **urb:** city.

   Derivatives: *interurban, suburban, suburbanite, suburbs, urban, urbane, urbanism, urbanite, urbanity, urbanize.*

city
- To *urbanize* a district is to make it become like a _city_ _____ [(city)/ farm].

urb
- The three-letter Latin root that means *city* is u_rb_ _____.

interurban
- Buses that travel between *cities* are *in_ter urban_* _____.

suburbs

■ On the outskirts of the *cities* lie the ___suburbs___ [subways / suburbs].

(a)

urbanities

■ An *urbane* fellow is (a) polished and suave, (b) countrified and crude. (*a*) He is accustomed to those *citified* refinements of manners known as the ___urbanities___ [gaucheries / urbanities].

18. **vac:** empty.

   Derivatives: *evacuate, vacancy, vacant, vacate, vacation, vacuity, vacuous, vacuum.*

evacuate

■ Floods made us e___vacuate___ our homes.

vacation

■ It rained during our ___vacati___ on abroad, and in the hotels we "got soaked" in more ways than one.

vacate

■ "Pay for your room or ___vacate___," growled the manager.

vac

vacuum

■ The three-letter root ___vac___ means *empty,* and nothing is *emptier* than a ___vacuum___ um.

vacancy

vacant

■ As soon as the landlord has a ___vacanc___ y, he'll rent us the ___vacan___ t apartment.

vacuous

■ Look alert. The professor will throw questions at you if you wear a ___vacuou___ s expression.

(b)

■ A reference to your "mental *vacuity*" should be taken as (a) a compliment, (b) criticism. (*b*)

19. **vit, viv:** life.

   Derivatives: *convivial, devitalized, revive, vital, vitality, vitals, vitamin, vivace, vivacious, vivid, vivify, viviparous, vivisection.*

vital

■ Desdemona was ___vital___ (essential) to his happiness, and because she was dead, Othello stabbed himself in the

vitals

___vita___ ls (heart, lungs, etc.).

devitalized

■ If you eat de___vitalized___ (energy-deprived) foods, you'd

vitamin

better take ___vitam___ in pills.

vitality

■ Buster is a bundle of ___vitali___ ty (energy).

convivial

■ Flo and Moe love food, friends, and *life.* In other words, they're con___vival___ people.

vivid
vivacious
vivace

■ I have a _____ **vivi** d (lifelike) memory of my
_____ **vivaci** ous (lively) grandmother tootling the
_____ **viva** ce (lively) movement of a Sousa march on her
piccolo.

■ Most mammals bring forth *living* young rather than eggs; in other
viviparous
words, they are _____ **vivipar** ous.

vivisection
revive

■ My pet was a laboratory victim of _____ **vivisection** (cutting a
live animal). We were unable to re**vive** _____ my beloved
cat.

20. **voc, vocat: call.**

Derivatives: *advocate, avocation, convocation, equivocal, evoke,
invoke, irrevocable, provoke, revoke, vocable, vocabulary, vocal,
vocation, vociferous.*

convocation

■ A *calling* together of students to assembly is a _____ **convocation**
[(convocation) / convection].

spoken
call

■ *Vocal* promises are _____ **spoken** [written / (spoken)]; after all,
the root *voc* means c **all** _____.

vocation

■ Your career job, or *calling,* is your _____ **vocat** ion.

avocation

■ Your hobby is your av **ocation** _____.

invokes

■ At the beginning of his epic, the poet Homer **invokes** _____
[(invokes) / inspires] the gods.

invocation

■ Today a minister usually gives the in**vocation** _____.

QUIZ

Write the meaning of each boldface Latin root.

1. twist
2. call
3. life
4. empty
5. city

1. dis**tort**ion   t **wist**
2. irre**voc**able   c **all**
3. de**vit**alized   l **ife**
4. **vac**uum   e**mpty**
5. sub**urb**an   c **ity**

Write True or False.

False	1. An *obsequious* person has a regal manner.
True	2. To *temporize* is to delay.
False	3. An *equivocal* remark is clear and vivid.
True	4. A *sanctuary* is a fairly safe place.
False	5. The *primrose* is a late bloomer.
True	6. *Nondescript* houses are quite undistinguished.
False	7. A *circumspect* fellow is reckless.

Write the meaning of each boldface Latin root. The first letter of each answer is given.

8. good re**son**ance   s _ound_

9. **urb**an problems   c _ity_

10. a Republican **reg**ime   r _ule_

11. a **rupt**ured lung   b _reak_

12. dis**tort**ed features   t _wist_

13. a game of **sol**itaire   a _lone_

14. to e**vac**uate the city   e _mpty_

15. inter**sect**ing highways   c _ut_

Write the letter that best completes the sentence.

(_d_) 16. *Respiration* refers to (a) the heart, (b) sweat, (c) first aid, (d) breathing.

(_b_) 17. An example of a *viviparous* creature is (a) an eagle, (b) a rabbit, (c) a chicken, (d) a butterfly.

(_b_) 18. To *disinter* a body is to take it out of (a) the water, (b) the earth, (c) a hospital, (d) wreckage.

(_c_) 19. *Portable* television sets are, by definition, (a) in color, (b) solid state (c) able to be carried, (d) manufactured abroad.

(_a_) 20. A *signet* ring has on it (a) a sign, (b) an emerald, (c) a diamond, (d) a curse.

Check your test answers with the following key. Deduct 5% per error from a possible 100%.

1. False	8. sound	15. cut
2. True	9. city	16. (d)
3. False	10. rule	17. (b)
4. True	11. break	18. (b)
5. False	12. twist	19. (c)
6. True	13. alone	20. (a)
7. False	14. empty	

Score:＿＿＿＿＿＿%

Latin Derivatives III

CHAPTER 5

Prefixes

ad, **1**	mis, **10**	semi, **19**
ante, **2**	multi, **11**	sub, **20**
bi, **3**	post, **12**	super, **21**
circum, **4**	pre, **13**	trans, **22**
co, **5**	pro, **14**	tri, **23**
contra, contro, counter, **6**	quadr, **15**	ultra, **24**
de, **7**	quasi, **16**	uni, **25**
inter, **8**	quint, **17**	
intra, intro, **9**	retro, **18**	

A knowledge of Latin prefixes is indispensable to a mastery of English vocabulary. Prefixes multiply the use we make of roots.

For example, we have seen that *scrib, script* mean "write," and that with prefixes we get combinations like *circumscribe, conscription, describe, inscribe, nondescript, postscript, prescribe, proscribe, subscribe,* and *transcribe.* These prefixes are a key to the meaning of such combinations.

Sometimes the spelling of a prefix is modified for the sake of pronunciation. For instance, the prefix *sub,* meaning "under," changes to *suc* in *succinct* and to *sup* in *supplant;* the prefix *ad,* meaning "to," changes to *af* in *affiliate* and to *an* in *annul.* The process is called *assimilation.*

Time has a way of changing the spelling, meaning, and application of words; so we should be ready to supplement our analysis of word parts by consulting a dictionary.

In this chapter, we will focus on twenty-five basic prefixes and their most common meanings.

Prefixes

1. **ad:** to; toward.

    Examples: *adhesive, admissible, advocate.*

adhesive

■ A substance such as tape that sticks *to* other things is _____ *adhesi* ve.

advocate

■ To speak in favor of a measure is to _____ *advocate* [advocate / deprecate] it.

may

■ *Admissible* evidence _____ *may* [may / may not] be brought into a court case.

■ The prefix *ad* is slippery and often changes to an "assimilated" form. It appears, for example, as *ac* in *accord* (because *adcord* would be hard to pronounce). Other assimilated forms of *ad*

al

an, as

   include *ag* in *aggressive*, _____ *al* _____ in *allude*, _____ *an* _____ in *annex*, and _____ *as* _____ in *assign*.

2. **ante:** before.

    Examples: *antebellum, antedate, anterior.*

before

■ *Antebellum* days came _____ *before* [before / after] the Civil War.

antedated

■ The Civil War _____ *antedated* [antedated / succeeded] World War I.

anterior

■ That which is toward the front or which comes *before* is _____ *anterior* [anterior / posterior].

3. **bi:** two.

    Examples: *bicameral, bifocal, bipartisan.*

two

■ A *bicameral* legislature has ___two___ [one / (two)] chambers.

bifocals

■ Glasses with *two* different focal lengths are called ___bifocals___ [monocles / bifocals].

bipartisan

■ A committee which represents *two* parties is ___bipartisan___ [bipartisan / partisan].

4. **circum:** around.

Examples: *circa, circumference, circumvent.*

circumference

■ The line *around* a circle is the ___circumference___ [(circumference) / diameter].

(a)

■ To *circumvent* the villain is ((a)) to get around him and outwit him, (b) to fall into his trap. (*a*)

about

■ Dante's *Divine Comedy* was written *circa* 1320, that is, ___about___ [after / (about)] 1320.

5. **co:** together.

Examples: *coagulate, coeducation, coexistence, coincidence.*

(a)

■ When blood or any other fluid *coagulates,* it ((a)) clumps together, (b) gets thinner. (*a*)

together

■ *Coeducation* refers to the teaching of male and female students ___together___ [together / separately].

coexistence

■ People of different religions and ideologies should strive for peaceful ___coexis ten___ ce (living together).

coincidence

■ My birthday and my bypass operation on the same day? What a co___Incidence___!

con, cor

■ The prefix *co* is assimilated as *com* in *compassion,* as *col* in *collate,* as ___con___ in *congenital,* and as ___cor___ in *correlate.*

Write the meaning of each boldface Latin prefix.

1. together
2. to
3. before
4. two
5. around

1. **co**operate   _together_
2. **ad**join   _to_
3. **ante**cedent   _before_
4. **bi**nomial   _two_
5. **circum**navigate   _around_

6. **contra, contro, counter:** against.

     Examples: _contraband, controvert, countercharge._

(b)

■ A _countercharge_ is (a) an admission of guilt, (b) a charge by the accused against the accuser. (**b**)

controvert

■ To argue _against_ a certain idea is to ___controvert___ [corroborate / controvert] it.

illegal

■ _Contraband_ is ___illegal___ [legal / illegal] merchandise.

7. **de:** away; down.

     Examples: _degradation, delusion, derision._

down

■ Those who live in _degradation_ are usually far ___down___ [up / down] on the socioeconomic ladder.

delusions

■ The lunatic was lured _away_ from reality by ___delusions___ [delusions / allusions] of grandeur.

(a)

■ An object of _derision_, Fulton was greeted by (a) jeers and ridicule, (b) warm applause. (**a**)

8. **inter:** between.

     Examples: _intercultural, interlinear, interregnum._

between

■ An _interlinear_ translation has the meaning inserted ___between___ [opposite / between] the lines.

between

■ The _interregnum_ is the period ___between___ [during / between] the rule of kings.

intercultural

■ Relations *between* cultural groups are said to be _interacultural_ [intercultural]/ subcultural].

9. **intra, intro:** within.

Examples: *intramuscular, intrastate, intravenous.*

within

■ *Intramuscular* pains are ___within___ [between / within] the muscles.

intravenous

■ An injection *within* a vein is ___intravenous___ [intervenous / intravenous].

Albany

■ *Intrastate* commerce goes on between New York City and ___Albany___ [Chicago / Albany].

10. **mis:** wrong, bad.

Examples: *misadventure, misdemeanor, misnomer.*

misadventure

■ We enjoyed our picnic, except for the ___misadventure___ (accident) involving the rattlesnake.

(a)

■ Overtime parking is *wrong* behavior of a minor sort. It is therefore classed as a (a) misdemeanor, (b) felony. (a)

(b)

■ Our plumber is called Speedy, but that's a *misnomer* (wrong name). He is actually very (a) fast, (b) slow. (b)

QUIZ

Write the meaning of each boldface Latin prefix.

1. within	1. **intra**state	w _ithin_
2. wrong	2. **mis**treat	w _rong_
3. between	3. **inter**change	b _etween_
4. against	4. **contra**dict	a _gainst_
5. away	5. **de**parture	a _way_

11. **multi:** many.

Examples: *multimillionaire, multiped, multitude.*

many

■ A *multiped* insect has ___many___ [many / two] feet.

are not

■ If your possessions are worth $3,469.12, you __are not__ [are /~~are not~~] a *multimillionaire*.

■ The ninety thousand frantic spectators at a soccer game are quite a __multitude__ [multitude / solitude].

multitude

12. **post:** after.

Examples: *posterior, posterity, posthumous.*

after

■ Mark Twain's *The Mysterious Stranger* was published *posthumously*, that is, __after__ [before /~~after~~] his death.

posterity

■ Those generations which come *after* us are our __posterity__ [ancestors /~~posterity~~].

posterior

■ That part of us which comes *after* us is our __posterior__.

13. **pre:** before.

Examples: *preamble, precedence, prejudice.*

before

■ That which has *precedence* comes __before__ [~~before~~/ after] the rest.

before

■ The word *prejudice* implies that a judgment is made __before__ [~~before~~ / after] the facts are studied.

preamble

■ The beginning of a constitution is a good place for the __preamble__ [amendments /~~preamble~~].

14. **pro:** forward; favoring.

Examples: *progeny, prognosis, prolabor.*

prognosis

■ The doctor noted gloomily that I had contracted leprosy and gave me his __prog n__is (medical forecast).

progeny
(a)

■ Those interested in their __proge__ ny (offspring) tend to look ~~(a)~~ forward, (b) backward. (a)

prolabor

■ Gary and Mary argue constantly because he is promanagement and she is __prolab__ or (favorable to workers).

15. **quadr:** four.

Examples: *quadrangle, quadrant, quadruplets.*

quadrants

- The pie graph was equally divided into four _____ *quadran* ts.

quadruplets

- After taking a fertility drug the woman gave birth to _____ *quadruple* ts.

four, four

- A *quadrangle,* as on a college campus, is an area with _____ *four* _____ sides and _____ *four* _____ angles.

QUIZ

Write the meaning of each boldface Latin prefix.

1. many
2. before
3. four
4. after
5. forward

1. **mult**itude _____ m *any*
2. **pre**natal _____ b *efore*
3. **quad**rangle _____ f *our*
4. **post**pone _____ a *fter*
5. **pro**pel _____ f *orward*

---

16. **quasi** (kwā′sī): seemingly but not actually.

Examples: *quasi-antique, quasi-poetry, quasi-scientific.*

does not

- A writer who refers to "the *quasi-scientific* mumbo-jumbo of astrology" _____ *does not* [does / (does not)] believe that astrology is a true science.

quasi-poetry

- At Gettysburg, Lincoln's words—noble and rhythmical—were _____ *quasi* -poetry.

(b)

- Sandstorms battered our new desert home, quickly turning it into (a) a genuine antique, ((b)) a quasi-antique. (*b*)

17. **quint:** five.

Examples: *quintessence, quintet, quintuplets.*

quintet

- Our woodwind _____ *quinte* t (five musicians) played Mozart, and I think Mozart lost.

fifth

- Their first kiss was the *quintessence*—that is, the ultimate or _____fifth_____ [third / (fifth)] essence—of happiness.

quintuplets

- "I'm pooped," said the stork. "I just brought Mrs. Shlep a set of _____quintuple*ts*_____" (five offspring).

18. **retro:** back.

   .Examples: *retroactive, retrogress, retrorocket.*

(b)

- If civilization is *retrogressing*, it is (a) improving (b) going back to a worse condition. (*b*)

retard

- A *retrorocket* tends to _____retard_____ [speed up / (retard)] a space ship.

retroactive

- A law or ruling which affects an earlier period is _____retroactive_____ [(retroactive) / radioactive].

19. **semi:** half.

   Examples: *semicentennial, semidiameter, semilunar.*

half

- A *semilunar* shape is like that of the _____half_____ [full / (half)] moon.

fifty

- *Semicentennials* celebrate a period of _____fifty_____ years.

radius

- The *semidiameter* of a circle is equal to its _____radius_____ [(radius) / circumference].

20. **sub:** under.

   Examples: *subconscious, subcutaneous, subtrahend.*

under

- The *subconscious* operates _____under_____ [within / (under)] the conscious mind.

under

- A *subcutaneous* infection is _____under_____ [on / (under)] the skin.

subtrahend

- In subtraction the number written *under* the other number is called the _____subtrahend_____ [(subtrahend) / minuend].

Write the meaning of each boldface Latin prefix.

1. five
2. half
3. under
4. not actually
5. back

1. **quint**et   _five_
2. **semi**tone   _half_
3. **sub**marine   _under_
4. **quasi**-bargain   _not actually_ a
5. **retro**spect   _back_

---

21. **super:** above; beyond.

     Examples: *supersensory, supersonic, superstructure.*

beyond

- *Supersensory* impressions are ___*beyond*___ [within / (beyond)] the normal limits of the senses.

above

- The *superstructure* of a warship is ___*above*___ [(above) / below] the main deck.

supersonic

- Speeds *beyond* the speed of sound are ___*super*___sonic.

22. **trans:** across.

     Examples: *transgress, transpolar, transversal.*

across

- A *transpolar* flight goes ___*across*___ [around / (across)] the pole.

transversal

- In geometry a line that cuts *across* two other lines is called a ___*transversal*___ [tangent / (transversal)].

(b)

- To *transgress* is (a) to respect the rules ((b)) to step across the rules or violate them. (*b*)

23. **tri:** three.

     Examples: *tricuspid, trilingual, triplicate.*

triplicate

- Two copies weren't enough for my boss. No, everything had to be in ___*triplica*___te (three copies).

tricuspid

- Dr. Pullem, my dentist, triumphantly held up a bloody, *three-* pointed tooth known as a ___*tricusp*___id.

trilingual

■ My Swiss friend speaks French, German, and English. He's
_____ *trilingual*.

24. **ultra:** very; beyond.

Examples: *ultraconservative, ultramodern, ultraviolet.*

beyond

■ *Ultraviolet* rays are invisible because they lie __beyond__
[(beyond)/ inside] the violet end of the visible spectrum.

■ Mr. Skraggs bitterly fought equal pay for women, social security,
"and all them other radical notions." Skraggs was an

ultraconservative

__ultra conserva__*tive.*

ultramodern

■ The Gelts had a dream kitchen—the latest in __ultra__
modern equipment—but they always ate out.

25. **uni:** one.

Examples: *unicameral, unicorn, unicycle.*

unicameral

■ A legislature with *one* chamber is __unicameral__ [(unicameral)/
bicameral].

one

■ The horns on a *unicorn* reach the grand total of __one__.

unicycle

■ A tricycle has three wheels; a bicycle has two wheels; a
__unicycle__ has *one* wheel.

QUIZ

Write the meaning of each boldface Latin prefix.

1. three
2. above
3. one
4. very
5. across

1. **tri**angle	*three*	
2. **super**saturated	*above*	
3. **uni**ty	*one*	
4. **ultra**fastidious	*very*	
5. **trans**port	*across*	

Write True or False.

False	1. To *advocate* a policy is to speak against it.
True	2. The Revolutionary War *antedated* the War of 1812.
True	3. A *semimonthly* magazine comes out twice a month.
True	4. To *retrogress* is to go back to an earlier condition.
False	5. Opera stars strive to win the audience's *derision*.
True	6. *Binoculars* are used by two eyes at the same time.
True	7. *Profeminists* usually favor women's rights.
False	8. Phone calls from Boston to Seattle are *intercontinental*.
False	9. *Quasi-Chinese* music is the native music of China.
True	10. The killer's nickname, "Gentle John," is a *misnomer*.

Write the meaning of each boldface Latin prefix. The first letter of each answer is given.

11. an unusual **circum**stance   _around_

12. **com**passion for the blind   _together_

13. a **contro**versial issue   _against_

14. problems in **tri**gonometry   _three_

15. a **multi**tude of unpaid bills   _many_

16. **quint**essence of greed   _five_

17. Chapman's **trans**lation   _across_

18. to run **inter**ference   _between_

19. **sub**zero weather   _under_

20. the campus **quad**rangle   _four_

Write the letter that indicates the best completion.

(**b**) 21. A *postmortem* is held on a person who is (a) old, (b) dead, (c) diseased, (d) dying.

(**a**) 22. The *preamble* to a document comes (a) at the beginning, (b) in the middle, (c) at the end, (d) in the amendments.

(b) 23. The Latin prefix that means *above* is used in which word?—(a) anteroom, (b) supernatural, (c) retrorocket, (d) submerge.

(c) 24. The prefix in *united* and in *unification* means (a) nation, (b) states, (c) one, (d) peace.

(d) 25. The Latin prefix for *beyond* is used in what word?—(a) navigate, (b) submit, (c) infrared, (d) ultraviolet.

KEY TO REVIEW TEST

Check your test answers with the following key. Deduct 4% per error from a possible 100%.

1. False	10. True	19. under
2. True	11. around	20. four
3. True	12. together	21. (b)
4. True	13. against	22. (a)
5. False	14. three	23. (b)
6. True	15. many	24. (c)
7. True	16. five, fifth	25. (d)
8. False	17. across	
9. False	18. between	

Score: _____ %

LATIN DERIVATIVES

 SUPPLEMENTARY EXERCISE

One derivative of each Latin root is given. Write three more derivatives. If in doubt about a word, check its etymology in a dictionary.

Root	Meaning	Derivatives
1. *anim*	spirit	animosity, *animated*, *animation*, *animator*
2. *arm*	weapon	armistice, *armament*, *armor*, *armada*
3. *art*	craft	artificial, *artisan*, *article*, *articulate*
4. *bel, bell*	war	rebel, *beleaguer*, *belittle*, *belligerent*
5. *ben, bene*	well	benefit, *benefaction*, *beneficial*, *beneficiary*
6. *carn*	flesh	incarnate, *carnage*, *carnal*, *carnivore*
7. *cord*	heart	cordial, ~~cordless~~ concord, *discord*, *courage*
8. *dent*	tooth	indent, *dental*, *dentate*, *dentin*
9. *du*	two	duet, *duel*, *duo*, *duplex*
10. *ego*	I	egotist, *egocentric*, *egoism*, *egotistical*
11. *fin*	end; limit	define, *final*, *finalist*, *finalize*
12. *grat*	please	gratify, *gratitude*, *gratuity*, *gratis*
13. *junct*	join	adjunct, *juncture*, *conjuction*, *junction*
14. *labor*	work	collaborate, *laboratory*, *laborious*, *labored*
15. *leg*	law	legal, *legalism*, *delegate*, *legislation*
16. *min*	little; less	minimum, *miniature*, *minimal*, *minimize*
17. *par*	equal	parity, *parabola*, *parallel*, *parliament*
18. *pater, patr*	father	patron, *paternal*, *paternity*, *patronage*
19. *rect*	right	direct, *rectify*, *rectitude*, *recto*
20. *simil*	like	simile, *similarity*, *simulate*, *similitude*

CHAPTER 6

Greek Derivatives I

Roots

anthrop, **1**	crypt, **8**	hetero, **15**
astr, **2**	cycl, **9**	hydr, **16**
auto, **3**	dec, **10**	log, **17**
bibli, **4**	dem, **11**	neur, **18**
bio, **5**	derm, **12**	pan, **19**
chrom, **6**	dyn, **13**	path, **20**
chron, **7**	gram, graph, **14**	

Socrates never heard of a *telephone* or an *astronaut* or *psychiatry*—and yet those words are derived from Greek roots. As more scientific discoveries are made year after year, the chances are good that new names will continue to be built on the old Greek stems and prefixes. Knowing the meaning of these Greek forms can throw a high-wattage light on many English words.

Historically, Greek and Latin came flooding into our language in three waves: (1) religious terms at the beginning of the Christian era; (2) literary and cultural terms during the Renaissance, the revival of learning of the fifteenth and sixteenth centuries; and (3) scientific terms in recent centuries.

This chapter deals with some important Greek terms and their clusters of derivatives. First, memorize the Greek term and its definition, given at the beginning of each frame. Next, note carefully the example derivatives that follow. Try to understand the connection between each of these derivatives and its Greek root. Then fill in the blanks.

EXERCISES

Roots

1. **anthrop:** man.

   Derivatives: *anthropocentric, anthropogenesis, anthropogeography, anthropoid, anthropology, anthropometry, anthropophagy, misanthropy, philanthropy.*

anthropoids
- The *man*-like apes are called _____*anthro*_____poids.

anthrop
- The Greek root for *man* is a*nthrop*_____.

anthropology
- The study of *humans* is _____*anthropology*_____ [philology / anthropology].

anthropophagy
- Cannibalism, or the eating of human flesh, is known as *anthropophagy* [anthropophagy / herbivorousness].

man
- *Anthrop* means ___*man*_____.

anthropocentric
- A *man*-centered universe is obviously _____*anthropocentr*ic.

misanthrope
- One who hates *mankind* is a _*misanthrope*_ [misanthrope / metronymic].

philanthropist
anthrop, man
- A charitable fellow is a _____*philanthrop*ist (from *phil*, meaning loving and a*nthrop*_____, meaning m*an*_____).

2. **astr:** star.

   Derivatives: *aster, asterisk, asteroid, astral, astrobiology, astrodome, astrogate, astrolabe, astrology, astrometry, astronaut, astronomy, astrophysics, disaster.*

stars
- *Asteroids* are tiny planets that look like _____*stars*_____ [apes / stars].

astr
- The Greek root for *star* is a*str*_____.

astronomy
astrology
- The scientific study of the *stars* is *astronomy*_my, and fortune-telling by the *stars* is _____*astrolo*gy.

astrogate
astronauts

- Those who fly toward the *stars* are said not to navigate but to
_____ *astro* _____ gate, and the fliers themselves are called
_____ *astronauts* _____ [dreadnaughts / (astronauts)].

asterisks

- Printer's *stars* (as in **H*Y*M*A*N K*A*P*L*A*N**) are called
_____ *asterisks* _____.

disaster

- The word *dis* *aster* _____ hints that the *stars* were contrary.

3. **auto:** self.

   Derivatives: *autobiography, autocrat, autogenesis, autograph,
   autohypnosis, autoinfection, automat, automation, automaton,
   automobile, autopsy, autosuggestion.*

self

- An *autobiography* is written by one's _____ *self* _____ [critic /
(self)].

self

- *Autosuggestion* is given by one's *self* _____ [doctor / self].

auto

- The Greek root for *self* is *a* *uto* _____.

automation

- A system of *self*-operating machinery is called
_____ *automat* ion.

automat

- A *self*-operating restaurant service is an _____ *autom* at.

autocrat
automobile
autograph

- I can't admire any _____ *auto* crat (dictator, having *self*-
power) riding in his bullet-proof _____ *automobile* _____, but I might ask
him for his _____ *autograph* (self-written name).

4. **bibli:** book.

   Derivatives: *Bible, Biblicist, bibliofilm, bibliography, bibliolatry,
   bibliomania, bibliophile, bibliopole.*

bibli

- The Greek root for *book* is *b* *ibli* _____.

bibliography

- A list of *book* sources is called a _____ *bibliogra* phy.

bibliomania

- A craze for collecting *books* is _____ *bibliomania* [numismatics /
bibliomania].

bibliophile
bibliopole

- The _____ *biblio* phile (book-lover) gets *books* from a
_____ *biblio* pole (book-dealer).

bibliofilm

- Scholars record rare *books* on special microfilm known as
_____ *bibliofilm* [movifilm / (bibliofilm)].

book	■ The root *bibli* means ___book___.
	5. **bio:** life.
	Derivatives: *biochemist, biodynamics, biogenesis, biography, biology, biolysis, biometrics, biophysics, biopsy.*
life	■ *Biology* deals with plant and animal ___life___ [(life) / fiction].
bio	■ The three-letter Greek root for *life* is ___bio___.
biography	■ The written account of a *life* is a ___biography___ *phy*.
biopsy	■ The diagnostic examination by microscope of a piece of *living* tissue is a ___bio___ *psy*.
biophysics	■ The branch of physics that deals with *living* matter is ___biophysi___ *cs*.
biochemistry	■ The branch of chemistry that deals with *life* processes is ___biochemis___ *try*.
(a)	■ *Biogenesis* is the theory that living things can come from (a) living things only, (b) lifeless matter. (a)

QUIZ

Write the meaning of each boldface Greek root.

1. book	1. **bibli**ography	b___ook___
2. self	2. **auto**infection	s___elf___
3. life	3. anti**biotics**	___life___
4. man	4. **anthro**pocentric	m___an___
5. star	5. **astr**onaut	s___tar___

6. **chrom:** color.

Derivatives: *chromatic, chromatology, chrome, chromium, chromosome, chromosphere, panchromatic, polychrome.*

polychromatic	■ A many-colored print is ___polychromatic___ [polyglot / polychromatic].

color	■ A lens with *chromatic* aberration distorts ___color___ [sound / color].
chrom	■ The Greek root for *color* is ch___rom___.
chromosphere	■ The *colorful* gases seen around the sun during a total eclipse are called the ___chromosphere___ [biolysis / chromosphere].
color	■ *Chrom* means ___color___.
chromosomes	■ Our hereditary markings depend on tiny ___chromo___ somes.

7. **chron:** time.

Derivatives: *chronic, chronicle, chronograph, chronological, chronology, chronometer, chronometry, chronoscope, synchronize.*

time	■ *Chronological* order is ___time___ (time / place) order.
time	■ *Chron* means ___time___.
synchronized	■ A motion picture film and its sound effects should be *timed* together, or *syn*___chronized___.
chronometer chronometry	■ A watch or clock is sometimes called a ___chrono___ *meter*, and the scientific measurement of *time* is ___chronometry___.
chron	■ The Greek root for *time* is ___chron___.
chronic	■ If your back aches for a long *time* you have a ___chronic___ backache.

8. **crypt:** secret.

Derivatives: *crypt, cryptic, cryptogram, cryptographer, cryptography, cryptology, cryptonym.*

secret	■ A *cryptic* remark has a ___secret___ [clear / secret] meaning.
crypt	■ The Greek root for *secret* is cr___ypt___.
cryptogram cryptographer	■ A *secret*, coded message is a ___crypto___ *gram*, and the fellow who decodes it is a ___cryptographer___.
cryptonym	■ A *secret* name is a ___cryptonym___ [cognomen / cryptonym].

crypt

■ Bodies were often hidden away in a ___crypt___ [chromosphere / (crypt)].

9. **cycl:** circle; wheel.

Derivatives: *cycle, cyclograph, cycloid, cyclometer, cyclone, cyclorama, cyclotron, encyclical, encyclopedia.*

(b)

■ An *encyclopedia* gives instruction in (a) science only, ((b)) the *circle* of arts and sciences. (*b*)

cycl

■ The Greek root for *circle* or *wheel* is c_ycle_____.

cyclone

■ A storm that has *circling* winds is called a ___cyclone___.

cyclorama

■ A *circular* room with large pictures is a ___cyclorama___ ama.

■ An apparatus that accelerates atomic particles in *circles* is a

cyclotron

___cyclotr___ on.

wheel

■ A *cyclometer* measures ___wheel___ [(wheel) Russian]

motorcycle

revolutions and might be useful on a ___motorcycle___ [foot / (motorcycle)].

10. **dec:** ten.

Derivatives: *decade, decagon, decaliter, Decalogue, Decameron, decameter, decasyllable, decathlon, decennial, decimal, decimate.*

decade,

■ *Ten* years equal a ___deca___ de, *ten* liters equal a

decaliter, decameter

___decalit___ er; *ten* meters equal a ___decamet___ er.

dec

■ The Greek root for *ten* is d_ec_____.

ten

■ A *decathlon* consists of ___ten___ [five / (ten)] athletic events.

ten

■ A *decennial* celebrates ___ten___ years.

Decalogue

■ The *Ten* Commandments are called the ___Decalogue___ [Heptateuch / (Decalogue)].

■ Boccaccio's tales were supposedly told during a plague by *ten*

Decameron

people on *ten* days—hence, they are entitled the ___Decameron___ [Pentateuch / (Decameron)].

Write the meaning of each boldface Greek root.

1. secret
2. ten
3. wheel
4. color
5. time

1. **crypt**ogram _secret_
2. **dec**imal _t en_
3. bi**cycle** _w heel_
4. **chrom**atics _c olor_
5. **chron**ology _t ime_

---

11. **dem:** people.

Derivatives: *demagogue, demiurge, democracy, democrat, demography, endemic, epidemic, pandemic.*

democracy
- Government by the *people* is called ____ _demo cra_cy.

demagogue
- One who uses false claims and emotional appeals to stir up the common *people* is a ____ _demago_ gue.

people
- The Greek root *dem* means ____ _people_ .

endemic
- A disease restricted to *people* in one locality is _endemic_ [(endemic) / cycloid].

epidemic
pandemic
- A disease that spreads among *people* is epi_demic_ ____, and if it hits *people* over a very wide area it is _pandemic_ [panoramic / (pandemic)].

people
- *Demography* is a study of how ____ _people_ [(people) // cattle] are distributed.

dem
- The Greek root for *people* is ____ _dem_ .

12. **derm:** skin.

Derivatives: *dermatitis, dermatoid, dermatologist, dermatophyte, epidermis, hypodermic, pachyderm.*

skin
- *Dermatitis* is an inflammation of the ____ _skin_ [joints / (skin)].

dermatologist
- A *skin* infection should be treated by a ____ _dermatolog_ ist.

derm
- The Greek root for *skin* is d_erm_ ____ .

pachyderms	■ Thick-*skinned* animals, like elephants and rhinoceroses, are ___pachyderms___ [anthropoids / (pachyderms)].
epidermis	■ Our outermost layer of *skin* is the *epi*dermis___.
hypodermic	■ An under-the-*skin* injection is a *hypo* dermic___.

13. **dyn:** power.

Derivatives: *dynamic, dynamism, dynamite, dynamo, dynamometer, dynasty, dyne, electrodynamics, hydrodynamics, thermodynamics.*

(b)	■ A *dyne* is a unit of (a) time (b) force or power. (*b*)
dynamometer	■ Mechanical *power* can be measured by a ___dynamometer___ meter.
dyn	■ The Greek root for *power* is *dyn*___.
dynamic	■ An energetic person is said to be ___dynamic___ ic.
dynasty	■ A *powerful* family which has ruled for some generations is a ___dyna___ sty.
power	■ *Dyn* means ___power___.
power	■ The *dynamos* at Niagara produce electrical ___power___.
dynamite	■ One *powerful* explosive is ___dynamite___.

14. **gram, graph:** write.

Derivatives: *autograph, biography, calligraphy, cryptogram, diagram, epigram, geography, graffiti, gramophone, grammar, graphic, graphite, graphology, holograph, lithograph, mimeograph, photograph, seismograph, telegram, typography.*

writing	■ *Graphite* is used in pencils for ___writing___ [erasing / (writing)].
write	■ The Greek roots *gram* and *graph* mean ___write___ [heavy / (write)].
calligraphy	■ One's penmanship, or *handwriting,* is called ___calligraphy___ [calliope / (calligraphy)].

seismograph

(b)

(b)

grandma

other
(a)

other

heterodox

heteroplasty,
heterograft

■ Seismic disturbances, or earthquakes, are *recorded* on the
seis **mograph** _____.

■ *Graphology* tries to analyze character by means of (a) head
bumps (b) handwriting. (**b**)

■ The *graffiti* found on walls are (a) insects, (b) rude sketches and
writing. (**b'**)

■ Which word wandered into the wrong line-up?—*epigram,
telegram, grammar, grandma, lithograph.* __**grandma**__

15. **hetero:** other.

   Derivatives: *heterodox, heterodyne, heterogeneous, heterograft,
   heteromorphic, heteronym, heteroplasty, heterosexual.*

■ *Hetero* means ____**other**____. Members of a *heterogeneous*
group are (a) of various types, (b) all alike. (**a**)

■ A *heterosexual* person is attracted to the ____**other**____ [same /
other] sex.

■ Religious or political beliefs that are *other* than the usual kind are
____**hetero**__dox.

■ Surgery in which the grafted tissue comes from *another* person is
called ____**hetero**____*plasty* or ____**hetero**__*graft.*

QUIZ

Write the meaning of each boldface Greek root.

1. skin
2. write
3. power
4. other
5. people

1. pachy**derm**   s **kin**
2. litho**graph**   w **write**
3. **dyn**amism   p **ower**
4. **heter**ogeneity   o **ther**
5. **dem**ocracy   p **eople**

16. **hydr:** water.

   Derivatives: *hydraulics, hydrocarbon, hydrocephaly, hydrogen,
   hydrography, hydrokinetics, hydrometer, hydropathy,
   hydrophobia, hydroponics, hydrotherapy.*

water	■ *Hydraulics* deals with the mechanical properties of w __ater__ and other liquids.
water	■ *Hydropathy* and *hydrotherapy* involve treatment of disease by use of w __ater__ .
hydr	■ The Greek root for *water* is h __ydr__ .
hydrophobia	■ Because rabies brings on a fear of *water*, the disease is also known as ___ __hydropho__ bia.
hydrocephaly	■ Excessive fluid in the skull is called ___ __hydrocephaly__ [hydrocephaly / heteroplasty].
fluids	■ *Hydroponics* is the science of growing plants in ___ __fluids__ [sand / fluids].

17. **log:** word; study.

Derivatives: *apology, biology, decalogue, dialogue, doxology, embryology, eulogy, geology, hydrology, logic, logorrhea, mineralogy, monologue, philology, prologue, tautology, theology.*

study	■ *Biology* is the ___ __study__ [breeding / study] of plant and animal life.
study	■ *Mineralogy* is the s __tudy__ of minerals.
log	■ The Greek root for *study* is l __og__ .
hydrology	■ The *study* of water and its distribution is __hydrology__ [hydrolysis / hydrology].
embryology	■ The *study* of embryo development is __embryology__ [embryology / embryectomy].
word	■ The root *log*, as in *monologue, dialogue,* and *eulogy,* means ___ __word__ (word / log).

18. **neur:** nerve.

Derivatives: *neural, neuralgia, neurasthenia, neurocirculatory, neurogenic, neurologist, neuromotor, neuromuscular, neuron, neurosis, neurotic.*

nervous	■ A *neurotic* suffers from a ___ __nervous__ [speech / nervous] disorder.

nerves

- *Neuritis* is a painful inflammation of the __nerves__ [skin / (nerves)].

neur

- The Greek root for *nerve* is n __eur__.

neurosis

- The *neurotic* has what is called a __neurosis__ [(neurosis) / psychosis].

neurasthenia

- If you develop fatigue, worries, and pains without apparent cause, your condition is called __neurasthe__ nia.

neurologist

- If you need a *nerve* specialist, go to a __neurologist__ ist.

19. **pan:** all.

   Derivatives: *panacea, Pan-American, Pan-Asiatic, panchromatic, pancreas, pandemic, pandemonium, panegyric, Panhellenic, panorama, pantheism, pantheon, pantomime.*

all

- *Panchromatic* film is sensitive to __all__ [no / (all)] colors.

all

- A *panacea* is a supposed cure for __all__ [one / (all)] disease or trouble.

pan

- The Greek root for *all* is p __an__.

panorama

- A picture with a view in *all* directions is a __panorama__ ama.

pandemic

- A disease that is very widespread is __pandemic__ ic.

Panhellenic

- A league of *all* the campus Greek-letter (Hellenic) fraternities and sororities is __Panhellenic__ ic.

Pantheon

- A temple for *all* the gods was the __Pantheon__ [Colosseum / (Pantheon)].

all

- *Pan* means __all__.

20. **path:** disease; feeling.

   Derivatives: *antipathy, apathy, empathy, neuropathy, osteopathy, pathetic, pathologist, pathos, psychopath, sympathy, telepathy.*

path

- The Greek root p __ath__ means *feeling.*

pathetic

- A *feeling* of pity is aroused by *pathos* or that which is __pathetic__ ic.

sympathy

empathy

diseases

psychopath

■ Your compassion for another person is *sym*__pathy_____, and your complete projection of yourself into the *feelings* of another person is *em*__pathy_____.

■ The root *path* means *feeling,* but it can also mean *disease;* thus, a *pathologist* is a specialist in ___diseases_____ [paths and trails / diseases].

■ A serious mental disorder would be found in a __psychopath___ [psychopath / bibliopole].

QUIZ

Write the meaning of each boldface Greek root.

1. word	1. dia**logue**	w__ord__
2. feeling	2. a**path**etic	feeling
3. all	3. **pan**acea	a__ll__
4. water	4. **hydr**aulics	wat__er__
5. nerve	5. **neur**on	n__erve__

Write True or False.

True	1. *Cryptography* deals with secret writing.
False	2. *Bibliomania* refers to excessive use of alcohol.
True	3. *Graphite* can be used to write with.
False	4. *Autosuggestion* requires two or more people.
True	5. *Dermatology* deals with the skin.
False	6. *Neurasthenia* refers to a hardening of the arteries.
True	7. A wristwatch is a type of *chronometer.*

Write the meaning of each boldface Greek root. The first letter of each answer is given.

8. an **anthrop**omorphic god   m _an_

9. **pan**hellenic organizations   a _ll_

10. suffering from de**hydr**ation   w _ater_

11. the Dewey **dec**imal system   t _en_

12. the **chrom**osome number   c _olor_

13. overuse of anti**biot**ics   l _ife_

14. faith in **dem**ocracy   p _eople_

15. the **hetero**doxies of Berkeley   o _ther_

Write the letter that indicates the best completion.

(**b**) 16. An *asterisk* is a printing symbol that looks like (a) a number, (b) a star, (c) a slanted line, (d) a question mark.

(**a**) 17. *Pathogenesis* has to do with the origin of (a) a disease, (b) a path, (c) God, (d) sin.

(**c**) 18. A *dynamometer* measures (a) speed of rotation, (b) spark, (c) power, (d) sound.

(**c**) 19. The Greek root for *circle* is used in which word?—(a) cryptic, (b) cardiac, (c) encyclical, (d) eclipse.

(**b**) 20. The Greek root which is common to both *geology* and *proctology* means (a) earth, (b) study, (c) tunnel, (d) the end.

Check your test answers with the following key. Deduct 5% per error from a possible 100%.

1. True	8. man	15. other
2. False	9. all	16. (b)
3. True	10. water	17. (a)
4. False	11. ten	18. (c)
5. True	12. color	19. (c)
6. False	13. life	20. (b)
7. True	14. people	

Score: _____ %

Greek Derivatives II

Roots		Prefixes	
phil, **1**	therm, **10**	kilo, **19**	
phon, **2**	amphi, **11**	meta, **20**	
physi, **3**	anti, **12**	mono, **21**	
pseudo, **4**	arch, **13**	neo, **22**	
psych, **5**	dia, **14**	peri, **23**	
pyr, **6**	epi, **15**	poly, **24**	
soph, **7**	eu, **16**	syn, sym, **25**	
tele, **8**	hyper, **17**		
the, **9**	hypo, **18**		

Chapter 7 continues our study of Greek derivatives. Follow the same procedure as in Chapter 6.

EXERCISES

Roots

1. **phil:** loving.

   Derivatives: *Anglophile, bibliophile, Francophile, philander, philanthropy, philatelist, philharmonic, philodendron, philogynist, philology, philoprogenitive, philosophy, philter.*

phil
- The Greek root for *loving* is *phil* __*phil*__ .

bibliophile
- One who *loves* books (*bibli*) is a _____ *bibliophile*.

- One with *love,* or charity, for man (*anthrop*) is called a
philanthropist
   _____ *philanthrop* ist.

philosopher
- One who *loves* wisdom (*soph*) is a _____ *philosopher.*

philogynist
- One who *loves* women (*gyn*) is a _____ *philogynist;* but if he
philanderer
   trifles with their *love,* he may be called a *philanderer*
   [demagogue / philanderer].

philharmonic
- If you *love* musical harmony, you might join a _____ *philharmonic*
   orchestra.

Francophile
- If you *love* or admire the French, you are a *Francophile*
   [Francophobe / Francophile].

philatelist
- If you *love* stamps and collect them, you are a *philatelist*
   [psychopath / philatelist].

2. **phon:** sound.

   Derivatives: *phoneme, phonetic, phonics, phonograph, phonology, phonometer, phonoscope, telephone.*

- The word *telephone* deals with *sound,* as is suggested by its Greek
phon
   root *p* __*hon*__ .

sound
- *Phonetic* spelling is based on the _____ *sound* ([sound]/
   general appearance] of words.

- In linguistics, a specific speech *sound* is called a
phoneme
   _____ *phoneme*.

■ *Phonics* deals with (a) picture transmission, (b) speech sound, especially as related to the teaching of reading and pronunciation. (b)

(b)

■ *Phon* means __sound__.

sound

3. **physi:** nature.

Derivatives: *physical, physician, physicist, physiocrat, physiognomy, physiography, physiology, physiotherapy.*

nature

■ A *physicist* studies the laws of __nature__ [poetry / nature].

physi

■ The Greek root for *nature* is ph __ysi__.

physiography

■ The description of *nature* and natural phenomena is sometimes called __physiography__ [empathy / physiography].

nature

■ *Physi* means __nature__.

physiology

■ The branch of biology that deals with the parts and the functions of the body is __physilogy__ gy.

physiognomy

■ Your face is your __physiognomy__ nomy.

4. **pseudo:** false.

Derivatives: *pseudoaquatic, pseudoclassic, pseudomorph, pseudonym, pseudopod, pseudoscience.*

pseudonym

■ An author's fictitious or *false* name, such as *Mark Twain* or *George Eliot* or *Lewis Carroll,* is a __pseudonym__ [surname / pseudonym].

false

■ *Pseudo* means f__alse__.

■ When a critic refers to a novel as "a pseudoclassic," he or she means that it is (a) a genuine classic, (b) not a genuine

(b)

classic. (b)

pseudosciences

■ Unreliable studies such as phrenology and astrology are actually __pseudosciences__ [social sciences / pseudosciences].

is not

■ A *pseudoaquatic* plant __is not__ [is / is not] genuinely aquatic.

- A *pseudomorph* is a mineral which looks like another one—for example, copper pyrites, known as "fools' gold"—and the word literally means ___*false*___.

  false

5. **psych:** mind; spirit.

   Derivatives: *psyche, psychedelic, psychic, psychiatrist, psychoanalysis, psychodrama, psychograph, psychology, psychometry, psychoneurosis, psychopath, psychosis, psychosomatic, psychotherapy.*

- *Psychiatry* treats disorders of the ___*mind*___ [eye / (mind)].

  mind

- Freudian analysis to cure the *mind* is *psychoanaly*sis.

  psychoanalysis

- The Greek root for *mind* is ps*ych*___.

  psych

- A chart of one's personality traits is a *psychograph* [(psychograph) / pseudomorph].

  psychograph

- A *psychic* shock or trauma has a permanent effect on the ___*mind*___ [heart / (mind)].

  mind

- Drugs like LSD which affect the *mind* are ___*psyche de* lic.

  psychedelic

QUIZ

Write the meaning of each boldface Greek root.

1. love
2. sound
3. mind
4. false
5. nature

1. **phil**harmonic — *love*
2. **phon**ograph — *sound*
3. **psych**osis — *mind*
4. **pseudo**pod — *false*
5. **physi**cian — *nature*

6. **pyr:** fire.

   Derivatives: *pyre, pyretic, Pyrex, pyrexia, pyrites, pyritology, pyrochemical, pyrogenic, pyrolysis, pyromancy, pyromaniac, pyrometry, pyrophobia, pyrosis, pyrostat, pyrotechnics.*

- A *pyromaniac* has a compulsion to *start fires* [steal things / (start fires)].

  start fires

fireworks	■ *Pyrotechnics* is the art of making and displaying *fireworks* [advertisements /(fireworks)].
pyr	■ The Greek root for *fire* is p *yr*.
pyre	■ Hindu widows used to be cremated on their husband's funeral *pyr* e.
Pyrex	■ American cooks use heat-resistant glassware called *Pyre* x.
fever	■ A child with *pyrexia* is suffering from *fever* [chills /(fever)].
pyrophobia	■ An irrational fear of *fire* is called *pyrophobia*.
unhappy	■ A *pyromaniac* and a *pyrophobe* would probably be *unhappy* [happy /(unhappy)] together.

7. **soph:** wisdom.

Derivatives: *gymnosophist, philosophy, Sophia, sophism, sophisticated, sophistry, Sophocles, sophomore, sophomoric, theosophy.*

wise sophomoric	■ The word *sophomore* has two Greek roots: *soph,* which means *wise* [(wise)/ strong], and *mor* (as in moron), which means *foolish.* Therefore an immature person who acts like a know-it-all is said to be *sophomoric* [(sophomoric)/ heterogeneous].
sophistry	■ Since the *sophists* were notorious for their clever but deceptive logic, a misleading argument is sometimes called a *sophist* ry.
sophisticated	■ People who are *worldly-wise* are *sophisticat* ed.
sophisticated	■ A rocket or electronic device that is very subtle and complicated in design is also said to be *sophisticat* ed.
wisdom	■ According to its Greek roots, the word *philosophy* means *the love of w isdom.*

8. **tele:** far.

Derivatives: *telecast, telegenic, telegraph, telekinesis, telemechanics, telemeter, telepathy, telephone, telephoto, telescope, telethermometer, telethon, teletype, television.*

far, writing

■ The word *telephone* literally means *far + sound.* Similarly, *telegraph* means *far* ___far___ + *writing* ___writing___.

far, seeing

■ *Television* means ___far___ + ___seeing___ [advertising / (seeing)].

tele

■ The Greek root for *far* is t ___ele___.

■ A thermometer that measures temperature from *afar* is a ___telethermomet___er.

telethermometer

telephoto

■ Photos can be taken from *afar* by ___telephotos___.

telepathy

■ Transmitting thoughts without use of the five senses is called ___tele___*pathy*

9. **the:** god.

Derivatives: *atheism, monotheism, pantheism, pantheon, polytheism, theism, theocentric, theocracy, theology, theosophy.*

God

■ *Theism* and *monotheism* generally refer to a belief in ___God___.

polytheism

■ Belief in many *gods* is *pol* ___ytheism___.

atheism

■ Belief in no *god* is *a* ___theism___.

the

■ The Greek root for *god* is t ___he___.

theocracy

■ Puritan New England, ruled by *God* and the church, was a ___theocracy___ [democracy / (theocracy)].

theology

■ The study of *God* and religious doctrines is called ___theology s___.

god

■ *The* means ___god___.

10. **therm:** heat.

Derivatives: *diathermy, hydrothermal, isotherm, thermal, thermocouple, thermodynamics, thermograph, thermometer, thermonuclear, thermopile, thermos, thermostat.*

heat

■ In a *thermonuclear* blast the nuclear fission releases ___heat___ [psychic waves /(heat)].

(a)

■ A *thermostat* controls ((a)) heat, (b) water. (**a**)

(b)

■ The word *hydrothermal* literally means (a) electric power, ((b)) hot water. (**b**)

isotherm

■ A line on the weather map between points of equal temperature is an ___isotherm___ (isotherm / isobar].

thermodynamics

■ The relations between *heat* and other forms of energy are dealt with in ___thermodynam___ics.

thermos

■ Coffee keeps its *heat* in a ___thermos___ jug.

QUIZ

Write the meaning of each boldface Greek root.

1. fire
2. god
3. far
4. heat
5. wisdom

1. **pyr**otechnics ___fire___
2. **the**ology ___god___
3. **tele**gram ___far___
4. dia**therm**y ___heat___
5. **soph**omore ___wisdom___

Prefixes

11. **amphi:** around; on both sides.

Examples: *amphibians, amphibolous, amphitheater.*

amphibians

■ Since frogs live *both* on land and in water, they are ___amphibians___ [bisexuals /(amphibians)].

amphitheater

■ An arena with spectators seated *around* it is an ___amphithea___ter.

amphibolous

- A statement with two possible meanings—such as "The Duke yet lives that Henry shall depose"—is *amphibolous* [amphibolous)/ anthropomorphic].

12. **anti:** against.

    Examples: *antibiotic, antipathy, antithesis.*

against

- An *antipathy* is a feeling __against__ [for /(against)] something.

contrast

- In *antithesis* the two parts of a sentence present a __contrast__ [similarity / (contrast)].

(b)

- A substance such as penicillin or streptomycin that works *against* certain germs and viruses is known as (a) insulin, (b) an antibiotic. (**b**)

13. **arch:** chief.

    Examples: *archangel, archfiend, architect.*

chief

- An *archangel* is a __chief__ [common / (chief)] angel.

(b)

- In Milton's *Paradise Lost* the *archfiend* is (a) a run-of-the-mill devil, (b) Satan himself. (**b**)

architect

- The *chief* worker in charge of designing a building is the __architect__ [stonemason /(architect)].

14. **dia:** through.

    Examples: *diabetes, diameter, diathermy.*

through

- *Diathermy* sends heat __through__ [(through)/ around] one's body.

diameter

- The distance *through* a circle is called the __diameter__.

(b)

- A disease associated with excess sugar passing *through* the body is (a) carditis, (b) diabetes. (**b**)

15. **epi:** upon; beside.

    Examples: *epicenter, epidermis, epitaph.*

upon

- The *epidermis* is the outer, nonsensitive layer that lies ___upon___ [(upon)/ below] the true skin.

epicenter

- The point above and *upon* the center of an earthquake is the ___epicenter___ [seismograph /(epicenter)].

epitaph

- The inscription *upon* a tomb is an ___epitaph___ [anagram / (epitaph)].

16. **eu:** good; well.

Examples: *eulogy, eupepsia, euphoria, euthanasia.*

well-being

- *Euphoria* is a feeling of ___well-being___ [pain / (well-being)].

good

- *Eupepsia* means ___good___ [(good)/ bad] digestion.

praises

- A *eulogy* ___praises___ [(praises)/ condemns].

euthanasia

- Mercy killing is known as ___euthanasia___ [asphyxia / (euthanasia)]

17. **hyper:** excessive.

Examples: *hypercritical, hyperopia, hyperthyroidism.*

hypercritical

- One who finds fault with an *excessive* number of details is ___hypercritical___ [hypocritical / (hypercritical)]

hyperopia

- A person whose eyes can see an *excessive* distance probably has ___hyperopia___ [myopia /(hyperopia)].

excessive

- *Hyperthyroidism,* marked by rapid pulse and sleeplessness, may be caused by ___excessive___ [insufficient /(excessive)] activity of the thyroid gland.

18. **hypo:** under.

Examples: *hypocrite, hypothermia, hypothesis.*

below

- A patient with *hypothermia* has a temperature ___below___ [above /(below)] normal.

hypothesis

- An assumption which *underlies* an investigation is called a ___hypothesis___ [(hypothesis) / prosthesis].

hypocrite

■ A person who pretends to be sincere, honest, or good but *under* it all is insincere, dishonest, or evil is a _____hypocrite___.

19. **kilo:** thousand.

   Examples: *kilocycle, kilometer, kilowatt.*

thousand

■ A *kilocycle* equals one _____thousand____ [hundred / (thousand)] cycles per second.

kilometer

■ One *thousand* meters equal one _____kilometer_____ .

one

■ Problem: One *thousand* watts of electrical energy used for sixty minutes equal _____one_____ [(one) / 60,000] kilowatt-hour[s].

20. **meta:** change; after.

   Examples: *metabolism, metamorphic, metempsychosis.*

metamorphic

■ Rocks such as marble which have *changed* their form under pressure are _____metamorphic___ [anthropomorphic / (metamorphic)].

metabolism

■ The body's chemical and physical *changes,* with release of energy, are aspects of _____metabolism___ [morphology / (metabolism)].

(b)

■ *Metempsychosis* assumes that at one's death one's soul (a) also dies, (b) makes a change, passing into another body. (b)

21. **mono:** one.

   Examples: *monodrama, monogamy, monomania.*

monogamy

■ Being married to only *one* person at a time is called _____monogamy___ [polygamy / (monogamy)].

monodrama

■ A play with *one* performer is a _____monodrama___ [(monodrama) / melodrama].

monomania

■ Captain Ahab's irrational interest in *one* subject, Moby Dick, amounts to _____monomania___ [bipolarity / (monomania)].

22. **neo:** new.

   Examples: *neoclassicism, neologism, neophyte.*

new	■ A *neophyte* in a religious order is a ___ *new* ___ [new / elderly] member.
neologism	■ A *new* word, freshly coined, is a ___ *neologism* ___ [neologism / hyperbole].
neoclassicism	■ A period of a *new* version, or revival, of classical literary style is known as ___ *neoclassicism* ___ [romanticism / neoclassicism].

23. **peri:** around.

   Examples: *perimeter, periphrasis, periscope.*

around	■ The *perimeter* of a ranch is the distance ___ *around* ___ [across / around] it.
(b)	■ An optical instrument used in submarines for looking *around* an obstruction is known as a (a) stereoscope. (b) periscope. (*b*)
(a)	■ *Periphrasis* is a *roundabout* way of phrasing, as in (a) "I did dance and Joe did shout," (b) "I danced and Joe hollered." (*a*)

24. **poly:** many.

   Examples: *polygon, polysyllable, polytechnic.*

many	■ A *polytechnic* institution offers courses in ___ *many* ___ [one or two / many] technical fields.
polygon	■ A plane figure with *many* sides is a ___ *polygon* ___ [polygon / mastodon].
(b)	■ A *polysyllable* has *many* (at least three) syllables, like the word (a) "logic," (b) "transcendentalism." (*b*)

25. **syn, sym:** together.

   Examples: *synchronize, syndrome, synthesis.*

(a)	■ *Synthesis* involves (a) bringing things together, (b) taking things apart. (*a*)
synchronized	■ Actions that are timed *together* are ___ *synchronized* ___ [acclimated / synchronized].
syndrome	■ Symptoms which occur *together* and indicate a specific disease are called a ___ *syndrome* ___ [syndrome / eupepsia].

Write *True* or *False*.

True	1. The *archdeacon* has a higher rank than the deacon.
False	2. *Hyperacidity* refers to a lack of enough stomach acid.
True	3. *Metamorphic* rocks have undergone a change of form.
False	4. A *polytheist* believes in the oneness of God.
False	5. The feminine name *Sophia* originally meant "stupid."
True	6. An *amphibian* plane can take off from land or sea.
False	7. *Antipathy* is warm affection.
True	8. A *phonoscope* enables one to see certain characteristics of sounds.
True	9. *Synchronized* movements are timed together.
False	10. A *kilogram* weighs one thousand pounds.

Write the meaning of each boldface Greek root or prefix. The first letter of each answer is given.

11. a **pseudo**medieval ballad   f _alse_
12. a jutting **peri**scope   a _round_
13. the doctor's **dia**gnosis   t _hrough_
14. cooking with **Pyr**ex   f _ire_
15. the actor's **mono**cle   o _ne_
16. **neo**-impressionism in art   n _ew_
17. the gentle **phil**osopher   l _ove_
18. suffering from **hypo**glycemia   u _nder_
19. a sensitive **therm**ocouple   h _eat_
20. cutting the **epi**cardium   u _pon_

Write the letter that indicates the best completion.

(a) 21. *Euphoria* refers to a feeling of (a) well-being, (b) weariness, (c) drowsiness, (d) hunger.

(c) 22. *Physics* is the study of (a) diseases, (b) chemicals, (c) nature, (d) beauty.

(d) 23. *Psychosurgery* involves cutting into (a) the lungs, (b) the face, (c) the muscles, (d) the brain.

(c) 24. *Tele* means (a) sound, (b) star, (c) far, (d) sight.

(b) 25. The Greek root which is common to both *pantheism* and *theology* means (a) all, (b) god, (c) study, (d) nature.

KEY TO REVIEW TEST

Check your test answers with the following key. Deduct 4% per error from a possible 100%

1. True	10. False	19. heat
2. False	11. False	20. upon
3. True	12. around	21. (a)
4. False	13. through	22. (c)
5. False	14. fire	23. (d)
6. True	15. one	24. (c)
7. False	16. new	25. (b)
8. True	17. loving	
9. True	18. under	

Score: _____%

GREEK DERIVATIVES

SUPPLEMENTARY EXERCISE

One derivative of each Greek root is given. Write three more derivatives. If in doubt about a word, check its etymology in a dictionary.

Root	Meaning	Derivatives
1. *cosm*	world; order	cosmic, _cosmopolitan_, _cosmogony_, _cosmology_
2. *crac, crat*	power	plutocrat, _autocrat_, _aristocrat_, _theocracy_
3. *gam*	marriage	monogamy, _polygamy_ _bigamy_, _theocracy_
4. *gen*	race; kind	genetics, _genesis_, _genealogy_, _pathogen_
5. *geo*	earth	geometry, _geography_ _geocentric_, _geology_
6. *gon*	angle	hexagon, _polygon_, _octagon_, _pentagon_
7. *gyn*	woman	gynecology, _mysoginist_ _gynecologist_ _ob-gyn_
8. *iso*	same	isobar, _isotope_, _isometric_, _isocline_
9. *lith*	rock	monolith, _lithosphere_, _microlith_, _Neolithic_
10. *mega*	great	megaphone, _megalopolis_ _megacycle_, _megaton_
11. *micro*	small	microbe, _microscope_, _microfilm_, _microwave_
12. *necr*	dead	necrosis, _necrology_, _necrological_, _necrotic_
13. *nom*	law; order	economy, _nomarchy_, _nomenclatural_, _nomological_
14. *onym*	name	antonym, _synonym_, _homonyms_, _synonimous_
15. *ped*	child	pedant, _pedology_, _pediatrics_, _pedodontist_
16. *phos, phot*	light	photograph, _photoactive_ _photosynthesis_ _photopic_
17. *poli*	city	police, _metropolis_, _politics_, _megalopolis_
18. *scop*	see; watch	episcopal, _telescope_, _microscope_, _stethoscope_
19. *techn*	art; skill	technique, _technical_, _technology_, _techno_
20. *zoo*	animal	zoo, _zoology_, _zodiac_, _zoomorphism_

Words in Context

adage, **1** ennui, **11** indigent, **21**
authenticate, **2** erudite, **12** innuendo, **22**
bigot, **3** exhume, **13** jeopardize, **23**
bovine, **4** fetid, **14** maim, **24**
cardiac, **5** fiasco, **15** nonchalant, **25**
clandestine, **6** gawk, **16** nonplused, **26**
contaminate, **7** glib, **17** noxious, **27**
denigrate, **8** iconoclastic, **18** predatory, **28**
docile, **9** inane, **19** prevaricate, **29**
duress, **10** indemnity, **20** rabid, **30**

Baby Joey is born with a vocabulary of zero. By the time little Joey is three, he knows hundreds of words. How did he learn those words? No, he didn't look them up in the dictionary, although that's certainly one of the best ways to improve one's vocabulary. He learned words by noticing the way they are used.

Joey's uncle yells, "Get the blazes off the sofa, you lousy rascal!" Little Joey has never heard the word *sofa* before. *Sofa* is not in his vocabulary. But he has often been told to get the blazes off a table or a dresser, so he quickly figures out that this furniture under his muddy shoes is called a "sofa." He also gets a distinct feeling that "lousy rascal" is not a term of endearment.

Like Joey, we learn most words in context, that is, by the way the words are used by speakers and writers. For instance, we read: "Violin virtuoso Itzhak Perlman played two Mozart sonatas in Carnegie Hall." Maybe we've never seen the word *virtuoso* before. *Virtuoso* is not in our vocabulary. But we realize from the sentence that Perlman is no hillbilly scratching out a polka on a fiddle. This is a concert violinist playing demanding compositions by Mozart—and at famous Carnegie Hall. That's enough. We assume, quite correctly, that a virtuoso is a highly gifted musician.

In this chapter we'll practice learning new words by analysis of context. We'll try to grasp the meaning of an unfamiliar word by deduction—by close study of the passage in which it occurs. If we look at the clues, we can usually make an intelligent guess.

To get a more complete and exact definition of words in this chapter, we should, of course, consult our desk dictionary. (A dictionary that looks brand new probably belongs to a lazy student. Riffle those pages!)

EXERCISES

1. **adage** (ad′ij): Grandmother was fond of repeating the *adage:* "Don't count your chickens before they're hatched."

■ *Adage* means (a) the total, (b) poem, (c) proverb, (d) falsehood. (*c*)

2. **authenticate:** Before you accuse the senator of accepting bribes, be sure you can *authenticate* the charge.

■ *Authenticate* means to (a) repeat, (b) explain it like an author, (c) apologize for, (d) prove true or genuine. (*d*)

3. **bigot** (big′ət): His sneering remarks about minority groups were what one would expect from that *bigot.*

■ A *bigot* is (a) a big national leader, (b) someone intolerant of other creeds, races, or beliefs, (c) the faucet of a beer keg, (d) a man with two wives. (*b*)

■ I'll buy this expensive painting if you can *authenticate* it as a genuine Picasso and not just a clever imitation. I believe in the

adage ___: "Better be safe than sorry."

■ The prejudices of the elderly *bigot* ___ were dipped in cement. He never tried to *authenticate* ___ his wild accusations. He illustrated the *adage* ___: "There's no fool like an old fool."

■ The signature on this big check looks genuine but I'd like to *authenticate* ___ it.

■ A person strongly prejudiced against other religions or ethnic groups is a *bigot* ___.

■ Please forgive me, darling. Remember the *adage* ___: "To err is human; to forgive, divine."

4. **bovine** (bō′vīn): On the dance floor the stout farmers moved like their own cattle, and with the same *bovine* clumsiness.

■ *Bovine* means (a) catlike, (b) cowlike, (c) doglike, (d) admirable. (*b*)

5. **cardiac:** The death of John Jones, 79, was due to *cardiac* arrest. He had complained of chest pains.

(a)

- *Cardiac* refers to (a) heart, (b) automobile, (c) gin rummy, (d) police officers. (*a*)

6. **clandestine** (klan-des'tin): Because churches were outlawed in Soviet Russia, some sects held *clandestine* prayer meetings in homes at night.

(c)

- *Clandestine* means (a) formal, (b) showy, (c) secret, (d) musical. (*C*)

(c)

- A person with "*bovine* intelligence" is (a) alert, (b) sly, (c) dull, (d) a genius. (*c*)

(d)

- *Clandestine* meetings would probably be held by (a) baseball teams, (b) an orchestra, (c) a town forum, (d) spies. (*d*)

(b)

- *Cardiac* surgery may involve (a) kidney stones, (b) a triple bypass, (c) reshaping the nose, (d) a sex change. (*b*)

clandestine
cardiac

- When she learned of her husband's cl*andestine*_____ romance with Lulu, Mrs. Grimm had a ca*rdiac*_____ attack.

bovine

- Our dairy manager depended on Dr. Schnapps, the veterinarian, to handle any bo*vine*_____ ailments.

QUIZ

Write the letter that indicates the best definition.

1. (c)
2. (d)
3. (f)
4. (a)
5. (b)
6. (e)

(*c*) 1. bovine		a. to prove genuine
(*d*) 2. adage		b. kept secret; furtive
(*f*) 3. bigot		c. a cow; like a cow
(*a*) 4. authenticate		d. a proverb
(*b*) 5. clandestine		e. of the heart
(*e*) 6. cardiac		f. an intolerant person

7. **contaminate:** If we continue to *contaminate* the air, the water, and the soil, humankind will pass away like the dinosaur.

(d)

- *Contaminate* means to (a) devour, (b) kill, (c) use, (d) pollute. (*d*)

8. **denigrate** (den′ə-grāt′): It became fashionable among biographers to *denigrate* the reputation of our national heroes, emphasizing their sins, weaknesses, and sex lives.

(c)

- *Denigrate* means to (a) praise, (b) whitewash, (c) defame or put down, (d) investigate. (C)

9. **docile** (dos′əl): Alice expected her young students to be noisy and unruly, but found them, on the contrary, to be quiet and *docile.*

(d)

- *Docile* means (a) highly argumentative, (b) of low intelligence, (c) handsome, (d) easy to handle and teach. (d)

(a)

- We *contaminate* some foods with (a) pesticides, (b) high prices, (c) dishonest advertising, (d) boiling. (a)

(c)

- The drama critic *denigrates* our class comedy when he refers to it as (a) amusing, (b) gripping, (c) amateurish, (d) hilarious. (C)

denigrate
docile

- I do not wish to *den igrate*_____ the character of Hank's pit bull, but that dog is not exactly *do cile*_____. It likes visitors, especially if they are soft and tender.

contaminate
denigrate

docile

- Traffic fumes *co ntaminate*_____ the atmosphere of Azusa. I have no desire to *de nigrate*_____ the good name of our city, but to curb this menace we must become active fighters, not *do cile*_____ spectators.

10. **duress** (dyoo-res′): The judge ruled that the contract was not valid because the widow had been forced to sign under *duress.*

- *Duress* means (a) without a dress, (b) compulsion or pressure, (c) bad weather conditions, (d) an unlucky astrological

(b)

sign. (b)

11. **ennui** (än-wē′): The rich man's son had seen and experienced everything at an early age. "Life," he complained, "is dullsville." He was overwhelmed by *ennui* and weariness of spirit.

(c)

- *Ennui* means (a) hunger, (b) turbulent emotions, (c) boredom, (d) financial greed. (C)

12. **erudite** (er′yoo-dīt): For such obscure facts we always turned to Professor Smeeby, an *erudite* fellow with thick glasses.

(c)

- *Erudite* means (a) handsome, (b) jolly and fun-loving, (c) scholarly and learned, (d) athletic. (C)

ennui
erudite

- A lesser man cooped in that silent private library might have suffered from *ennui* _____; but to the scholarly and *erudite* _____ Judge Jenkins it was as exciting as a gymnasium.

duress

- The great mathematician felt no *duress* _____ to act and dress like the rest of us. He had no social life, preferring to bury

erudite
ennui

himself in his *erudite* _____ equations, yet he was quite free of spiritual discontent or *ennui* _____.

duress

- Mama was too busy to be bored. Those under *duress* _____ to make a living while raising a family had no time for

ennui

ennui _____.

QUIZ

Write the letter that indicates the best definition.

1. (d)
2. (a)
3. (e)
4. (b)
5. (c)
6. (f)

(d) 1. **erudite**   a. tame; easy to handle
(a) 2. **docile**   b. pollute; befoul; render impure
(e) 3. **duress**   c. boredom; weariness of spirit
(b) 4. **contaminate**   d. learned; scholarly
(c) 5. **ennui**   e. compulsion by threat; coercion
(f) 6. **denigrate**   f. defame; disparage; blacken

---

13. **exhume** (eks-hyōōm′): The officials decided to *exhume* the long-buried corpse of Mrs. Bluebeard and check it for skull fractures.

(b)

- *Exhume* means (a) cover with dirt, (b) dig up, (c) burn, (d) hold services for. (b)

14. **fetid** (fet′id): With the clothespin on her nose, Nancy didn't mind the *fetid* odor of the pigpen, but the clothespin slipped and Nancy fainted.

(a)

- *Fetid* means (a) stinking, (b) strange, (c) interesting, (d) fragrant. (a)

15. **fiasco** (fē-as′kô): A warm sun melted the ice rink and turned our long-awaited hockey game into a ridiculous *fiasco*.

(a)

- *Fiasco* means (a) complete failure, (b) exciting spectacle, (c) triumph, (d) money-maker. (a)

fiasco

fetid

exhume

fiasco

fetid, exhume

fiasco

- Dingbat High lost its first basketball game 87 to 21, a real _fiasco_.

- The Dingbat players stuffed their sweaty gym clothes into their lockers, and by Monday the room had acquired a ripe, _fetid_ odor.

- The neighbor's dog tore up my daisies while trying to _exhume_ an imaginary, hidden pork chop.

- My cousin spent his life savings trying to market "no-calorie pizza," but his investment ended in a _fiasco_.

- From under the rose bushes, of all places, came a _fetid_ odor, leading the police to _exhume_ the slain bodies; and so the killer's "perfect crime" proved to be a _fiasco_.

16. **gawk** (gôk): On this busy corner the visitors to New York would stand open-mouthed and *gawk* at the Empire State Building.

(d)

- *Gawk* means (a) criticize, (b) throw stones at, (c) sneer, (d) stare stupidly. (_d_)

17. **glib:** Murphy was a *glib* sports commentator who drowned his listeners each evening in a rapid shower of words.

(a)

- *Glib* means (a) fast-talking, (b) learned, (c) conceited, (d) popular. (_a_)

18. **iconoclastic** (ī-kon′ə-klas′tik): Monarchies, religions, and cherished beliefs—all were attacked by the *iconoclastic* Thomas Paine.

(c)

- *Iconoclastic* means (a) peace-loving, (b) quiet and humble, (c) smashing revered ideas, (d) patriotic. (_c_)

glib

- I kicked the tires, and before I knew it a _glib_ used-car salesman had talked me into buying the jalopy.

iconoclastic

- In 1492 the belief that the earth is flat was challenged by an _iconoclastic_ navigator named Columbus.

gawk

glib

- At the county fair we would gather and _gawk_ at a salesman who assured us with a _glib_ tongue that his snake oil cured arthritis, baldness, and cancer.

gawk

glib, iconoclastic

- In "The Music Man" the villagers g*awk*_____ at the
  g*lib*_____ young stranger with his *ic onoclastic*_____
  theories about creating band music through will power.

QUIZ

Write the letter that indicates the best definition.

1. (c)
2. (f)
3. (d)
4. (b)
5. (e)
6. (a)

(*C*) 1. **glib**	a. gape; stare stupidly
(*f*) 2. **fiasco**	b. smashing popular beliefs
(*d*) 3. **exhume**	c. fast-talking; fluent
(*b*) 4. **iconoclastic**	d. dig up; disinter
(*e*) 5. **fetid**	e. having a foul odor; stinking
(*a*) 6. **gawk**	f. a complete failure

19. **inane** (i-nān'): I made some empty-headed comment, and the
    chairperson kindly ignored my *inane* remark.

(d)

- *Inane* means (a) wise, (b) unexpected, (c) clever, (d) silly. (*d*)

20. **indemnity** (in-dem'ni-tē): Our insurance company will pay you a
    huge *indemnity* if you are hit by a comet while you are riding in a
    public bus on a Thursday.

(c)

- *Indemnity* means (a) apology, (b) trial expenses, (c) compensation
  for damages, (d) hospital bills. (*C*)

21. **indigent** (in'di-jənt): The country doctor often received no
    payment at all from his *indigent* patients, or perhaps only a
    skinny chicken or two.

(a)

- *Indigent* means (a) very poor, (b) exasperated, (c) unmarried,
  (d) generous. (*a*)

inane

- Everything seemed funny at the slumber party, and we giggled at
  the most *in ane*_____ remark.

indigent

- At Thanksgiving our town provided turkey dinner for the
  homeless and the *indigent*_____, then ignored them the rest
  of the year.

indemnity

indigent

- When his Cadillac hit a cow on the highway, Mr. Biggs agreed to
  pay a small *in demnity*_____ to the penniless owner, who was
  indignant as well as *indigent*_____.

inane

indigent

indemnity

(b)

(a)

(c)

innuendo
jeopardize

maim
jeopardize

innuendo
maim

■ Hedda Lettis hated her husband's stupid, *inane* _____ small talk. How long could she endure this poverty, this *indigent* _____ existence? There on the edge of the cliff with him she thought of his insurance policy: "Double *indemnity* _____ for accidental death."

22. **innuendo** (in'yoo-en'dō): I resented Kay's catty remarks, especially her *innuendo* that my Uncle Waldo liked the bottle.

■ *Innuendo* means (a) written statement, (b) indirect insult, (c) song, (d) compliment. (b)

23. **jeopardize** (jep'ər-diz'): Dr. Schmaltz warned the pregnant woman that her smoking would *jeopardize* the health of her baby.

■ *Jeopardize* means (a) endanger, (b) improve, (c) affect, (d) the baby would be born with yellow fingers. (a)

24. **maim:** The wrestler twisted my leg until I screamed and was sure he would *maim* me.

■ *Maim* means (a) cure, (b) hurt, (c) cripple, (d) defeat. (c)

■ Smith's nasty *innuendo* _____ about my connections with the Mafia may *jeopardize* _____ my chances of winning this election.

■ Our football rivals would love to *maim* _____ our star quarterback and thus *jeopardize* _____ our scoring threats.

■ Louie the Lump is very sensitive, and if he hears your *innuendo* _____ about his not exactly being a genius, he'll probably crush your legs with a bat and *maim* _____ you.

QUIZ

Write the letter that indicates the best definition.

1. (f)
2. (a)
3. (e)
4. (d)
5. (c)
6. (b)

(f) 1. **innuendo**
(a) 2. **indigent**
(e) 3. **maim**
(d) 4. **indemnity**
(c) 5. **inane**
(b) 6. **jeopardize**

a. needy; poor; impoverished
b. to imperil; risk; endanger
c. senseless; silly; empty
d. compensation for loss or damage
e. to cripple; injure physically
f. a slur; an indirect insult

25. **nonchalant** (non'shə-länt'): I envied Karen's carefree manner and wished I could be as *nonchalant* as she was.

(a)

- *Nonchalant* means (a) cool and casual, (b) excitable, (c) sincere, (d) attractive. (a)

26. **nonplused** (non'plust): I was so *nonplused* by the accusing tone of the traffic officer that I could hardly remember my name.

(c)

- *Nonplused* means (a) pleased, (b) angered, (c) confused, (d) hurt. (c)

27. **noxious** (nok'shəs): We inhaled *noxious* fumes from a bus in front of us and learned what it is like to die in a gas chamber.

(d)

- *Noxious* means (a) unusual, (b) harmless, (c) like after-shaving cologne, (d) injurious to health. (d)

nonchalant

- The girls who pose for bikini ads usually look skinny and elaborately *non* chalant .

noxious

- The rat poison contained cyanide and other *no* xious ingredients that would persuade a rodent to depart for rodent heaven.

nonchalant, nonplused

- Bomber Benjy entered the ring, confident and *non* chalant , but he was quickly *non* plused when Windmill Willy flattened his nose.

nonchalant noxious nonplused

- I tried to act calm and *non* chalant as I began the chemistry experiment, but when the *n* oxious vapors appeared I was completely *n* onplused .

28. **predatory** (pred'ə-tōr'ē): Mrs. Hawkins reports that her pet Pekingese, Fifi, was attacked and eaten by *predatory* animals.

(c)

- *Predatory* means (a) friendly and neighborly, (b) fur-bearing, (c) habitually preying on others, (d) prehistoric. (c)

29. **prevaricate** (pri-ver'ə-kāt'): When it comes to making up fish stories, a long-armed fisherman can *prevaricate* better than a fisherman with short arms.

(b)

- *Prevaricate* means (a) catch fish, (b) lie, (c) swim, (d) eat. (b)

30. **rabid** (rab'id): Oakland had won the World Series!—and the grandstands became a madhouse of leaping, screaming, *rabid* fans.

(a)

prevaricate
rabid

predatory
prevaricate

prevaricate,
predatory
rabid

1. (c)
2. (e)
3. (a)
4. (d)
5. (b)
6. (f)

- *Rabid* means (a) raving and possibly crazy, (b) extremely hungry, (c) swift-moving, (d) like a rabbi. (*a*)

- Honestly, the squirrel that bit me had shaving cream dripping from its fangs. Why would I *pre varicate* ? I'm sure that squirrel is nutty—I mean *rabid* .

- Warn Aunt Martha not to buy more junk bonds from that *pre datory* (hunting for prey) financier. I've heard him *pre varicate* (lie) about "sure" profits, and she believes him because he has blue eyes.

- President Lincoln was called Honest Abe because he did not *pre varicate* . A more *pr edatory* (wolfish) leader would have leapt upon the fallen South and gobbled its resources. But Lincoln, unlike his *rabid* (maddened) associates, desired reconciliation, not revenge.

QUIZ

Write the letter that indicates the best definition.

(c) 1. **predatory**   a. to lie; tell a falsehood

(e) 2. **nonplused**   b. raging; mad; furious

(a) 3. **prevaricate**   c. preying on others

(d) 4. **nonchalant**   d. calm; unexcited; casual

(b) 5. **rabid**   e. confused; perplexed; bewildered

(f) 6. **noxious**   f. harmful; injurious; pernicious

Write a word studied in this chapter that can take the place of the words in italics.

noxious	1. inhaling *unhealthful, injurious* crop dust [no-]
glib	2. a *fast-talking but rather shallow* witness [gl-]
iconoclastic	3. a *tradition-attacking* scientist [ic-]
bovine	4. wore a *dull, stolid, oxlike* expression [bo-]
prevaricate	5. witnesses who *distort the truth* [pr-]
nonphused	6. to be *utterly puzzled and confused* [no-]
ennui	7. overcome by *boredom and lack of interest* [en-]
nonchalant	8. strolled in with a *casual, unconcerned* air [no-]
bigot	9. a *man intolerant of other races and creeds* [bi-]
fiasco	10. What a *completely ridiculous failure!* [fi-]
innuendo	11. guilty of *hinting something nasty* [in-]
adage	12. to quote the *familiar proverbial saying* [ad-]
fetid	13. the *strong offensive* odor of rotted fish [fe-]
erudite	14. an extremely *learned and scholarly* lady [er-]
exhume	15. to *dig away and bring up* the buried gems [ex-]
predatory	16. He was always *stalking innocent victims.* [pr-]
indemnity	17. received insurance *payment for damages* [in-]
cardiac	18. performed *problems-of-the-heart* surgery [ca-]
authenticate	19. to *prove the genuineness of* this painting [au-]
inane	20. their *silly, empty-headed* chatter [in-]
clandestine	21. *secret* meetings in Lovers' Lane [cl-]
indigent	22. food and shelter for *penniless* families [in-]
docile	23. a *teachable, easily managed* pony [do-]
jeopardize	24. to *risk the loss of* your health [je-]
rabid	25. bitten by a *crazed, hydrophobic* dachshound [ra-]

Check your test answers with the following key. Deduct 4% per error from a possible 100%.

1. noxious
2. glib
3. iconoclastic
4. bovine
5. prevaricate
6. nonplused
7. ennui
8. nonchalant
9. bigot

10. fiasco
11. innuendo
12. adage
13. fetid
14. erudite
15. exhume
16. predatory
17. indemnity
18. cardiac

19. authenticate
20. inane
21. clandestine
22. indigent
23. docile
24. jeopardize
25. rabid

Score: _____ %

Descriptive Words I

affable, **1**
altruistic, **2**
ambidextrous, **3**
aromatic, **4**
asinine, **5**
astute, **6**
bawdy, **7**
bellicose, **8**
berserk, **9**
bizarre, **10**
buoyant, **11**
buxom, **12**

cadaverous, **13**
candid, **14**
craven, **15**
dastardly, **16**
deft, **17**
defunct, **18**
destitute, **19**
diabolic, **20**
discreet, **21**
disenchanted, **22**
dogmatic, **23**
droll, **24**

dubious, **25**
eccentric, **26**
enigmatic, **27**
erotic, **28**
exorbitant, **29**
feasible, **30**
fluent, **31**
frugal, **32**
furtive, **33**
gullible, **34**
impeccable, **35**
impromptu, **36**

The right descriptive word can be worth diamonds in a composition. Of course, as Mark Twain said, it must be the right word, not its second cousin. Naturally, if you know thirty ways to describe a woman or a voice or a smile instead of only five ways, you have a wider selection and your chances of picking an effective word are much improved.

These descriptive words should be part of the stock-in-trade of any writer of themes or reader of literature. **Study carefully the definitions at the beginning of each frame. Then fill in the blanks with words defined in that frame, unless other choices are offered.**

EXERCISES

1. **affable** (af′ə-bəl): easy to talk to; amiable.
2. **altruistic** (al′trōo-is′tik): unselfish; concerned for the welfare of others.

(b)

■ An *affable* professor is (a) hostile, (b) friendly. (b)

(a)

■ An *altruistic* woman is one who sacrifices to help (a) others, (b) only herself. (a)

affable

■ We found Homer in a friendly, talkative mood, in fact, quite *affable* _____.

altruistic

■ Devoted to public charities, Straus was certainly *altruistic* _____.

affable

■ In *A Tale of Two Cities,* the executioner stands grim and silent, hardly an *affable* _____ fellow. Then Sydney Carton gives his life—loses his head, in fact—to save a friend. What an

altruistic

altruistic _____ deed!

3. **ambidextrous** (am′bə-dek′strəs): able to use both hands with equal ease.
4. **aromatic** (ar′ə-mat′ik): fragrant; spicy; sweet-smelling.

(b)

■ *Aromatic* plants are (a) odorless, (b) pleasantly scented. (b)

ambidextrous

■ A basketball player who shoots baskets with either hand is *ambidextrous* [ambidextrous / paraplegic].

ambidextrous

■ Wilma bats the baseball equally well from either side of the plate because she is *ambidextrous* _____.

aromatic

■ Her boudoir was *aromatic* _____ with subtle perfumes and incense.

aromatic
ambidextrous

■ At harvest these orchards are *aromatic* _____, and the owner hires a few fast, cheap, *ambidextrous* _____ pickers.

5. **asinine** (as′ə-nīn′): stupid; silly; ass-like.
6. **astute** (ə-stōot′): shrewd; keen in judgment; cunning.

(a)

■ The baseball fan's *asinine* comments made it clear that he was (a) a knucklehead, (b) a deep thinker. (a)

astute

■ Our nation needs _astute_ _____ [astute / asinine] diplomats.

astute

- Not everyone is shrewd enough to make as _astute_ investments.

asinine

- Trusting the strange door-to-door salesman with all my savings was an as _inine_ thing to do.

astute
asinine

- Even the most ast _ute_ student can make a mistake, but to keep repeating the same mistakes is as _inine_ .

✚ QUIZ

Write the letter that indicates the best definition.

1. (e)
2. (c)
3. (b)
4. (f)
5. (a)
6. (d)

(e) 1. affable	a. very stupid
(c) 2. altruistic	b. using both hands equally well
(b) 3. ambidextrous	c. completely unselfish
(f) 4. aromatic	d. keenly intelligent
(a) 5. asinine	e. warm and friendly
(d) 6. astute	f. sweet-scented

7. **bawdy** (bô′dē): indecent; obscene.
8. **bellicose** (bel′ə-kōs′): hostile; eager to fight; warlike.

(b)

- _Bawdy_ shows can be expected at (a) Sunday schools, (b) Las Vegas. (b)

bellicose

- World tension is increased when national leaders exchange _bellicose_ [affable / bellicose] remarks.

bellicose

- Bouncing his knuckles off my nose seemed to me a be _llicose_ gesture.

bawdy

- The minister's daughter blushed at the ba _wdy_ anecdote.

bawdy
bellicose

- When I tried to hush the drunken stranger who was singing a vulgar, ba _wdy_ song in our church, he became quite be _llicose_ .

9. **berserk** (bər-sûrk′): crazed; in a destructive frenzy.
10. **bizarre** (bi-zär′): odd in appearance; grotesque; queer. (Don't confuse with _bazaar_—a market or sale.)

bizarre

- Halloween masks are usually _bizarre_ [bazaar / bizarre].

(a)

berserk

bizarre

bizarre
berserk

- People who go *berserk* belong in (a) asylums, (b) crowded buses. (*a*)

- The brand-new straitjacket looks stylish on the man who went *ber_serk_____*.

- The green wig gave my aunt a *bi_zarre_____* appearance.

- The painting was so *bi_zarre_____* that Twain thought it depicted a cat going *_berserk_____* in a platter of tomatoes.

11. **buoyant** (boi′ənt): tending to float; light of spirit; cheerful.
12. **buxom** (buk′səm): healthily plump; full-bosomed; attractive.

(a)

buxom

buxom
buoyant

buoyant

buxom
buoyant

- When drowning, grab a *buoyant* material, like (a) cork, (b) a lead pipe. (*a*)

- The Flemish women painted by Rubens tend to be fleshy—that is, *___buxom____* [buxom / buoyant].

- After a week at the health spa, Amy lost her *_____buxo_m* figure, and her step became *_____byoya_nt*.

- The balloonist said that hydrogen was lighter and more *_____buoya_nt* than helium, and that he got a bigger bang out of using it.

- The astronauts looked *_____buxo_m* in their space suits, and they floated about in *_____buoyant* weightlessness.

QUIZ

Write the letter that indicates the best definition.

1. (b)
2. (d)
3. (f)
4. (e)
5. (a)
6. (c)

(*b*) 1. bawdy
(*d*) 2. bellicose
(*f*) 3. berserk
(*e*) 4. bizarre
(*a*) 5. buoyant
(*c*) 6. buxom

a. tending to float; cheerful
b. off-color; indecent
c. attractively plump
d. warlike; pugnacious
e. peculiar in appearance
f. destructively enraged

13. **cadaverous** (kə-dav′ər-əs): gaunt; haggard; corpse-like.
14. **candid:** frank; unprejudiced; outspoken.

(b)

- A *cadaverous* person should probably (a) reduce, (b) put on weight. (*b*)

candid

- I want the unvarnished truth, so give me a *candid* [candid / candied] report.

candid

- The editor said that my poems stank. He was quite _*candid*_.

cadaverous

- After forty days of fasting, Maximilian looked pale and *cadaverous*.

cadaverous
candid

- The sick hermit was so wasted and *cadaverous* that, to be *candid*, the doctor hardly knew whether to feed him or bury him.

15. **craven:** cowardly; timid; chicken-hearted.
16. **dastardly:** sneaky and mean; brutal.

(b)

- It was *dastardly* of Punky Jones to (a) chase the cattle rustlers, (b) trip and rob the blind man. (*b*)

(a)

- It was *craven* of me (a) to flee from the dachshund, (b) to challenge the bully. (*a*)

craven

- Amid flying bullets one tends to develop a timid, even a *craven* spirit.

dastardly

- Beating his infants was *dastardly*, even if they did pour syrup on his stamp collection.

dastardly, craven

- Who painted the captain's horse blue? Private Jubbs did the *dastardly* deed, but he was too *craven* to admit it.

17. **deft:** skilled and neat in action; adroit; dexterous.
18. **defunct** (di-fungkt′): dead; deceased; no longer existing.

(a)

- One must be particularly *deft* to (a) do needlework, (b) ride escalators. (*a*)

(a)

- A *defunct* enterprise belongs to (a) the past, (b) the future. (*a*)

deft

- I found that to play Chopin's "Minute Waltz" in less than five minutes requires quick, *deft* fingers.

defunct

- Alas, poor Yorick, whose skull I hold—he is _____ _defun_ct.

deft, defunct

- To walk across this boulevard of speeding cars, you must be _____ _deft_ or soon you'll be _____ _defunct_.

QUIZ

Write the letter that indicates the best definition.

1. (d)
2. (f)
3. (a)
4. (b)
5. (e)
6. (c)

(_d_) 1. craven	a. mean, villainous
(_f_) 2. deft	b. haggard; like a corpse
(_a_) 3. dastardly	c. frank; open and sincere
(_b_) 4. cadaverous	d. cowardly; timid
(_e_) 5. defunct	e. dead; functioning no more
(_c_) 6. candid	f. skillful

19. **destitute** (des′ti-tōōt′): extremely poor; lacking the necessities of life.
20. **diabolic** (dī′ə-bol′ik): devilish, fiendish.

(a)

- His *diabolic* ambition was to destroy (a) humankind, (b) disease. (_a_)

(b)

- The *destitute* have more than their share of (a) money, (b) poverty. (_b_)

destitute

- Her husband died three days after his insurance lapsed, and she was left *des_titute_*.

diabolic

- King Edward IV plotted to have his brother Clarence stabbed and drowned in a barrel of wine. How *dia_bolical_*!

destitute, diabolic

- The melodrama dealt with a penniless old couple—absolutely *des_titute_*—the victims of a _diabolic_ villain who foreclosed on the mortgage.

21. **discreet:** prudent; tactful; careful not to talk or act unwisely.
22. **disenchanted:** set free from one's rosy illusions.

disenchanted

- Those who expected to find fat gold nuggets lying on the Yukon snowbanks were quickly _disenchanted_ [vindicated / disenchanted].

(a)

- A *discreet* roommate (a) keeps a secret, (b) blabs about confidential matters. (_a_)

discreet

■ This juicy story should not be publicized, fellows, so please be
dis _creet_ .

disenchanted

■ Those who trusted Stalin's promises were soon
dis _enchanted_ .

discreet

■ After marriage William was less dis_creet_ in his
drinking; and his bride, stumbling among his bottles, was

disenchanted

disenchanted.

23. **dogmatic** (dog-mat'ik): asserting opinions in a dictatorial way;
positive; strongly opinionated.
24. **droll** (drōl): comical; quaintly amusing.

(b)

■ A _droll_ fellow at the circus is (a) the tiger, (b) the clown. (_b_)

(b)

■ Highly _dogmatic_ conversationalists are usually (a) popular,
(b) obnoxious. (_b_)

droll

■ The audience laughed at Will Rogers' dr_oll_ remarks.

dogmatic

■ Military men often become opinionated and dog_matic_ .

dogmatic
droll

■ Our landlord kept ordering us in do_gmatic_ fashion to
clean our rooms; nor did he smile at Bill's dr_oll_
remark that the garbage disposal must have backfired.

QUIZ

Write the letter that indicates the best definition.

1. (f)
2. (c)
3. (b)
4. (a)
5. (e)
6. (d).

(_f_) 1. destitute
(_c_) 2. diabolic
(_b_) 3. discreet
(_a_) 4. disenchanted
(_e_) 5. dogmatic
(_d_) 6. droll

a. losing one's romantic beliefs
b. prudent in speech and conduct
c. fiendish; outrageously wicked
d. comical; whimsically amusing
e. opinionated; dictatorial
f. needy; penniless

25. **dubious** (doo'bi-əs): doubtful; vague; skeptical; questionable.
26. **eccentric** (ik-sen'trik): odd; peculiar; unconventional; offcenter.

■ The bearded gentleman skating around in the drugstore is thought

eccentric

to be rather _eccentric_ [eccentric / conventional].

dubious

■ Although madman Columbus said the world was round, his listeners could see it was flat, and so they were naturally ___dubious___ [dubious / delusive].

eccentric

■ Mrs. Doodle often takes her Flemish rabbit for a walk on a leash—another one of her *eccentricities* ~~habits~~.

dubious

■ The drug addict claimed he could fly from the hotel roof, but the police officers were *dubious*.

eccentric, dubious

■ The farmer decided that the nudists were either crazy or highly *eccentric*; he was *dubious* about them.

27. **enigmatic** (en'ig-mat'ik): puzzling; perplexing; mysterious.
28. **erotic** (i-rot'ik): pertaining to sexual love; amatory.

erotic

■ "Adult movies" are usually more ___erotic___ [prudish / erotic] than "family movies."

(b)

■ We refer to Mona Lisa's smile as *enigmatic* because it is (a) dazzling, (b) puzzling. (b)

enigmatic

■ I was mystified by the *enigmatic* warning.

erotic

■ The sexy passages in *Tropic of Cancer* were so *erotic* that they gave off blue smoke.

erotic

■ If you cut all the *erotic* passages from Noodle's last novel, the book would disappear. When asked why he wrote it,

enigmatic

Noodle winked in *enigmatic* fashion.

29. **exorbitant** (ig-zôr'bə-tənt): extravagant; excessive in price; unreasonable.
30. **feasible** (fē'zə-bəl): capable of being done; practicable; suitable.

exorbitant

■ Five dollars an egg, as paid by those early miners, would ordinarily seem *exorbitant* [cheap / exorbitant].

not feasible

■ To build a bridge across the Pacific is at present ___not feasible___ [feasible / not feasible].

feasible

■ Your plan to feed the whole world is charitable, but is it *feasible*?

exorbitant

- "Fifty dollars to clip my dog is an *exorbitant*_____ fee—you've clipped me, too!"

exorbitant
feasible

- Gasoline prices rose to *exorbitant*_____ levels, and Archy decided that riding a skateboard might be *feasible*_____.

QUIZ

Write the letter that indicates the best definition.

1. (f)
2. (c)
3. (b)
4. (a)
5. (d)
6. (e)

(f) 1. exorbitant   a. doubtful; skeptical
(c) 2. feasible   b. mysterious
(b) 3. enigmatic   c. practicable; reasonable
(a) 4. dubious   d. having to do with sexual desire
(d) 5. erotic   e. peculiar; having odd traits
(e) 6. eccentric   f. too high-priced

31. **fluent** (floo′ənt): able to speak or write readily; flowing smoothly.
32. **frugal** (froo′gəl): costing little; spending little; meager; scanty.

(b)

- A tongue-tied immigrant who learned English from a book will probably (a) be fluent, (b) not be fluent. (b)

(a)

- A *frugal* meal (a) is cheap and plain, (b) contains fruit. (a)

frugal

- On his tiny pension Mr. Snurd eked out a *frugal*_____ existence.

fluent

- To make the debate squad you should be a *fluent*_____ speaker.

frugal
fluent

- For thirty years the woman saved, suffered, lived a *frugal*_____ life, for her dream was to become a lawyer and to deliver *fluent*_____ speeches in court.

33. **furtive:** stealthy; sly; done in secret; clandestine.
34. **gullible** (gul′ə-bəl): easily cheated or tricked; credulous.

gullible

- Brooklyn Bridge has often been sold to the _*gullible*_ [gullible / sophisticated] visitor.

furtive

- A stealthy gesture is said to be _furtive_ [ambidextrous / (furtive)].

furtive

- Mike stole a *fur tive* glance at the blonde.

gullible

- The con man got rich selling swampland to *gullible* investors.

- Nancy believed the handsome stranger's promises, for she was innocent and *gullible*; and she gave his hand a

gullible
furtive

furtive squeeze.

35. **impeccable** (im-pek′ə-bəl): faultless; without sin or error.
36. **impromptu** (im-promp′to͞o): done on the spur of the moment; offhand.

impeccable

- Banks should hire employees of _impeccable_ [dubious / (impeccable)] honesty.

(a)

- *Impromptu* remarks are (a) spontaneous, (b) planned in advance. (*a*)

impromptu

- Called on unexpectedly, Daniel Webster delivered a brilliant _impromp tu_ talk.

impeccable

- Our eminent minister was presumably of *im mpeccable* moral character.

impromptu

- College freshmen must often quickly scribble an _impromptu_ theme in class; and naturally the professor feels insulted if the

impeccable

production is not brilliant and _impecc able_.

QUIZ

Write the letter that indicates the best definition.

1. (c)
2. (e)
3. (a)
4. (d)
5. (f)
6. (b)

(C) 1. fluent   a. sly; stealthy
(e) 2. frugal   b. improvised; spur of the moment
(a) 3. furtive   c. smooth flowing in speech
(d) 4. gullible   d. easily swindled
(f) 5. impeccable   e. meager and costing little
(b) 6. impromptu   f. flawless

Write the word studied in this chapter that will complete the sentence.

berserk

buoyant

dubious

disenchanted

defunct

exorbitant

affable

discreet

eccentric

aromatic

impromptu

candid

bellicose

altruistic

fluent

destitute

dastardly

erotic

1. The waiter screamed and threw soup at us. He'd gone [ber-].

2. My hungry uncle found his false teeth just as the banquet began, and his spirits were now [bu-].

3. The widow distrusted Mr. Finn because of his [du-] reputation.

4. Those who expected modern plumbing in Morocco were soon [dis-].

5. Our lease had expired. It was as [def-] as Benedict Arnold.

6. Nine dollars for a dish of prunes? Isn't that a bit [ex-]?

7. The swindler had been talkative and friendly, an [af-] fellow.

8. Discuss this untidy affair with no one. Try to be [dis-].

9. Uncle Phil was an oddball; in fact, he was downright [ec-].

10. He slipped into the vat of cologne and smelled quite [ar-].

11. Was that an [imp-] speech, or had you rehearsed it for a week?

12. Please be frank. I want your [ca-] opinion.

13. The taxi driver swore and raised his fists in [bel-] fashion.

14. She donated a kidney to save her sister. An [alt-] act!

15. Don't stammer. With self-confidence you can be smooth and [fl-].

16. The fire and flood left the old widow [des-].

17. Tripping and robbing that feeble man was a [das-] act.

18. Knute likes sexy soap operas, the more [er-] the better.

Matching. Write the letter that indicates the best definition.

(C) 19. asinine
(e) 20. deft
(i) 21. bizarre
(j) 22. diabolic
(g) 23. gullible
(h) 24. dogmatic
(a) 25. feasible

a. capable of being done
b. birdlike
c. stupid as a donkey
d. pertaining to washing canines
e. dextrous; skillful in action
f. a church money-raiser sale
g. easily fooled
h. opinionated
i. odd in appearance
j. devilishly wicked

KEY TO REVIEW TEST

Check your test answers with the following key. Deduct 4% per error from a possible 100%.

1. berserk
2. buoyant
3. dubious
4. disenchanted
5. defunct
6. exorbitant
7. affable
8. discreet
9. eccentric

10. aromatic
11. impromptu
12. candid
13. bellicose
14. altruistic
15. fluent
16. destitute
17. dastardly
18. erotic

19. (c)
20. (e)
21. (i)
22. (j)
23. (g)
24. (h)
25. (a)

Score _____ %

Fill in the blank with the descriptive word that fits the definition.
Although these words were not defined in this chapter, you should recognize most of them.
Check your answers with the key at the end of the exercise. Use your dictionary to study any unknown words.

■ abstemious, articulate, astute, auspicious, bland

1. _bland_ — mild; nonstimulating; insipid
2. _astute_ — shrewd; clever; cunning
3. _abstemious_ — temperate; eating and drinking sparingly
4. _auspicious_ — favorable; propitious; of good omen
5. _articulate_ — able to express oneself well; clearly presented

■ caustic, compatible, copious, culpable, deferential

6. _compatible_ — able to get along well together
7. _deferential_ — very respectful; courteous
8. _culpable_ — at fault; deserving blame
9. _caustic_ — corrosive; stinging; sarcastic
10. _copious_ — very plentiful; abundant

■ delectable, delusive, derisive, disgruntled, disoriented

11. _derisive_ — ridiculing; mocking
12. _disgruntled_ — disappointed; displeased; sulky
13. _delusive_ — misleading; false; deceptive
14. _delectable_ — delicious; enjoyable
15. _disoriented_ — confused; out of adjustment to one's environment

■ dissident, dormant, dyspeptic, erudite, exotic

16. _exotic_ — strangely beautiful; foreign and fascinating
17. _dyspeptic_ — grouchy and gloomy because of indigestion
18. _dormant_ — as if asleep; inactive
19. _dissident_ — not agreeing; differing; dissenting
20. _erudite_ — learned; scholarly

■ heinous, illicit, immaculate, imperturbable, impotent

21. _immaculate_ pure; flawless; completely clean
22. _heinous_ atrocious; extremely wicked
23. _impotent_ powerless; helpless; without virility
24. _imperturbable_ calm; unruffled
25. _illicit_ unlawful; improper

KEY TO SUPPLEMENTARY EXERCISE

1. bland
2. astute
3. abstemious
4. auspicious
5. articulate
6. compatible
7. deferential
8. culpable
9. caustic

10. copious
11. derisive
12. disgruntled
13. delusive
14. delectable
15. disoriented
16. exotic
17. dyspeptic
18. dormant

19. dissident
20. erudite
21. immaculate
22. heinous
23. impotent
24. imperturbable
25. illicit

Score: _____ %

CHAPTER 10

Descriptive Words II

indomitable, **1**

inept, **2**

innate, **3**

inscrutable, **4**

insidious, **5**

intrepid, **6**

lethal, **7**

lethargic, **8**

lucid, **9**

lunar, **10**

myopic, **11**

naive, **12**

nebulous, **13**

nostalgic, **14**

occult, **15**

ominous, **16**

opaque, **17**

ostentatious, **18**

picayune, **19**

prolific, **20**

pusillanimous, **21**

raucous, **22**

sagacious, **23**

sedentary, **24**

senile, **25**

sinister, **26**

stoical, **27**

succinct, **28**

taciturn, **29**

toxic, **30**

venerable, **31**

verbose, **32**

verdant, **33**

vicarious, **34**

vindictive, **35**

zealous, **36**

This chapter continues our study of descriptive words.

Follow the same procedure as in the previous chapter.

EXERCISES

1. **indomitable** (in-dom′i-tə-bəl): unconquerable; unyielding.
2. **inept:** clumsy; incompetent; not suitable.

(a)
- An *indomitable* fighter (a) fights on and on, (b) quits. (a)

inept
- A pianist wearing mittens would probably be _inept_ [impeccable / inept].

indomitable
- Every nation speaks of its soldiers' *ind omitable* courage.

inept
- The Dodgers made five errors in the field and were just as _inept_ pl at the plate.

indomitable
inept
- Wanda climbed to the peak, for her spirit was *indomitable* ble; but I slipped off a boulder, for I was _inept_.

3. **innate** (i-nāt′): inborn; natural, not acquired.
4. **inscrutable** (in-skrōō′tə-bəl): mysterious; not able to be understood.

not innate
- One's political beliefs are _not innate_ [innate / not innate].

cannot
- When we speak of "*inscrutable fate,*" we mean that we _cannot_ [can / cannot] easily foresee the future.

inscrutable
- At one time no mystery melodrama was complete without its slinking and *in scrutable* foreign butler.

innate
- Ducklings seem to have an *innate* attraction to water.

innate

inscrutable
- At age five Capablanca had already shown an *in nate* talent for chess; and his face over the tournament board was tight-lipped and *inscrutable*.

5. **insidious** (in-sid′ē-əs): treacherous; crafty; more dangerous than is apparent.
6. **intrepid** (in-trep′id): very brave; dauntless; bold.

insidious
- Traitors who bore from within are _insiduous_ [innate / insidious].

intrepid
- Courageous aviators are said to be _intrepid_ [intrepid / craven].

intrepid

- Only hardy and *intrepid* _____ men could reach the North Pole.

insidious

- Socrates was accused of corrupting the Athenian youths with *insiduous* _____ doctrines.

intrepid
insidious

- Sam danced into the lion's cage to prove how _____ *intrep* id he was, but some *ins iduous* _____ fellow had left a banana peel on the floor.

QUIZ

Write the letter that indicates the best definition.

1. (f)
2. (d)
3. (b)
4. (c)
5. (a)
6. (e)

(f) 1. indomitable   *a.* stealthily treacherous
(d) 2. inept   *b.* inborn
(b) 3. innate   *c.* mysterious; beyond understanding
(c) 4. inscrutable   *d.* awkward; clumsy
(a) 5. insidious   *e.* fearless; brave
(e) 6. intrepid   *f.* unable to be defeated

7. **lethal** (lē′thəl): causing death; deadly; fatal.
8. **lethargic** (li-thär′jik): sluggish; dull; drowsy.

chlorine

- A *lethal* gas used in World War I was *chlorine* [oxygen / chlorine].

lethal

- A gun, a knife, an automobile—any of these may be considered a _____ *lethal* al weapon in a court case.

lethargic

- Basketball coaches don't want *lethargic* [ambidextrous / lethargic] athletes.

lethargic

- Having swallowed the pig, the snake became *le thargic* and sleepy.

lethargic
lethal

- This heavy smog has slowed me up, and I feel _____ *lethargic*; I hope the stuff is not _____ *lethal*.

9. **lucid** (lōō′sid): clear; easily understood; mentally sound.
10. **lunar** (lōō′nər): pertaining to the moon.

(b)

- A *lunar* eclipse blots out (a) the sun, (b) the moon. (b)

lucid
- Technical directions ought to be ___lucid___ [enigmatic / (lucid)].

lunar
- On the moon the astronauts conducted certain _____lunar experiments.

lucid
- Velma says her friend is crazy but that he has his _____lucid moments.

lucid
lunar
- The friendly astronomer gave us a _____lucid description of the _____lunar landscape.

11. **myopic** (mī-op′ik): nearsighted.
12. **naive** (na-ēv′): childlike; artless; lacking in worldly wisdom.

myopic
- Nearsighted people are ___myopic___ [(myopic) / hyperopic].

naive
- Anyone who thinks that concert artists don't have to practice is pretty ___naive___ [(naive) / astute].

myopic
- Benny sat in the front row and strained to see the movie. He was quite *myopic* _____.

naive
- College freshmen range from the very sophisticated to the very *naive* _____.

QUIZ

Write the letter that indicates the best definition.

1. (f)
2. (b)
3. (c)
4. (e)
5. (a)
6. (d)

(f) 1. lethal   a. nearsighted
(b) 2. lethargic   b. slow-moving; sluggish
(c) 3. lucid   c. easy to understand; clear
(e) 4. lunar   d. childlike; unsophisticated
(a) 5. myopic   e. of the moon
(d) 6. naive   f. deadly

13. **nebulous** (neb′yōō-ləs): cloudy; vague; indefinite.
14. **nostalgic** (nŏs-tal′jik): homesick; yearning for what is past or far away.

(b)
- *Nebulous* plans are (a) clearly detailed, (b) vague. (b)

(b)
- A *nostalgic* line is (a) "Brevity is the soul of wit," (b) "Gone, gone, are the lovely lasses of yesteryear." (b)

nostalgic

■ Recalling his three happy years in the fifth grade, Grandpa became _nostalgic_ .

nebulous

■ Through the Los Angeles smog we could make out the _nebulous_ outline of the city hall.

nostalgic
nebulous

■ Dad sings "When You and I Were Young, Maggie" and other _nostalgic_ songs; meanwhile his prospects for finding a job are _nebulous_ .

15. **occult** (ə-kult′): beyond human understanding; mysterious.
16. **ominous** (om′ə-nəs): threatening; menacing.

(b)

■ _Occult_ subjects include (a) geometry, (b) astrology. (b)

occult

■ Telepathy and reincarnation belong to those puzzling areas known as the _occult_ .

(b)

■ An _ominous_ gesture is (a) friendly, (b) threatening. (b)

ominous

■ Over the ball park hung dark and _ominous_ clouds.

occult
ominous

■ A spiritualist with _occult_ powers evoked a baritone ghost—it made _ominous_ predictions that curled our hair.

17. **opaque** (ō-pāk′): not letting light through; obscure; unintelligent.
18. **ostentatious** (os′tən-tā′shəs): showy and pretentious so as to attract attention.

(a)

■ _Opaque_ glass is sometimes used in (a) bathrooms, (b) automobile windshields. (a)

(b)

■ An _ostentatious_ living room seems to say, (a) "I'm simple and comfortable," (b) "Look, look—see how grand and expensive I am!" (b)

ostentatious

■ It was a bit _ostentatious_ of Mrs. Schmaltz to go shopping for groceries (a) in her pink Cadillac with chauffeur, (b) on her Schwinn bicycle. (a)

(a)

opaque

■ Such a dolt! His mind is absolutely _opaque_ .

opaque

■ My dusty glasses were practically _opaque_ , yet I saw that Diamond Jim was wearing six or eight sparkling rings. Hmm, somewhat _ostentatious_ , I thought.

ostentatious

Write the letter that indicates the best definition.

1. (c)
2. (d)
3. (e)
4. (f)
5. (a)
6. (b)

(c) 1. ominous   a. sentimental about the past
(d) 2. opaque   b. supernatural; beyond understanding
(e) 3. ostentatious   c. threatening
(f) 4. nebulous   d. not transparent
(a) 5. nostalgic   e. showy to attract attention
(b) 6. occult   f. vague; misty

---

19. **picayune** (pik′ē-yōon′): petty; trivial; contemptible.
20. **prolific** (prō-lif′ik): fruitful; fecund; producing many works.

- Agatha Christie, who wrote mystery novels by the dozen, was obviously very __prolific__ [phlegmatic / (prolific)].

prolific

- Charging extra for toothpicks in a restaurant is pretty __picayune__ [(picayune) / petulant].

picayune

- Rats multiply fast. They are *prolific*.

prolific

- The holdup netted sixty cents, or some such *picayune* amount.

picayune

- Your fat batch of poems proves that you are *prolific*, and my criticism of the spelling in your inspired poetry will seem *picayune*.

prolific

picayune

21. **pusillanimous** (pū′sə-lan′ə-məs): cowardly; fainthearted.
22. **raucous** (rô′kəs): rough-sounding; hoarse; boisterous.

- The foghorn that awakened me was merely the sergeant's __raucous__ [pusillanimous / (raucous)] voice.

raucous

- On the battlefield the braggart Falstaff was actually timid—in fact, (a) pusillanimous, (b) raucous. (a)

(a)

- Pancho is shy. He wants to marry Rosa, but he is too *pusillanimous* to pop the question.

pusillanimous

- One distrusts car salespeople who are pushy and *raucous*.

raucous

raucous
pusillanimous

- A bumblebee chased me out of the park, and I heard *raucous* laughter from those who thought me *pusillanimous*.

23. **sagacious** (sə-gā′shəs): shrewd; sound in judgment.
24. **sedentary** (sed′ən-ter′i): involving sitting; physically inactive.

(a)

- A *sagacious* decision is (a) wise, (b) stupid. (a)

(a)

- *Sedentary* work is done by (a) bookkeepers, (b) bricklayers. (a)

sagacious

- Advertising your umbrellas for sale just before the rainy weekend was *sagacious*.

sedentary

- The cowboy did not want office work or any other *sedentary* job.

sagacious
sedentary

- Old folks are not necessarily *sagacious*; some are just *sedentary*. Some are wise and some otherwise.

QUIZ

Write the letter that indicates the best definition.

1. (e)
2. (c)
3. (b)
4. (f)
5. (a)
6. (d)

(e) 1. sagacious
(c) 2. prolific
(b) 3. sedentary
(f) 4. pusillanimous
(a) 5. raucous
(d) 6. picayune

a. rough-sounding; harsh
b. involving sitting
c. producing in abundance
d. petty; trivial
e. having sound judgment
f. timid; cowardly

---

25. **senile** (sē′nīl): aged and infirm; showing the mental and bodily weaknesses of old age.
26. **sinister** (sin′is-tər): hinting of imminent danger; threatening harm.

- *Senile* people are often cared for in a home for (a) the aged, (b) wayward girls. (a)

(a)

senile

- The day our old neighbor wandered away from home in his nightgown, we felt he was getting *senile*.

(b)

sinister

senile

sinister

- If you were confronted by *sinister* strangers, you would probably be (a) amused, (b) worried. (*b*)

- The conspirators hatched a *sinister* _____ plot.

- The druggist, who was old and *senile* _____, saw nothing *sinister* _____ in Beulah's purchase of a quart of arsenic.

27. **stoical** (stō′i-kəl): indifferent to pain or pleasure.
28. **succinct** (sək-singkt′): concise; terse; brief and meaningful.

succinct

- Cablegrams at three dollars a word should be _succinct_ [*succinct*/ redundant].

succinct

- Wordiness is boring, so be *succinct* _____.

(a)

- Even during childbirth she was *stoical*: in other words, she was (a) calm and uncomplaining, (b) screaming her head off. (*a*)

stoical

- The captured warrior endured the ritual of torture with *stoical* _____ calm.

stoical

succinct

- Mr. Koltz sat quiet and *stoical* _____ during most of Buster's birthday party, but finally he made a *succinct* _____ announcement: "Shut up!"

29. **taciturn** (tas′i-tûrn′): not inclined to talk; uncommunicative.
30. **toxic** (tok′sik): poisonous.

(a)

- *Taciturn* people tend to (a) be silent, (b) talk your arm off. (*a*)

toxic

- Pesticides are usually _toxic_ [*toxic*/ nutritious].

toxic

- Wilbur said he wasn't afraid of *toxic* _____ fumes. We bury him on Tuesday.

taciturn

- Chess players are inclined to be reflective and *taciturn* _____.

toxic

taciturn

- "I filled my tires with smoggy, *toxic* _____ New Jersey air," I explained, "and they died." Replied the *taciturn* _____ Vermont mechanic: "Hm-m-mp."

Write the letter that indicates the best definition.

1. (c)
2. (e)
3. (b)
4. (d)
5. (f)
6. (a)

(*c*) 1. taciturn   a. showing no emotions
(*e*) 2. senile   b. poisonous
(*b*) 3. toxic   c. not talkative
(*d*) 4. sinister   d. ominous; threatening
(*f*) 5. succinct   e. old and feeble
(*a*) 6. stoical   f. concise; brief

---

31. **venerable** (ven′ər-ə-bəl): aged and worthy of reverence.
32. **verbose** (vər-bōs′): wordy; long-winded.

venerable

■ Ulysses was a wise and __venerable__ [venerable / venereal] warrior.

(b)

■ *Verbose* statements contain too many (a) ideas, (b) words. (*b*)

verbose

■ Trim your theme; it is *v__erbose__* .

venerable

■ We gazed at the *ven__erable__* statue of Abraham Lincoln.

venerable
verbose

■ Every evening my white-haired and *ven__erable__* military friend gave me a __*ver b ose*__ account of how he won the war.

33. **verdant** (vûr′dənt): green; covered with grass; unsophisticated.
34. **vicarious** (vī-kâr′i-əs): participating by imagination in another's experience.

(a)

■ *Verdant* fields are (a) grassy, (b) covered with boulders. (*a*)

vicarious

■ By identifying yourself with your movie hero you have __vicarious__ [venerable / vicarious] pleasure.

verdant

■ William Wordsworth trod these *ver__dant__* meadows.

vicarious

■ From the adventures of D'Artagnan, Jane Eyre, and Martin Arrowsmith we derive a *vi__carious__* thrill.

verdant
vicarious

■ Novels take us from foamy seas to *ver__dant__* hills; they let us live a thousand *vi__carious__* lives.

35. **vindictive** (vin-dik′tiv): revengeful; spiteful.
36. **zealous** (zel′əs): ardently devoted to a cause; enthusiastic.

■ To spite me, Bart bored a hole in my rowboat. It was a _vindictive_ [(vindictive)/ venerable] act.

vindictive

■ The boy who burned your garage to get even with you has a _vindictive_ nature.

vindictive

(b)

■ A *zealous* reader reads with (a) reluctance (b) enthusiasm. (b)

■ A town orchestra or museum often exists because of a few _zealous_ supporters.

zealous

zealous
vindictive

■ My roommate, a _zealous_ musician, played his violin all night until a _vindictive_ neighbor threw a can of beans through our window.

QUIZ

Write the letter that indicates the best definition.

1. (e)
2. (d)
3. (b)
4. (f)
5. (a)
6. (c)

(e) 1. venerable   a. inclined to revenge; spiteful
(d) 2. verbose   b. green with vegetation
(b) 3. verdant   c. fervent; ardently active
(f) 4. vicarious   d. wordy; talkative
(a) 5. vindictive   e. commanding respect because of age
(c) 6. zealous   f. sharing the feelings of others

Write the word studied in this chapter that will complete the sentence.

ominous   1. The storm clouds looked black and [om-].

inept   2. Thirty errors! Our ball team was incredibly [in-p-].

sagacious   3. What a wise choice! You are quite [sag-].

verbose   4. Five pages for a simple message? Joe is too [v-b-s-].

occult   5. Astrologers are steeped in supernaturalism and the [occ-].

picayune   6. The bloody fight was for a jellybean or other [pic-] item.

ostentatious   7. Her mink coat and flashy jewelry are a bit [ost-].

naive   8. Junior thinks babies grow under rocks. How [n-v-]!

lunar   9. Last night Moe kissed Flo during the [lu-] eclipse.

sedentary   10. I buy two-trouser suits because of my [sed-] occupation.

intrepid   11. The astronauts reached the moon. What an [int-p-] crew!

stoical   12. The condemned man showed no emotion. He was [sto-].

verdant   13. The coalminer dreamed of trees and [ver-] meadows.

senile   14. I'm losing my shingles. I'm old, feeble, and [sen-].

succinct   15. Cables are expensive. Keep the message [suc-].

myopic   16. Hold the book closer. I'm [my-].

prolific   17. Schubert wrote hundreds of songs. He was [pro-].

nostalgic   18. The old man wallowed in sweet [nost-] memories of college.

Matching. Write the letter that indicates the best definition.

(i) 19. venerable   a. an unmarried woman

(f) 20. zealous   b. stony; mountainous

(g) 21. pusillanimous   c. deadly

(d) 22. raucous   d. harsh-sounding

(j) 23. sinister   e. like a smelly animal

(c) 24. lethal   f. enthusiastic; dedicated to a cause

(h) 25. lucid   g. cowardly

     h. easy to understand; clear

     i. old and highly respected

     j. threatening danger

Check your test answers with the following key. Deduct 4% per error from a possible 100%.

1. ominous
2. inept
3. sagacious
4. verbose
5. occult
6. picayune
7. ostentatious
8. naive
9. lunar

10. sedentary
11. intrepid
12. stoical
13. verdant
14. senile
15. succinct
16. myopic
17. prolific
18. nostalgic

19. (i)
20. (f)
21. (g)
22. (d)
23. (j)
24. (c)
25. (h)

Score: _____ %

Fill in the blank with the descriptive word that fits the definition.
Although these words were not defined in this chapter, you should recognize most of them.
Check your answers with the key at the end of the exercise. Use your dictionary to study any unknown words.

■ inclement, indolent, indefatigable, insipid, luminous

1. _insipid_ — without flavor; tasteless; dull
2. _inclement_ — stormy; without leniency
3. _luminous_ — shining; clear; bright
4. _indefatigable_ — tireless
5. _indolent_ — lazy; idle

■ morbid, oblivious, ornate, precocious, ruthless

6. _ornate_ — overdecorated; flowery
7. _oblivious_ — unaware of; unmindful; forgetful
8. _ruthless_ — cruel; pitiless
9. _precocious_ — maturing early; bright for its age
10. _morbid_ — excessively interested in gruesome matters

■ salutary, scurrilous, skeptical, spasmodic, squalid

11. _skeptical_ — doubting; questioning; not easily convinced
12. _spasmodic_ — occurring now and then; fitful
13. _squalid_ — wretched; poverty-stricken in appearance
14. _scurrilous_ — foul-mouthed; grossly abusive
15. _salutary_ — beneficial; having a good effect

■ squeamish, staid, stalwart, suave, subtle

16. _stalwart_ — strong; valiant; unyielding
17. _suave_ — smoothly pleasant and polite, urbane
18. _squeamish_ — oversensitive; prudish, easily disgusted
19. _subtle_ — cunning, crafty; delicately skillful
20. _staid_ — sedate and settled

■ sullen, surreptitious, tepid, terse, voracious

21. _surreptitious_ secret; stealthy; sneaky
22. _sullen_ gloomy and resentful; glum; morose
23. _terse_ concise; to the point
24. _voracious_ greedy; gluttonous; insatiable
25. _tepid_ lukewarm

KEY TO SUPPLEMENTARY EXERCISE

1. insipid
2. inclement
3. luminous
4. indefatigable
5. indolent
6. ornate
7. oblivious
8. ruthless
9. precocious

10. morbid
11. skeptical
12. spasmodic
13. squalid
14. scurrilous
15. salutary
16. stalwart
17. suave
18. squeamish

19. subtle
20. staid
21. surreptitious
22. sullen
23. terse
24. voracious
25. tepid

Score: _____ %

CHAPTER 11

Action Words

abscond, **1**	disconcert, **13**	orient, **25**
acquit, **2**	disparage, **14**	ostracize, **26**
adulterate, **3**	disseminate, **15**	pander, **27**
alienate, **4**	elucidate, **16**	procrastinate, **28**
blaspheme, **5**	expurgate, **17**	prognosticate, **29**
bungle, **6**	extradite, **18**	rant, **30**
canonize, **7**	haggle, **19**	raze, **31**
canvass, **8**	heckle, **20**	recant, **32**
cauterize, **9**	immobilize, **21**	simulate, **33**
condone, **10**	impeach, **22**	slander, **34**
decimate, **11**	intimidate, **23**	smirk, **35**
deify, **12**	laud, **24**	supersede, **36**

The verb is the beating heart of the sentence. A strong, meaningful verb often lets you cut out prepositional phrases that clutter and suffocate a sentence. One student writes, "The temperatures were now at a much lower level than during the previous period." Another writes, "The temperatures plunged." The good writer gets considerable mileage from vigorous, well-selected action words (verbs).

This chapter focuses on action words. The drill technique is the same as with the descriptive words.

Study carefully the words and definitions at the top of each frame; then try to fill in the blanks without looking back or at the answers.

EXERCISES

1. **abscond** (ab-skond′): to depart hastily and secretly, especially to escape the law.
2. **acquit** (ə-kwit′): to declare innocent; to absolve.

■ If *acquitted* of a crime you are legally (a) guilty, (b) innocent. (   )

■ The prisoner was so pretty that the Yukon jury voted unanimously to *ac*_____ her.

■ A company clerk known as Honest Jim has _____ [absconded / abdicated] with our money.

■ Our bank teller, who was five feet tall and ten thousand dollars short, has _____ed.

■ Although the treasurer did *ab*_____ one night with the union funds, his lawyer managed later to get him _____ed.

3. **adulterate** (ə-dul′tə-rāt): to cheapen by adding inferior ingredients; to corrupt.
4. **alienate** (āl′yə-nāt′): to make unfriendly; to estrange.

■ Adding sawdust to sausage meat _____ [fortifies / adulterates] it.

■ Insulting your friends in public is usually a good way to _____ [alienate / captivate] them.

■ If Linus flirts with everybody, he'll soon *al*_____ his girlfriend.

■ Chemical additives often *ad*_____ our food.

■ Many bakeries add generous amounts of artificial preservative to their bread and thus *ad*_____ it; such practices *al*_____ health-minded customers.

(b)

acquit

absconded

absconded

abscond

acquitted

adulterates

alienate

alienate

adulterate

adulterate
alienate

5. **blaspheme** (blas-fēm′): to speak profanely of God or sacred things; to curse.
6. **bungle:** to botch; to perform clumsily.

bungled

- If her surgeon had been sober, he would not have _____ [bungled / misfired] that operation.

(a)

- Those who *blaspheme* are (a) cursing, (b) praying. (   )

blaspheme

- The priest shuddered to hear the atheist bl_____ near the cathedral.

bungle

- If you *bu*_____ your baking, the upside-down cake may come out rightside-up.

bungle
blaspheme

- Although the clumsy carpenter had to cut only one board, he managed to *b*_____ the job; then he began to *bl*_____.

QUIZ

Write the letter that indicates the best definition.

1. (b)	( ) 1. abscond	a. to add inferior ingredients
2. (e)	( ) 2. acquit	b. to flee from the law
3. (a)	( ) 3. adulterate	c. to do imperfectly
4. (f)	( ) 4. alienate	d. to use profanity
5. (d)	( ) 5. blaspheme	e. to declare not guilty
6. (c)	( ) 6. bungle	f. to make hostile

7. **canonize** (kan′ə-nīz′): to declare a dead person to be a saint.
8. **canvass** (kan′vəs): to go through a district asking for votes, opinions, or orders.

canvass

- We'll get Dooley elected even if we have to _____ [canvas / canvass] the whole town.

(b)

- The Catholic Church has *canonized* (a) Columbus, (b) Saint Joan of Arc. (   )

canonize

- Live like a saint and maybe the Church will *can*_____ you.

canvass

- "To sell tickets for—pardon the expression—*Gotterdammerung*," said Silas, "we had to can_____ the county."

canvass
canonize

- When Bobo hit that grand slam home run, he became an instant saint; you didn't have to _____ss the crowd to know they would practically _____ze him.

9. **cauterize** (ko′tə-rīz′): to sear with a hot iron, as to cure wounds.
10. **condone** (kən-dōn′): to pardon or overlook a fault.

(a)

- Infected wounds can be *cauterized* by (a) burning, (b) ice cubes. (   )

condone

- When a father shrugs off his son's vandalism, he is said to _____ [condone / canonize] it.

cauterize

- A white-hot needle was used to *cau*_____ the ugly scratch.

condone

- Though Gauguin was an inspired artist, many cannot *con*_____ his desertion of his family.

cauterize
condoned

- The army surgeon's failure to *c*_____ Fenwick's bullet wound cannot be _____ed.

11. **decimate** (des′ə-māt′): to kill many of.
12. **deify** (dē′ə-fī′): to make a god of; to exalt and idealize.

deify

- We tend to _____ [decimate / deify] our top athletes.

deify

- A heavyweight champion is not a god, and we should not *d*_____ him.

decimate

- With the hydrogen bomb any two nations can _____ [decimate / deify] each other more efficiently.

decimate

- We gave the South Sea natives the benefits of our modern "syphilization" and managed to *dec*_____ them.

deify

- It was the habit of the ancient Greeks to *de*_____ the sun, the moon, and the winds; it was also their habit to *dec*_____ their enemies.

decimate

Write the letter that indicates the best definition.

1. (d)
2. (b)
3. (e)
4. (a)
5. (c)
6. (f)

(   ) 1. canonize   a. to shrug off a fault
(   ) 2. canvass   b. to check opinions of an area
(   ) 3. cauterize   c. to slay large numbers
(   ) 4. condone   d. to raise to sainthood
(   ) 5. decimate   e. to sear a wound
(   ) 6. deify   f. to treat as a god

---

13. **disconcert** (dis'kən-sûrt'): to embarrass; to confuse; to upset.
14. **disparage** (dis-par'ij): to belittle; to speak of with contempt.

disparage

- To belittle an effort is to _____ [condone / disparage] it.

disconcert

- Jeering at a speaker tends to _____ [deify / disconcert] him.

disconcert

- Finding half a worm in my apple was enough to *dis*_____ me.

disparage

- Don't *dis*_____ the restaurant coffee—it's quite good compared to the doughnut.

disparage,
disconcert

- The clarinet duet sounded like cats fighting, but let's not _____*ge* it or we may _____*ert* the young artists.

15. **disseminate** (di-sem'ə-nāt'): to scatter everywhere; to spread, as if sowing.
16. **elucidate** (i-loo'si-dāt'): to make clear; to explain.

(b)

- To *elucidate* a literary passage is (a) to disparage it, (b) to clarify its meaning. (   )

(b)

- To *disseminate* propaganda is (a) to stifle it, (b) to spread it. (   )

elucidate

- This poem sounds like jabberwocky. Please *el*_____ it, Sheldon.

disseminate

- A helicopter was used to drop and *dis*_____ circulars advertising Anti-Litter Week.

disseminate

- The Internal Revenue Service loved to *dis*_____ among common citizens a tax form that only a genius could
elucidate

*el*_____.

17. **expurgate** (ek′spər-gāt′): to remove obscene or objectionable matter; to purge.
18. **extradite** (ek′strə-dīt′): to return a fugitive to another state or nation.

(a)

- The PTA members *expurgated* our class play. In other words, they (a) cleaned it up, (b) added a few dirty words. (   )

(b)

- France promised to *extradite* Killer McGee. This means he will be (a) executed there, (b) shipped back to us. (   )

extradite

- Argentina was requested by Israel to *ex*_____ a Nazi war criminal.

expurgate

- Censors used a blue pencil to *ex*_____ the naughty lines.

extradite
expurgate

- Some countries refuse to *ex*_____ political refugees; some show Hollywood films but will *ex*_____ the kissing scenes.

■ QUIZ

Write the letter that indicates the best definition.

1. (d)
2. (e)
3. (a)
4. (f)
5. (c)
6. (b)

(   ) 1. elucidate   a. to return a fugitive across borders
(   ) 2. expurgate   b. to spread everywhere
(   ) 3. extradite   c. to speak slightingly of
(   ) 4. disconcert   d. to clarify
(   ) 5. disparage   e. to eliminate objectionable passages
(   ) 6. disseminate   f. to embarrass

19. **haggle:** to argue in petty fashion about terms and prices.
20. **heckle:** to harass with questions and sarcastic remarks.

(b)

- Those who *haggle* at a garage sale are probably discussing (a) politics, (b) prices. (   )

(a)

- To *heckle* the chairman is to shower him with words of (a) sarcasm, (b) praise. (   )

haggle	■ Natives in the marketplace would *hag*＿＿＿＿＿＿ ten minutes over the price of a fish.
heckle	■ Spectators in Hyde Park who disagree with speakers will mercilessly *hec*＿＿＿＿＿＿ them.
heckle haggle	■ The crowd began to *h*＿＿＿＿＿＿ the orator; meanwhile, the peddler and the hippie continued to *h*＿＿＿＿＿＿ for the overripe cantaloupe.

21. **immobilize** (i-mō′bə-līz′): to make unable to move; to fix in place.
22. **impeach:** to accuse an official of wrongdoing.

(b)	■ President Andrew Johnson was *impeached;* this means that he was (a) guilty, (b) accused. (　)
impeach	■ If the governor has misused the funds, we should *imp*＿＿＿＿＿＿ him.
(b)	■ To *immobilize* a broken leg is (a) to exercise it, (b) to keep it from moving. (　)
immobilize	■ The police officer pulled Nick's arms back so as to *im*＿＿＿＿＿＿ him.
impeach immobilize	■ One columnist predicts that we will *im*＿＿＿＿＿＿ Senator Swindle, convict him, and send him to a prison cell to *im*＿＿＿＿＿＿ him.

23. **intimidate** (in-tim′i-dāt′): to make timid; to control action by inducing fear.
24. **laud** (lôd): to praise.

intimidate	■ Bugsy's scowl and brass knuckles were enough to ＿＿＿＿＿＿ [intimate / intimidate] me.
(a)	■ If critics *laud* your performance, they are (a) praising it, (b) knocking it. (　)
laud	■ Some artists have to die before anyone will *l*＿＿＿＿＿＿ them for their accomplishments.
intimidate	■ Drive a compact car in heavy traffic and the huge trucks will *int*＿＿＿＿＿＿ you.

laud
intimidate

■ Belinda saved the hikers' lives, and our newspapers all
l_____ her bravery. She did not let the grizzly bears
*int*_____ her.

QUIZ

1. (e)
2. (b)
3. (d)
4. (a)
5. (c)
6. (f)

( ) 1. impeach   a. to quibble about prices
( ) 2. intimidate   b. to control by fear
( ) 3. laud   c. to annoy with sarcastic remarks
( ) 4. haggle   d. to heap praises on
( ) 5. heckle   e. to accuse of misconduct
( ) 6. immobilize   f. to eliminate movement

25. **orient** (ôr′ē-ənt): to adjust to a situation.
26. **ostracize** (os′trə-sīz′): to exclude from society; to banish.

ostracized

■ When a person is shunned by others, he is said to be
_____ [extradited / ostracized].

orient

■ In your first days of work at the stock exchange, you will try to
_____ [alienate / orient] yourself.

oriented

■ The new clerk at the department store didn't know a lace curtain
from a lace panty. He was not yet _____ed.

ostracize

■ Jasper was a sneak and a tattletale, so his fellow workers began to
*os*_____ him.

orient

ostracized

■ Every year this college must *or*_____ a new class of
freshmen and must hope that each newcomer will be accepted, not
_____ed, by campus groups.

27. **pander:** to help satisfy the base desires of others.
28. **procrastinate** (prō-kras′tə-nāt′): to delay, to postpone action.

pander

■ Dope pushers, bootleggers, and prostitutes _____
[pander / don't pander] to the vices of others.

pander

■ No lust or desire is so low but that someone will
*pa*_____ to it.

(b)

procrastinate

procrastinate
pander

- Elmer *procrastinates,* repeating, (a) "Let's do it now," (b) "Let's wait." (   )

- Huge term reports are due soon, so don't *pro*_____.

- Our town drunkard gets up early; he does not *pr*_____. By nine a.m. he has found a bartender to *pa*_____ to his thirst.

29. **prognosticate** (prog-nos′tə-kāt′): to predict; to foretell.
30. **rant:** to speak wildly; to rave.

(a)

(b)

rant

prognosticate

rant
prognosticate

- Every day the newspaper *prognosticates* (a) the weather, (b) accidents and crimes. (   )

- To *rant* is to speak (a) logically, (b) loudly and wildly. (   )

- Julius mounted the soapbox and began to fling his arms around and *ra*_____.

- Madame Zaza used a crystal ball to *pro*_____ the misfortunes ahead.

- Professor Schluck would glare at us and *r*_____ about our lack of discipline; then he would *pro*_____ our final reward—on the gallows.

QUIZ

Write the letter that indicates the best definition.

1. (b)
2. (e)
3. (d)
4. (c)
5. (f)
6. (a)

( ) 1. procrastinate	a. to serve the low desires of others
( ) 2. prognosticate	b. to put off taking action
( ) 3. rant	c. to adjust to surroundings
( ) 4. orient	d. to talk wildly and noisily
( ) 5. ostracize	e. to predict future events
( ) 6. pander	f. to shut out from society

31. **raze** (rāz): to tear to the ground; to demolish.
32. **recant** (ri-kant′): to renounce formally one's previous statements.

(b)

■ To *recant* is (a) to add overwhelming evidence, (b) to take back one's words. (   )

raze

■ To improve our city we should first _____ [raise / raze] more condemned tenements.

recant

■ Galileo asserted that the earth revolved around the sun, but he was forced by the Church to *re*_____.

raze

■ Let's *ra*_____ the old barn, Hiram, and build a newfangled garage.

raze

■ Mayor Gronk promised to *ra*_____ all unsafe buildings, but when his own hotel was condemned, he decided to

recant

*re*_____.

33. **simulate** (sim′yə-lāt′): to pretend; to imitate; to counterfeit.
34. **slander:** to utter falsehoods injuring someone's reputation.

(b)

■ "Real simulated pearls," recently advertised for $15.95, are (a) genuine pearls, (b) imitations. (   )

simulate

■ Death and agony, says Emily Dickinson, are genuine and not easy to *sim*_____.

slander

■ To print damaging lies about somebody is to libel; to speak such lies is to *sla*_____.

slander

■ Call the tax assessor a "bribe-happy reptile" and he'll sue you for *sl*_____.

simulate
slander

■ Thomas Paine had many enemies, and when he died a few tried to *sim*_____ grief and others continued to *sl*_____ him.

35. **smirk:** to smile in a conceited or affected manner.
36. **supersede** (soo′pər-sēd′): to take the place of; to replace; to supplant.

(b)

■ As a news reporter you would be insulting the guest of honor if you wrote that he (a) smiled, (b) smirked. (   )

(b)

■ If Plan X *supersedes* Plan W, then (a) both plans are in effect, (b) only Plan X is in effect. (   )

supersede

■ Yesterday's orders are void because today's orders
*sup*_____ them.

smirk

■ Posing for the camera, most tourists will stand in front of a
museum and *sm*_____.

supersede

smirk

■ When Dora told Moose, the big fullback, that he was going to
*su*_____ everybody else in her affections, he could only
scratch his ear and *sm*_____.

QUIZ

Write the letter that indicates the best definition.

1. (b)
2. (c)
3. (d)
4. (f)
5. (e)
6. (a)

(   ) 1. raze   a. to take the place of
(   ) 2. recant   b. to tear down
(   ) 3. simulate   c. to take back what was said
(   ) 4. slander   d. to imitate
(   ) 5. smirk   e. to smile in a silly way
(   ) 6. supersede   f. to utter defamatory remarks

Write the word studied in this chapter that will complete the sentence.

_____   1. Heat the iron! We must [ca-t-z-] the wound.

_____   2. This passage in Homer is Greek to me. Please [el-d-t-].

_____   3. Adding chicory will merely [ad-lt-] this pure coffee.

_____   4. Calling him a dirty thief is [sl-d-].

_____   5. My term paper is due. Oh, why did I [pr-c-t-]?

_____   6. Our governor is corrupt. We must [imp-] him.

_____   7. We ignore the live artist. He dies and we [l-d] his works.

_____   8. In Morocco one is expected to [h-gl-] over rug prices.

_____   9. I want a candid camera shot. Please don't [sm-k].

_____   10. Sally sprayed the ants and managed to [dec-] them.

_____   11. He'd become St. Buster if the Church would [can-] him.

_____   12. Your leg is broken. We'll use splints to [im-b-z-] it.

_____   13. Praise your spouse in public. Never [dis-ge] her.

_____   14. What a mimic! She can [sim-t-] the sound of a dog-cat fight.

_____   15. "Trigger" Sloan is a killer. Why did the jury [a-q-t] him?

_____   16. Ohio wants the fugitive and has asked Utah to [ex-d-] him.

_____   17. At a new school you need a week to [or-t] yourself.

_____   18. Never have so many economists tried to [prog-] future economic trends. We need an excess prophets' tax.

Matching. Write the letter that indicates the best definition.

(   ) 19. blaspheme   a. to taunt and annoy a speaker

(   ) 20. canvass   b. to put up a tent

(   ) 21. condone   c. to meditate

(   ) 22. heckle   d. to excuse a fault

(   ) 23. ostracize   e. to satisfy vulgar desires of others

(   ) 24. pander   f. to swear profanely

(   ) 25. rant   g. to lease to a tenant

               h. to check district opinions

               i. to shun socially

               j. to speak wildly

Check your test answers with the following key. Deduct 4% per error from a possible 100%.

1. cauterize
2. elucidate
3. adulterate
4. slander
5. procrastinate
6. impeach
7. laud
8. haggle
9. smirk
10. decimate
11. canonize
12. immobilize
13. disparage
14. simulate
15. acquit
16. extradite
17. orient
18. prognosticate
19. (f)
20. (h)
21. (d)
22. (a)
23. (i)
24. (e)
25. (j)

Score: _____ %

Fill in the blank with the verb that fits the definition. Although these verbs were not defined in this chapter, you should recognize most of them. Check your answers with the key at the end of the exercise. Use your dictionary to study any unknown words.

■ atrophy, belie, browbeat, corroborate, covet

1. _____ to bully; to intimidate
2. _____ to confirm; to make more certain
3. _____ to prove false
4. _____ to desire what belongs to another
5. _____ to wither; to waste away

■ decry, deploy, dismantle, edify, emulate

6. _____ to instruct; to enlighten spiritually
7. _____ to imitate so as to equal or excel
8. _____ to spread out forces according to plan
9. _____ to denounce; to condemn; to disparage
10. _____ to strip of equipment; to disassemble

■ epitomize, equivocate, implicate, impoverish, jettison

11. _____ to represent the essence of
12. _____ to be ambiguous purposely; to hedge; to mislead
13. _____ to make poor; to reduce to poverty
14. _____ to throw cargo overboard in an emergency
15. _____ to show to be involved; to entangle

■ mollify, osculate, rankle, retaliate, retrench

16. _____ to kiss
17. _____ to cause resentment; to fester; to irritate
18. _____ to pay back injury for injury; to revenge
19. _____ to make less angry; to soothe; to appease
20. _____ to cut expenses; to economize

- scrutinize, skulk, swelter, thwart, tipple

21. _____ to prevent from accomplishing a purpose; to hinder
22. _____ to drink liquor frequently
23. _____ to move about furtively; to lurk; to shirk
24. _____ to examine carefully; to look at closely
25. _____ to suffer or perspire from oppressive heat

KEY TO SUPPLEMENTARY EXERCISE

1. browbeat
2. corroborate
3. belie
4. covet
5. atrophy
6. edify
7. emulate
8. deploy
9. decry
10. dismantle
11. epitomize
12. equivocate
13. impoverish
14. jettison
15. implicate
16. osculate
17. rankle
18. retaliate
19. mollify
20. retrench
21. thwart
22. tipple
23. skulk
24. scrutinize
25. swelter

Score: _____ %

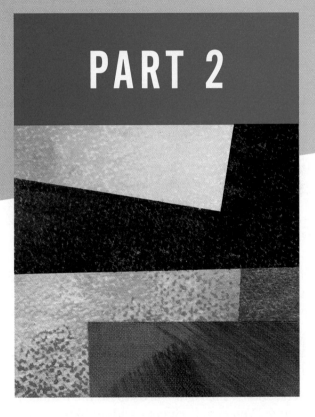

PART 2

Rhetoric

When you write English, you are a soldier crawling through a mined field. You have to recognize and avoid the traps and snares—clichés, redundancy, plagiarism, logical fallacies. You have to know and use the helpful devices, too—concreteness, analogy, parallelism, ellipsis, idioms. As a resourceful writer you study your craft to survive.

This chapter defines terms that deal with writing. Most frames present two definitions and the usual choices and completions.

As in previous chapters, choose the right words to fill the blanks. But you can do more than learn word meanings. You can, perhaps—without damage to your creativity— apply some concepts behind these terms to your own writing.

EXERCISES

1. **rhetoric** (ret′ə-rik): the art of using words persuasively and effectively in writing and speaking. *Rhetoric* involves grammar, logic, style, and figures of speech.
2. **redundancy** (ri-dun′dən-sē): wordiness; needless repetition; tautology. Examples: "Big in size," "in my opinion, I think," "at this point in time," "Jewish rabbi."

rhetoric

■ The art of composition is called _____ [rhetoric / redundancy].

redundancy

■ Padded phrases like "red in color" are examples of *re_____.*

redundancy
rhetoric

■ The phrase "necessary essentials" also illustrates _____ and is poor *rh_____.*

(a)

■ Mere *rhetoric* without sound ideas usually results in (a) empty eloquence, (b) a literary masterpiece. (   )

redundancy

■ Terms like *tautology, pleonism, verbiage, verbosity, circumlocution, diffuseness, periphrasis,* and *prolixity* refer to various aspects of wordiness, or *re_____.*

rhetoric

(b)

■ The master of effective writing, or *rh_____,* avoids *redundant* phrases such as (a) "a hot pastrami sandwich," (b) "edible food to eat." (   )

3. **malapropism** (mal′ə-prop-iz′əm): ridiculous misuse of a word for another one that sounds like it. Mrs. *Malaprop* in Richard Sheridan's play *The Rivals* (1775) spoke of "an allegory on the banks of the Nile."

malapropism

■ The misuse of a word for another one that sounds like it, as in "they won the world serious," is a _____.

(b)

■ Which of these two blunders involves a *malapropism?* (a) "Us boys went," (b) "The professor gave a lecher." (   )

malapropism

■ "Every morning my mother exercises her abominable muscles." This sentence contains a *m_____.*

malapropism

incandescent
frankincense
reservations
monarchy
an imaginary line

■ Cross out each ridiculous misuse, known as a *m*_____, and write the correct word above it:

Thomas Edison invented the indecent lamp.

The wise men brought gifts of myrrh and frankfurters.

Our government put the Indians into reservoirs.

The government of England is a limited mockery.

The equator is a menagerie lion that runs around the middle of the earth.

4. **euphemism** (yo͞o′fə-miz′əm): a mild expression substituted for a distasteful one. Examples: "a morals charge" for "rape," "resting place" for "grave," "stylishly stout" for "fat."

5. **triteness:** dullness in expression or content; lack of freshness and creativity. *Triteness* occurs in story plots ("theft of diamonds"), in greeting cards ("just a note to say I am thinking of you"), and in speeches ("Dr. Fossil needs no introduction, so without further ado. . . .")

euphemism

■ A mild, indirect expression to avoid a blunt, painful one is a *eu*_____.

euphemism
triteness

■ To say that an ailing cat was "put to sleep" is a *eu*_____. Also, the stale phrase is an example of *tr*_____.

Examples:
bathroom
washroom
powder room
restroom

■ Hardly anybody goes to the toilet any more. Give two euphemisms we usually use for "toilet."

_____   _____

Write *trite* in front of any dull, unoriginal lines.

_____ a. I have decided to write my theme on the subject of dogs.

_____ b. Last week I was attacked by a four-legged flea plantation known as man's best friend.

Trite: a, c

_____ c. Sooner or later, after all is said and done, a senior citizen must face the prospect of retirement.

euphemism
euphemisms
Examples: heck,
my gosh, egad,
holy jeepers,
jiminy crickets,
cripes

■ A substitute expression that avoids the naming of deity (ex., "holy gee," "for gosh sake," "by golly") is a *eu*_____. Cite three other such softened oaths known as *eu*_____

_____.

QUIZ

Write the letter that indicates the best definition.

1. (e)
2. (a)
3. (d)
4. (b)
5. (c)

(   ) 1. rhetoric   a. tautology; wordiness
(   ) 2. redundancy   b. a mild substitute expression
(   ) 3. malapropism   c. staleness in expression
(   ) 4. euphemism   d. a ridiculous word blunder
(   ) 5. triteness   e. art of effective communication

6. **acronym** (ak′rə-nim): a word made up from the initial letters or syllables of a title or phrase. Examples: MADD (Mothers Against Drunk Drivers), WAC (Women's Army Corps).

acronym

■ If you don't want a jail or a new mall built in your neighborhood, you are a NIMBY, which word is an *ac*_____ for "not in my back yard."

initial
acronym

■ The word "AWOL" is made up basically from the _____ [initial / final] letters of "absent without leave" and is called an *a*_____.

UFO
radar
UNESCO

■ _____ unidentified flying object (Give acronym)
■ _____ radio detecting and ranging
■ _____ United Nations Educational, Scientific, and Cultural Organization

7. **antonym** (an′tə-nim): a word of opposite meaning. "Tall" and "short," "fast" and "slow," "smart" and "stupid" are pairs of *antonyms*.

8. **homonym** (hom′ə-nim): a word that sounds like another word but has a different meaning and usually a different spelling. "Air" and "heir," "past" and "passed," "site" and "cite" are *homonyms*.

homonyms

■ Pairs of words like "principle" and "principal," "block" and "bloc," are called *ho*_____.

antonyms

■ Pairs of words like "beautiful" and "ugly," "rich" and "poor," are called *an*_____.

antonyms
homonyms

■ "Dear" and "hateful" are _____; "dear" and "deer" are _____.

homonyms
antonyms

■ "Bare" and "bear" are _____; "bare" and "clothed" are _____.

9. **concreteness:** quality of being specific and of referring to particular things. *Concreteness* adds clarity and power to writing.

10. **connotation:** the suggestiveness and emotional associations of a word, apart from its denotation, or literal meaning. Propagandists often use words that seem honest but which, by their *connotations,* arouse prejudice.

concreteness

- Clarity of detail is called *con*_____.

(b)

- Choose the *concrete* phrase: (a) "some young fellow," (b) "a shambling newsboy." (   )

(b)

- Choose the *concrete* phrase: (a) "an interesting animal," (b) "a blue-bottomed ape." (   )

connotation

- The feeling that surrounds a word is its *con*_____.

steadfast
staunch
unflinching

- Underline three words with favorable *connotations* to describe an ancestor who absolutely refused to change his opinions about anything: obstinate, pig-headed, steadfast, hidebound, bigoted, staunch, unflinching.

(b)

- Which news headline has unfavorable *connotations?* (a) "Mayor and Wife Invite Friends to Housewarming," (b) "Facts Bared About Mayor's New Love-Nest." (   )

Write the letter that indicates the best definition.

1. (d)
2. (e)
3. (b)
4. (a)
5. (c)

( ) 1. acronym	a. exactness; specificness
( ) 2. antonym	b. word with same sound
( ) 3. homonym	c. suggestive qualities; overtones
( ) 4. concreteness	d. word made from initials
( ) 5. connotation	e. word with opposite meaning

11. **prose:** writing or speech which is not poetry. Most communication—whether of newspapers, magazines, or conversation—is *prose.*

(a)

- *Prose* is the language of (a) ordinary conversation and writing, (b) Longfellow's "The Village Blacksmith." (   )

prose

- All of your life you have been talking in _____ [poetry / prose].

prose

■ Essays by Michael Montaigne, Charles Lamb, and Robert Benchley are all written in _____ [poetry / prose].

(b)

■ A *prose* composition requires (a) rhyming, (b) no rhyming. (   )

12. **exposition:** writing which explains or informs. *Exposition* is one of four traditional types of discourse, the others being *description, narration,* and *argumentation.*

13. **précis** (prā′sē): a short condensed version of a piece of writing. The *précis* is shorter than the original, but it maintains something of the same phrasing, tone, order, and proportion of ideas.

exposition

■ Writing that is explanatory is called _____ [narrative / exposition].

précis

■ Summarizing a composition but preserving the original phrasing and tone results in a *pr_____.*

(a)

■ The *précis* of a magazine article or essay (a) shortens it, (b) expands it. (   )

exposition
(b)

■ To set forth information is the function of *ex_____*; so the natural language of *exposition* is (a) poetry, (b) prose. (   )

(a)

■ Although the *précis* of a composition is much shorter than the original, it usually retains (a) some of the original phrasing and tone, (b) the minor details. (   )

14. **plagiarism** (plā′jə-riz′əm): copying the language or ideas of another author and presenting them as one's own; includes the lifting of phrases and sentences from research sources without using quotation marks. *Plagiarism* results in severe penalties at most colleges.

15. **paraphrase** (par′ə-frāz′): to restate a passage in different words. The researcher must *paraphrase* borrowed material or place it within quotation marks and in either case must credit the source.

plagiarism

■ Copying somebody else's writing without giving proper credit is called *pl_____.*

paraphrase

■ To restate a borrowed passage in one's own words is to *pa_____.*

credit

■ Whether one *paraphrases* a passage or quotes it, he or she should _____ [credit / ignore] the original source.

(a)

■ *Plagiarism* is (a) literary theft, (b) permissible borrowing. (   )

plagiarism

(b)

(b)

plagiarism

- To avoid the serious offense of _____, one might (a) change a word or two in borrowed material, (b) use quotes around each borrowed passage and credit the original writer. ( )

- If a line is too individual or clever for easy *paraphrasing,* the researcher should (a) steal it, (b) place it in quotation marks. ( ) Then, if the writer also credits the source, he or she will avoid *p*_____.

QUIZ

Write the letter that indicates the best definition.

1. (d)
2. (e)
3. (b)
4. (c)
5. (a)

( ) 1. prose	a. a restatement in one's own words
( ) 2. exposition	b. a condensation; a shortened version
( ) 3. précis	c. literary theft
( ) 4. plagiarism	d. ordinary nonpoetic language
( ) 5. paraphrase	e. informative writing; one type of essay

16. **ellipsis** (i-lip'sis): the omission of words, as from quoted material, usually indicated by three dots or asterisks. *Ellipsis* may be used to shorten a quoted passage but not so as to change the meaning or to remove surgically any damaging evidence.

(a)

- "But, in a larger sense, we cannot dedicate . . . this ground." The three dots indicate (a) an ellipsis, (b) a pause while Lincoln took a drink. ( )

ellipsis

- The omission of words from a quoted passage is called an *el*_____.

three

- The *ellipsis* is indicated by _____ [three / seven] dots.

improper
ellipsis

- If your research quote says, "Poe drank, although very infrequently, during this period" and you write it as "Poe drank . . . during this period," you are making _____ [proper / improper] use of _____.

17. **begging the question:** assuming what has yet to be proved. *Begging the question* is a fallacy of logic, as when we say, "Shouldn't all those crooks at City Hall be turned out of office?" or "It's a waste of money to give that murderer a trial—just string 'im up!"

18. **post hoc** (pōst hok′): assuming that one thing caused another merely because it happened earlier. This term for a fallacy of logic is from the Latin phrase *post hoc, ergo propter hoc,* which literally means "after this, therefore because of this."

begging

■ To take something for granted without proof is _____ *the question.*

question
"useless"

■ "Why must a useless course like history be made compulsory?" The word that *begs the* _____ and needs proving is _____ ["useless" / "course"].

■ When an Indian dance gets credit for causing the rain that falls the next day, the reasoning behind such credit is called

post hoc

   p_____ h_____.

■ The fallacy of assuming that two events that follow each other must have a cause-effect relationship is called _____

post hoc

   _____.

begs
(b)

■ "We must not permit a pornographic book like *The Catcher in the Rye* to be kept in our library." The word that _____ *the question* and needs proving is (a) "permit," (b) "pornographic." (   )

(a)

■ A young pugilist wearing a certain bathrobe scored a knockout in one round; thereafter he insisted on wearing that same robe, never cleaned, to every fight of his career. He believed in (a) *post hoc* reasoning, (b) hygiene. (   )

19. **ad hominem** (ad hom′ə-nəm): appealing to a person's prejudices or selfish interests rather than to his reason; attacking an opponent rather than sticking to the issue. The Latin phrase *argumentum ad hominem* means "argument at or to the man."

20. **non sequitur** (non sek′wi-tər): a conclusion that does not follow from the evidence presented. The Latin phrase *non sequitur* means "it does not follow."

hominem

■ In a debate about state lotteries, an attack on your moral character is an *ad* _____.

(a)

■ *Ad hominem* implies that the real issue of the argument gets (a) overlooked, (b) close attention. (   )

sequitur

■ "My husband loves Italian motion picture films, so I think he'll enjoy the chicken cacciatora I am going to cook for him." The reasoning here involves a *non* _____.

Chapter Twelve **161**

does not

non sequitur

ad hominem

- In a *non sequitur* the conclusion _____ [does / does not] follow from the evidence presented.

- "Schopenhauer was very pessimistic, and nobody should read his essays." The conclusion is not justified by the evidence, and we have a *n*_____ *s*_____.

- "Better vote against this school bill, Smedley; your kids have graduated already and you'll just get soaked for more taxes." The argument here is *a*_____ *h*_____.

1. (c)
2. (d)
3. (e)
4. (a)
5. (b)

( ) 1. ellipsis	a. appeal to prejudice
( ) 2. begging the question	b. an illogical conclusion
( ) 3. *post hoc*	c. omission of words
( ) 4. *ad hominem*	d. assuming without proof
( ) 5. *non sequitur*	e. after this, therefore because of this

bandwagon

win

bandwagon

(b)

21. **bandwagon device:** persuasion to join the popular or winning side. "To climb aboard the bandwagon" means to shift one's vote to the apparent winner.

- "Three out of four smoke Hempos!" Such ads that suggest that we join the majority use the *b*_____ *device*.

- The *bandwagon device* tells us to vote for Jim Snurd because he is going to _____ [lose / win] by a landslide.

- "Three million sold already!" Whether this pitch refers to Klunker cars, to horseburgers, or to albums by the Five Lunatics, it uses the *b*_____ *device* and it urges you to do (a) the rational thing, (b) what the crowd is doing. (   )

22. **faulty dilemma** (di-lem′ə): the offering of only two alternatives when more than two exist. "We must wipe out the Pootzians or we will perish." Such talk illustrates the *faulty dilemma,* since it ignores the possibility of peaceful coexistence.

23. **analogy** (ə-nal′ə-jē): an extended comparison to clarify an idea; a comparison of things which are alike in certain ways and therefore presumably alike in other ways. *Analogies* can illustrate an idea, but they do not prove it.

■ "Either the man is boss in a home or the woman will rule." Such logic presents a *faulty d_____.*

dilemma

■ Comparing man to an eagle that must rule its own nest is an *an_____.*

analogy

■ *Analogies* _____ [prove / illustrate] ideas.

illustrate

■ "The early bird catches the worm, so I'll be up at dawn and find a job." This is reasoning by _____.

analogy

■ "Don't touch alcohol or you'll end up in the looney bin." This choice is the *f_____ d_____.*

faulty dilemma

■ The *faulty dilemma* forces one to choose from _____ [two / all of the] possibilities.

two

■ Bede's *Ecclesiastical History* (eighth century) likens our life to the quick flight of a sparrow through a lighted hall at night. This is an *a_____.*

analogy

24. **Socratic irony** (sə-krat′ik): the device of pretending to be ignorant and asking questions in order to trap the opponent into obvious error. Socrates uses *Socratic irony,* for instance, to refute a husky Athenian who argues that might makes right.

■ The man who uses *Socratic irony* asks a series of innocent-sounding questions (a) because he is stupid, (b) because he is leading his opponent into self-contradiction. (   )

(b)

■ To employ *S_____ irony* one must (a) ask adroit questions to draw out the other fellow's ignorance, (b) talk constantly in an opinionated fashion. (   )

Socratic

(a)

■ If falsely accused of plagiarism you might use *Socratic* _____ to clear yourself by saying, (a) "I'm innocent, Teacher; I swear I'm innocent!" (b) "Very interesting—now where is this passage which I have stolen?" (   )

irony

(b)

QUIZ

Write the letter that indicates the best definition.

1. (b)
2. (d)
3. (a)
4. (c)

(   ) 1. bandwagon device   a. an extended comparison

(   ) 2. faulty dilemma   b. argument for joining the popular side

(   ) 3. analogy   c. refuting by means of clever but innocent-sounding questions

(   ) 4. Socratic irony   d. offering two alternatives when more exist

---

25. **fragment:** an incomplete sentence. *Fragments* are often considered the unpardonable sin in freshman themes, though they are acceptable in exclamations, dialogue, and certain types of informal writing.

26. **comma splice:** the use of a comma between main clauses where a period or semicolon should be used. Example: "Jack London wrote about supermen and superdogs, he became a rich socialist."

Before each of the following write *fragments, comma splice,* or *correct.*

comma splice

- _____ H. L. Mencken was pungent and opinionated, I never thought he was dull.

fragment

- _____ Alexandre Dumas being about the most imaginative novelist I had ever read.

correct

- _____ Elvis died.

comma splice

- _____ The British loved Kipling, however, he was never poet laureate.

fragment

- _____ A scholarly analysis, which reads like a detective story, of the Shakespeare sonnets, particularly those dealing with the Dark Lady.

correct

- _____ My brother can't write like Chaucer, but he spells like him.

27. **infinitive** (in-fin′i-tiv): a verbal form that consists usually of "to" plus a verb, as "to walk." The *infinitive* can do the work of a noun, adjective, or adverb.

28. **participle** (pär′ti-sip′əl): a verbal adjective. "Flying in a battered plane, I had some frightening moments." Here "flying," "battered," and "frightening" are *participles.*

infinitive

- A phrase like "to paint" is an *in*_____.

participile

- A verbal adjective—like "honking" in "honking geese"—is a *p*_____________.

participle
infinitive,
participle

- "Attacking his critics, James Fenimore Cooper began to waste valuable writing time." "Attacking" is a _____________, "to waste" is an _____________, and "writing" is a _____________.

infinitives

- "To strive, to seek, to find, and not to yield." This final line of Tennyson's poem "Ulysses" (1842) contains four _____________.

(a)

- Inserting words between "to" and the verb in an *infinitive* results in a *split infinitive,* a phrasing which often sounds awkward. Which phrase has a split infinitive? (a) "to as soon as possible analyze Chekhov's play," (b) "to analyze Chekhov's play as soon as possible. (   )

infinitive
participle

- "Shakespeare was able to find several gripping themes in the chronicles of Holinshed." Here "to find" is an *i*_____________ and "gripping" is a *p*_____________.

Write *dangler*–for "dangling participle" or *correct.*

dangler

- Becoming six years old, my mother got a divorce. _____________

correct

- Echoing Emerson, Walt Whitman spoke of man's divinity. _____________

dangler

- If stewed, you will enjoy these prunes. _____________

29. **parallelism** (par′ə-lel′iz-əm): similarity of grammatical structure given to similar ideas. *Parallelism* in phrasing brings out *parallelism* in ideas.

parallelism
yodeling

- Consider the sentence, "Fritz loves fishing, climbing, and to yodel." It has faulty *par*_____________ but would become acceptable if the phrase "to yodel" were changed to the word *y*_____________.

faulty

- "Gunder has vowed to work, to save money, and that he will succeed in business." This sentence has _____________ [acceptable / faulty] *parallelism.*

(b)

- Which has better *parallelism?* (a) "I came and after I saw the enemy they were conquered by me," (b) "I came, I saw, I conquered." (   )

for

parallelism

■ Lincoln referred to "government of the people, by the people, _____ [for / to help] the people" and achieved structural *pa_____.*

30. **idiom:** an accepted phrase that is contrary to the usual language pattern. *Idioms* are natural, supple, and often very informal. Examples: "catch cold," "give in," "hint at," "knock off work," "pick a fight."

idioms

■ Phrases like "comes in handy" and "takes after his father" are *id_____.*

(a)

■ Although *idioms* violate normal language construction, they are (a) proper and acceptable, (b) colorful but unusable. (   )

idiom
(b)

■ Another peculiar English phrasing, known as an *id_____* is (a) "walk with me," (b) "angry with me." (   )

(b)

■ Which is an *idiom?* (a) "became a loafer," (b) "went to the dogs." (   )

idiomatic

■ Ernest Hemingway achieved vigor and naturalness in his stories by using _____ [formal / idiomatic] English.

QUIZ

Write the letter that indicates the best example.

1. (e)
2. (c)
3. (a)
4. (d)
5. (f)
6. (b)

( ) 1. fragment	a. "*To err* is human."
( ) 2. comma splice	b. We grabbed a bite.
( ) 3. infinitive	c. "Here comes Lulu, get the hymn book."
( ) 4. participle	d. "'The Lottery' is a *terrifying* story."
( ) 5. parallelism	e. "Whereas Irving knew the Catskills."
( ) 6. idiom	f. He lived; he loved; he died.

Supply the missing word in each sentence.

1. Copying material without giving proper credit is *pl*_____.

2. The ridiculous misuse of a word for another that sounds like it is a *mal*_____.

3. A word like "WAVE," made up from the initials of a title, is an *ac*_____.

4. A mild word substituted for a blunt one is a *eu*_____.

5. Prose composition that explains or sets forth is *ex*_____.

6. Ordinary writing that is not poetry is called *pr*_____.

7. A word of opposite meaning is an *an*_____.

8. A word with the same sound but different meaning is a *ho*_____.

9. A conclusion which "does not follow" from the evidence is a *n*_____ *se*_____.

10. Needless repetition or wordiness is *re*_____.

11. An accepted phrase that defies normal language patterns is an *id*_____.

12. The verbal "grinning" in "grinning faces" is a *pa*_____.

13. An incomplete sentence is a *fr*_____.

14. Propaganda urging one to follow the crowd is the *b*_____ *device*.

15. An omission of words, indicated by three dots, is an *el*_____.

Write True or False.

_____ 16. *Concreteness* refers to the use of clear, specific detail.

_____ 17. *Post hoc* logic is considered valid in science.

_____ 18. *Begging the question* means assuming without proof.

_____ 19. An argument *ad hominem* sticks to the main issue.

_____ 20. *Triteness* adds color and vigor to one's style.

_____ 21. To use *Socratic irony* means to argue and fall into one's own trap.

_____ 22. In the *faulty dilemma* one must choose from an incomplete set of alternatives.

_____ 23. *Comma splice* refers to the omission of a comma.

_____ 24. The following contains *parallelism:* "We will fight with guns, with bombs, and with fists."

_____ 25. *Rhetoric* is the art of persuasive writing and speaking.

Write the letter that indicates the best completion.

(   ) 26. An *analogy* is (a) a proof, (b) an exaggeration, (c) a comparison, (d) a stale expression.

(   ) 27. An example of an *infinitive* is (a) "the critic Mencken," (b) "criticizing," (c) "to criticize," (d) "to critics."

(   ) 28. A *précis* is (a) an explanation, (b) an expansion, (c) a quotation, (d) a condensation.

(   ) 29. A *paraphrase* is (a) a restatement, (b) a quotation, (c) a line of poetry, (d) a wordy passage.

Match each word with its definition.

(   ) 30. participle   a. dull, worn-out phrasing
(   ) 31. triteness   b. suggestiveness
(   ) 32. connotation   c. verbal adjective
(   ) 33. plagiarism   d. literary theft

KEY TO REVIEW TEST

Check your test answers with the following key. Deduct 3% per error from a possible 100%.

1. plagiarism	12. participle	23. False
2. malapropism	13. fragment	24. True
3. acronym	14. bandwagon	25. True
4. euphemism	15. ellipsis	26. (c)
5. exposition	16. True	27. (c)
6. prose	17. False	28. (d)
7. antonym	18. True	29. (a)
8. homonym	19. False	30. (c)
9. *non sequitur*	20. False	31. (a)
10. redundancy	21. False	32. (b)
11. idiom	22. True	33. (d)

Score: _____ %

Diction

CHAPTER 13

Partial List

aggravate, **1**	lousy, **10**	that, **20**
cliché, **2**	majority, **11**	themselves, **21**
complexioned, **3**	nice, **12**	this, **22**
criteria, **4**	plus, **13**	try, **23**
enthusiastic, **5**	prejudiced, **14**	unique, **24**
etc., **6**	regardless, **17**	used to, **16**
funny, **7**	somewhere, **18**	which, **25**
have, **8**	supposed to, **15**	
lots of, **9**	suspicion, **19**	

A nearsighted farm boy didn't want his new girlfriend to find out how weak his eyes were. He pounded a nail into a tree a hundred yards away. That evening, to impress his new friend, he pointed to the distant tree and said, "I think I see a little nail in yonder tree." He started to walk toward the nail and tripped over a cow.

Similarly, we may hope to impress people with our far-ranging vocabulary, but if meanwhile we trip over common, everyday words, we'll impress nobody.

This chapter deals with phrases that are stumbling blocks to good compositions. It warns against using clichés—weary, worn-out expressions such as "last but not least," "strange as it seems," and "cool as a cucumber." It warns against verbal misdemeanors such as "irregardless," "complected," and "suspicioned." It warns, in short, that expanding our vocabulary is not enough—we must also guard against faulty expressions that threaten our writing style.

Common, trivial words can be a disaster area for the amateur writer.

Fill the blanks thoughtfully. Look to your grammar books for other slipshod expressions that should be avoided. Let the esoteric vocabulary come later.

✚ EXERCISES

1. **aggravate:** to make worse. "Sleeping in the snowbank will *aggravate* Joe's bronchitis." In formal English, we avoid using *aggravate* to mean "irritate." Bad conditions may be aggravated (worsened); people are *irritated,* not aggravated.

Write *aggravate* or *irritate*.

irritate

aggravate

■ Those howling dogs *irritate* _____ Alice. They seem determined to *aggravate* _____ her headache.

irritate

■ My former name, John Belch, used to *irritate* _____ me, so I changed it to Fred Belch.

irritate

irritate

aggravate

■ Chewing your bubble gum may *irritate* _____ your classmates. It will certainly *irritate* _____ your teacher. Those popping sounds will *aggravate* _____ his wrath.

irritate

aggravate

■ Smokers *irritate* _____ Mrs. Smith. The fumes *aggravate* _____ her cough, so she steps on cigarettes. Now she has cancer of the foot.

2. **cliché** (klē-shā'): a much overused expression: a trite phrase or idea. Clichés have lost their cleverness and may bore or irritate the reader. Examples: "last but not least," "strong as an ox," "doomed to disappointment."

In the following sentences, choose the ending that is *not* a cliché.

(b)

■ Harvard must win tomorrow—(a) that is the bottom line! (b) we will not accept defeat! (**b**)

(b)

■ Uncle Nick died (a) at a ripe old age, (b) on his ninety-third birthday, (c) when he was old as the hills. (**b**)

(b)

■ All of General Custer's men (a) bit the dust, (b) died in the battle, (c) met their Maker. (**b**)

(c)

■ Our soccer team intends to (a) bring home the bacon, (b) take the bull by the horns, (c) win this tournament. (**c**)

(c)

■ After crossing the border, we (a) breathed a sigh of relief, (b) were on cloud nine, (c) broke into happy conversation. (**c**)

Clichés are like old jokes—the reader knows the ending before it arrives. Show that you can predict the end of these clichés.

a. never
b. milk
c. blue
d. dogs
e. ado
f. seems

a. better late than ___never___
b. cry over spilt ___milk___
c. a bolt from the ___?.?___   *blue*
d. raining cats and ___dogs___
e. without further ___ado___
f. strange as it ___seems___

Draw a line through the cliché in each of the following sentences and write a substitute phrase above it.

Examples:
swindle us

to reform—

sailing the ocean
excited me.

■ The stranger managed to ~~pull the wool over our eyes~~. *fool us.*

■ The burglar promised to ~~walk the straight and narrow path~~ —which he did until tempted again. *~~~~ to reform*

■ The prospect of sailing the ~~briny deep blew my mind~~. *ocean   was exciting*

3. **complexioned** (kəm-plek'shənd): having a specified skin color (Avoid the colloquial *complected*.)

(a)

■ The Rose Bowl queen was fair- (a) complexioned, (b) complected. (*a*)

complexioned

■ After a day in the coal mine, the miners were sooty- *com**plexioned***

complexioned,
complexioned

■ Phineas claimed that his skin ointment was as good for light- *c**omplexioned*** people as for dark-c *omplexioned* people, and it probably was.

complexioned

■ The word *complected* is considered colloquial or dialectal, and most good writers prefer to use *complexioned*.

4. **criteria** (krī-tēr'ē-ə): standards of judgment; rules for testing anything. Note that *criteria* is the plural of *criterion*, and *criteria* takes a plural verb. "Several *criteria* were used in choosing our family dog."

criterion

■ The main *criterion* in hiring a bartender is that he be fairly honest.

criteria
criterion
criteria

- I judge a baseball pitcher by five *cr* _iteria_____ The first *cr* _iterion_____ is whether he can pitch strikes. If he can pitch strikes, the other four *cr* _iteria_____ don't matter.

criteria

criterion

- Hank rates a restaurant according to a few simple _criteria_____. Food must be cheap; food must be plentiful; and, final _criterion_____, the roaches must stay out of sight.

5. **enthusiastic:** eager; ardent. (Avoid using the colloquial *enthused.*)

enthusiastic

- The strip teaser performed before an _enthusiastic_ [enthused / (enthusiastic)] crowd.

was enthusiastic

- The Englishman _was enthusiastic_ [enthused / (was enthusiastic)] about the house with two bathrooms.

enthusiastic

- We were all _enthusiastic_ [enthused / enthusiastic] when Tom Mix untied his sweetheart from the railroad tracks.

(b)

- In formal writing the use of *enthused* is generally (a) acceptable, (b) undesirable. (**b**)

QUIZ

Circle the choice that results in the more acceptable sentence.

1. irritate
2. criterion

3. do assignments

4. complexioned
5. enthusiastic

1. Blowing on your soup may [aggravate / (irritate)] your girlfriend.
2. What is your [(criterion) / ~~criteria~~] for choosing a beauty queen?
3. The star halfback failed the course because he didn't [crack a book / (do assignments) / burn the midnight oil].
4. The fortune-teller told me to keep away from a reddish-[complected / (complexioned)] man with a knife in his hand.
5. The immigrant was [(enthusiastic) / enthused] about the rooms with the brand-new rattraps.

6. **etc.:** et cetera (et set′rə); and others; and so forth. (The abbreviation *etc.* is usually avoided in formal writing. Use its English equivalent.)

(b)

- Poe later wrote "The Tell-Tale Heart," "The Black Cat," (a) etc., (b) and other horror stories. (**b**)

(b)

■ If accepted at Harvard, I will take courses in physics, chemistry, (a) etc. (b) and mathematics. (*b*)

etc.

■ To pronounce and spell *etc.* correctly, you should think of the first three letters of *et cetera*—they give us the abbreviation ___*etc.*___ .

(a)

■ *Etc.* means "and so forth"—thus to write "and etc.," with its additional "and," is (a) incorrect, (b) correct. (*a*)

7. **funny:** comical, laughable; humorous. (Avoid *funny* in formal writing when you mean "strange, peculiar, odd.")

strange

■ We thought it was ___strange___ [funny / strange] that our low-salaried sheriff would buy a yacht.

unusual

■ When Hilda found the letters from John's three other wives, she realized that something ___unusual___ [funny / unusual] was going on.

funny

■ Mark Twain's lectures were extremely *funny* ___.

mournful

■ The widow sat near the casket with a ___mournful___ [mournful / funny] look on her face.

8. **have:** to possess. (Use *have* as an auxiliary verb in phrases like "should *have*," "could *have*," "might *have*," and avoid the nonstandard "should of," "could of," . . .)

Write *have* or *of* in the sentences that follow:

have
of

■ The material might ___have___ cost ten dollars a yard, but none ___of___ the bathers wore twenty cents' worth.

have
have

■ You should ___have___ warned me that Ambrose would sing here, so that I could ___have___ gone to the ball game instead.

of
have

■ Olaf washed the top windows ___of___ the building and must ___have___ stepped back to admire his work.

9. **lots of; a lot of:** many; a great deal. (The informal phrases "lots of" and "a lot of" are acceptable but tend to be used far too frequently; they should be avoided in formal writing. Incidentally, "a lot" is two words, not one.)

numerous

■ Shakespeare wrote ___numerous___ [a lot of / numerous] sonnets.

Many
considerable

- ■ _Many_ [Lots of / Many] farms were struck by the hailstorm and _considerable_ [lots of / considerable] damage was done.

many

- ■ Grandpa bought a few lots near the garbage dump and made _many_ [lots of / many] other bad investments.

informal
sparingly

- ■ The phrases "lots of" and "a lot of" are considered _informal_ [formal / informal] and should therefore be used _sparingly_ [sparingly / lots of times] in student research papers.

10. **lousy** (slangy, overused expression; try to use a more precise term in its place): dingy, unworkable, ugly, tasteless, moronic, unfashionable, shoddy, amateurish.

general

- ■ The slang word "lousy" expresses disapproval in a very _general_ [general / precise] way.

poorly paid

- ■ Our fry cook gave up his _poorly paid_ [poorly paid / lousy] job.

unromantic

- ■ The couple had a(n) _unromantic_ [lousy / unromantic] honeymoon.

Substitute a more precise word for "lousy."

Examples
indigestible
rainy
weedy

lousy meal: _inedible_ meal
lousy weather: _gloomy_ weather
lousy lawn: _dry_ lawn

11. **majority:** more than half of the total number; the excess over all the rest of the votes. (A *plurality,* however, refers to the excess of votes received by the leading candidate over the second of three or more candidates. Do not use *majority* to refer to most of a single thing. WRONG: "Bill ate the majority of the watermelon.")

most

- ■ The elderly couple were sick during _most_ [most / the majority] of the trip on the pleasure cruiser.

most

- ■ Myrtle did _most_ [most / the majority] of the engine design.

did

- ■ Anna had 80 votes; Ben, 40 votes; Clarence, 25 votes. Anna _did_ [did / did not] receive a majority of the votes.

15

She won the election by a majority of ___15___
[15 / 40 / 80].

did not

6

■ In another election, Alice had 95 votes; Bill, 89 votes; Chester, 72 votes. Alice __did not__ [did / did not] receive a majority of the votes. She won the election by a plurality of __6__ [6 / 13 / 95] votes.

majority

most

■ Mr. Grunt chopped down twelve of his twenty pine trees. He has, therefore, cut a *majority* of his trees. He will now spend _most_ [most / the majority] of the money he earns on a hernia operation.

12. **nice; cool** (informal, overused expressions; use more precise terms if you can): refreshing, comfortable, sunny, beautiful, cordial, delicious, attractive, pleasant, eye-catching.

(b)

(c)

(b)

The natives were (1) nice, (b) extremely friendly, (c) cool. (*b*)
My neighbor? He's (a) cool, ~~(b) nice,~~ (c) amusing. (*C*)
My room is now (a) pretty nice, (b) freshly painted, (c) cool, huh? (*b*)

Substitute a more descriptive word for "nice" or "cool."

Examples
expensive
inspirational
sunny
surrealistic

nice car: _____*flashy*_____ car
cool teacher: _____*young*_____ teacher
nice weather: _____*Sunny*_____ weather
cool short stories: *enthralling* short stories

QUIZ

Circle the choice that results in the more acceptable sentence.

1. most
2. biased

3. ominous
4. etc.
5. friendly
6. six
7. have

1. The widow left (most / the majority] of her money to Rover.
2. One sports writer attributed our loss to the [biased / lousy] decisions of the referee.
3. When Bluebeard's fifth wife was strangled, I knew something [funny / ominous] was going on.
4. Our pet hospital cared for dogs, cats, birds, (etc. / and etc.]
5. Rosa is a (friendly / nice] girl.
6. The Vanderpelts own [lots of / six] cars.
7. Mabel must (have / of] been a talented tuba player.

13. **plus:** in addition to. "Two *plus* two equals four." *Plus* should not be used as a conjunctive adverb in place of *also, moreover, furthermore,* or *besides,* despite the current fad in advertisements to misuse it that way. "We pay high interest; *also* [not *plus*] we give you a free checking account."

If plus is used incorrectly below, cross it out and write *also* above it. If plus is used correctly, write OK in front of the sentence.

a. also

_____ a. The convict was a drug addict; ~~plus~~ *also* he was a molester. A model citizen he wasn't.

b. OK

OK b. Sam gained twelve pounds on his vacation tour plus two pounds on his grapefruit diet.

c. OK
d. also

OK c. Critics said Josie had personality plus brains.

_____ d. These widgets, carefully crafted by Tibetan lamas, are $49.95 this week only; ~~plus~~ *also* you get a money-back guarantee.

e. also

_____ e. Joe Blitz earned twenty credits last semester; ~~plus~~ *also* he worked until dawn in a night restaurant. His funeral will be held tomorrow.

14. **prejudiced:** biased. "Tom was *prejudiced*" (not "was prejudice").
15. **supposed to:** "We are *supposed* to study (not "suppose to").
16. **used to:** "I *used* to be a dog-sitter" (not "use to").

used

■ Joe *used* to pass the crematorium and ask, "What's cooking?"

supposed

■ Students are s*upposed* to write compositions weekly, not weakly.

used, prejudiced

■ I u*sed* to be pr*ejudiced* against pigeons—but they're delicious.

supposed, used

■ You are not s*upposed* to loaf. Father u*sed* to say that even God put in a six-day week.

prejudiced
supposed

■ Smart shoppers are pre*judiced* against chemical preservatives. We are s*upposed* to read food labels carefully.

used, prejudiced

■ Whenever the Miltown Misfits lost a baseball game, their coach u*sed* to say the umpires were pr*ejudiced*.

17. **regardless:** heedless; in spite of; anyway. (Do not use the nonstandard term *irregardless.*)

regardless

- Use correct English _regardless_ [regardless / irregardless] of how it may shock a few illiterate friends.

regardless

- Americans must have equal opportunities, _regard_ less of sex, color, or creed.

(b)

- In the word *regardless,* the suffix *less* expresses a negative; therefore, the addition of the negative prefix *ir*—creating a double negative—is (a) logical, (b) illogical. (_b_)

an incorrect
regardless

- Adding the prefix *ir* to the word *regardless* would create _an incorrect_ [a correct / an incorrect] expression, _regard_ less of who used it.

18. **somewhere:** (Don't add an *s* to this word, nor to *anywhere* or *nowhere*). "We'll meet again *somewhere* (not *somewheres*)."

Somewhere

- Tex sang a mournful tune entitled, "_Somewhere_ in Old Wyoming," and he got a little applause, probably from his family,

somewhere

s _omewhere_ in the audience.

somewhere

- A teacher lost a nickel *s* _omewhere_ and began digging to find it. The result was the Grand Canyon. You must have heard

somewhere

about it *s* _omewhere_ .

Somewhere

- Doris warbled "The Beautiful Isle of _Somewhere_," and most of us wished she had stayed there.

QUIZ

Circle the choice that results in the more acceptable sentence.

1. supposed
2. used,
   somewhere
3. prejudiced
   regardless

4. also

1. You're [suppose / supposed] to take in less cholesterol.
2. Smith [use / used] to be penniless, but he got started [somewheres / somewhere] and now he owes a million dollars.
3. A good American isn't [prejudice / prejudiced], and he or she will judge people for what they are, [regardless / irregardless] of their ethnic origin or sex.
4. Mike is an able mechanic; [plus / also] he is fairly honest.

19. **suspicion:** distrust; doubt. (Avoid using the noun *suspicion* when the verb *suspect* is called for.)

suspected

- When the bank teller saw her customer holding a gun, she *suspected* [suspected / suspicioned] that he would request instant cash.

suspected

- The young couple often flung dishes and pounded heads against the wall, and we *suspected* [suspicioned / suspected] that they were solving some minor marital problems.

(a)

- In a detective story the butler was usually the first person to be (a) suspected, (b) suspicioned. (*a*)

(a)

- *Suspected* is a verb; *suspicion* is (a) a noun, (b) a verb. (*a*)

20. **that:** *That* is nonstandard when used to mean *very.* Avoid writing: "The game was not *that* exciting."

(b)

- We postponed lunch because we weren't (a) that hungry, (b) hungry. (*b*)

(b)

- The beauty contest losers claim that the winner is not (a) that cute, (b) exceptionally beautiful. (*b*)

easy

- "The Star-Spangled Banner" is not *easy* [easy / that easy] to sing.

(b)

- In a statement like "It's not that expensive," the word *that* is (a) clear and descriptive, (b) vague. (*b*)

21. **themselves** (reflexive and emphatic form of *them*). (Do not use nonstandard variations such as *theirselves* or *themselfs.*)

themselves

- Teachers don't fail students; students fail *themselves* [themselves / theirselves].

themselves

- Talented women must move *themselves* from the kitchen to the public arena.

themselves

- The salesmen *themselves* had more crust than a pie factory.

themselves
themselves

- The ministers *themselves* tell us that God helps those who help *themselves*.

22. **this.** (Refers to something nearby or just mentioned. Avoid the vague use of *this,* particularly in reference to something not yet mentioned.)

Write *Right* or *Wrong*, depending on whether the word *this* is used correctly. Assume that each sentence is the opening line of a theme.

Wrong

- ___WRONG___ This poem is about this Viking who elopes with this princess.

Right

- ___RIGHT___ Longfellow's "A Skeleton in Armor" is about a Viking who elopes with a princess; the poem describes the fate of this pair in America.

Wrong

- ___WRONG___ I still remember this boy in our schoolyard who threw this big snowball at me.

Wrong

- ___WRONG___ This friend of mine has this hobby of collecting Avon bottles.

23. **try:** to attempt. (Write "try to" instead of the informal "try and.")

to

- I will try ___to___ [to and] analyze how James Fenimore Cooper portrays women in his novels.

to

- The marriage vows should suggest that a couple try ___to___ [to and] live within their income.

(b)

- Careful writers prefer the phrase (a) "try and," (b) "try to." (b)

to
to

- Gunther will try ___to___ [to / and] do the triple somersault, and tomorrow I will try ___to___ [to / and] visit him at the hospital.

24. **unique:** the only one of its kind; peerless. "Poe's 'Ulalume' is *unique.*" (Avoid the somewhat illogical "more unique" and "most unique.")

unique

- The world has only one Taj Mahal; that beautiful building is ___unique___.

impossible

- Your right thumbprint is unique, the only one of its kind. It is, therefore, ___impossible___ [possible / impossible] for any other fingerprint to be more one-of-its-kind than that one.

exotic

- Sandra's Hawaiian muumuu is more ___exotic___ [unique / exotic] than her Macy's dress.

rare
unique

- Only two copies of Franklin's original *Almanack* are known to exist. Each copy is extremely __rare__ [unique / rare], but it is not __unique__ [unique / rare].

unique

- Suppose you had the only 1807 dollar of its kind in the world; that coin would be __unique__.

25. **which.** (Reference to a thing previously mentioned. But use *who* or *that,* not *which,* when referring to a person.) "A man *who* saw me coming sold me the horse *which* just died."

who

- This is the little boy __who__ [who / which] hit a home run through our window.

which

- Our cat is one creature __which__ [who / which] never cries over spilt milk.

who
which

- The man __who__ [who / which] lives in the apartment above us wears shoes __which__ [who / which] are made of wood.

which

- Alvin owns a parrot __which__ [who / which] doesn't talk but is a good listener.

who

- Boris is a barber __who__ [who / which] will take a big load off your mind.

QUIZ

Circle the choice that results in the more acceptable sentence.

1. a
2. which, feeble
3. suspected
4. startling
5. to
6. themselves

1. Once there was [this / a] gentleman named Mr. Piltdown.
2. I invested my savings in a racehorse [who / which] was not at all [feeble / that feeble] except for its legs.
3. Our sheriff [suspected / suspicioned] the man with the wooden leg.
4. Her fig leaf costume was extremely [unique / startling].
5. I try [to / and] fit the round tomatoes into the square sandwiches.
6. The visiting players saw us and laughed among [themselfs / themselves / theirselves].

REVIEW TEST

Write the correct words in full.

enthusiastic	1. Even Gloomy Gus, our coach, was [enthused / enthusiastic] about our prospects.
supposed	2. You aren't [supposed / suppose] to use my razor to cut linoleum.
many	3. Framers of our constitution had to solve [many / lots of] problems.
unusual	4. Kay held a pistol, and I knew something [unusual / funny] was going on.
used	5. My bank balance was so low I [use / used] to kneel to read it.
suspect	6. I [suspect / suspicion] that Scrooge wouldn't give a duck a drink if he owned the Atlantic Ocean.
themselves	7. Those who didn't vote can blame [themselves / themselfs].
prejudiced	8. People on juries should not be [prejudiced / prejudice].
to	9. As a surgeon, Nancy will try [and / to] carve out a career.
irritate	10. Screaming babies [irritate / aggravate] the library patrons.
have	11. When things looked dark, you should [have / of] sent them to the laundry.
and swimming	12. Mary excelled in soccer, volleyball, [etc. / and swimming].
complexioned	13. The funeral director, like the corpse, was dark-[complexioned / complected].
regardless	14. Buy the bagels [regardless / irregardless] of price.
rare	15. A snowstorm in Pasadena is extremely [unique / rare].
a	16. Hawthorne's novel deals with Hester Prynne and [a / this] villain named Arthur Dimmesdale.
which	17. The donkey is a small beast [who / which] carries a big load.
most	18. Rossini spent [a majority / most] of the winter in an asylum.
friendly	19. The Snerds have two girls and a [nice / friendly] dog.

criterion

20. When an essay is judged, the main [criterion / criteria] is not length but depth.

defeated

21. The Jurx team was [defeated / doomed to disappointment].

rushed back

22. We [beat a hasty retreat / rushed back].

staggered us

23. The bad news [came like a bolt from the blue / staggered us].

incredibly

24. The baby, [incredibly / strange as it seems], was unhurt.

hammering shingles

25. The carpenter was [busy as a bee / hammering shingles].

KEY TO REVIEW TEST

Check your test answers with the following key. Deduct 4% per error from a possible 100%.

1. enthusiastic
2. supposed
3. many
4. unusual
5. used
6. suspect
7. themselves
8. prejudiced
9. to

10. irritate
11. have
12. and swimming
13. complexioned
14. regardless
15. rare
16. a
17. which
18. most

19. friendly
20. criterion
21. defeated
22. rushed back
23. staggered us
24. incredibly
25. hammering shingles

Score: _____ %

Figures of Speech

Figures of Speech

Abraham Lincoln said that a man should preach "like a man fighting off a swarm of bees" (simile); that "we must save the good old ship of the Union on this voyage" (metaphor); that we must "bind up the nation's wounds" (personification). Figures of speech are a trademark of the imaginative writer. A random survey of William Shakespeare, Emily Dickinson, Herman Melville, or Dave Barry would reveal a galaxy of similes, metaphors, hyperboles, oxymorons.

Your familiarity with such terms can help you in two ways: As an analyst of literary passages, you can more ably identify and appreciate the stylistic devices used; as a creative writer you can gain sparkle and vigor by using a greater variety of figures of speech.

EXERCISES

1. **simile** (sim'ə-lē): a figure of speech comparing two unlike things, usually with "like" or "as." Example: "She has a figure like an hourglass—and not a minute of it wasted."
2. **metaphor** (met'ə-fôr'): a figure of speech in which one thing is said to be another thing, without "like" or "as," or in which a likeness is implied. Examples: "All the world's a stage"; "My boss barked out his orders."

metaphor
- _____ Boston was a beehive. (*simile* or *metaphor*?)

simile
- _____ Orville has a head like a granite block.

simile
- _____ Teacher's heart is as big and soft as an overripe pumpkin.

metaphor
- _____ My Aunt Bertha sailed into the room.

- An expressed comparison between unlike things, with "like" or

simile
metaphor
"as," is a _____; an implied comparison is a _____.

metaphor
- _____ Mabel was a dynamo, but she got short-circuited.

simile
- _____ He looks like a dishonest Abe Lincoln.

metaphor
- _____ The Buick purred down the freeway.

3. **alliteration:** the repetition of an initial sound in words or accented syllables close together. *Alliteration* abounds in "the big brutal battles of *Beowulf*."
4. **onomatopoeia** (on'ə-mat'ə-pē'ə): the use of words whose pronunciation suggests their meaning. *Onomatopoeic* words are common: *boom, hiss, murmur, zoom, moan, hum, chug, sizzle, cuckoo, glug.*

onomatopoeia
- Using words that sound like what they mean is *on*_____.

alliteration
- Using the same initial letter in neighboring words is *al*_____.

- Which line of poetry by Robert Herrick contains *alliteration?*
(a) "The liquefaction of her clothes," (b) "I sing of brooks, of

(b)
blossoms, birds and bowers." (   )

onomatopoeia
- _____ The locomotive snorted and hissed—then went chug-ah!

alliteration
- _____ What a tale of terror now their turbulency tells!

alliteration
- _____ That lazy, lovable lunatic.

onomatopoeia
- _____ He dived on his belly—plop, splash.

5. **hyperbole** (hī-pûr′bə-lē): a gross exaggeration for rhetorical effect. Example: "The new blonde typist made errors by the barrel, but nobody noticed."

6. **litotes** (lī′tə-tēz′): a figure of speech in which a point is made by a denying of its opposite; a kind of understatement; for example, "It's no small matter"; "Rockefeller was no pauper"; "The prisoner approached the electric chair without enthusiasm."

litotes

■ Denying the opposite of what you mean is *li*_____.

hyperbole

■ Gross exaggeration is *hy*_____.

■ A *hyperbole* might say that the village boozer (a) drank several bottles of beer, (b) made the local brewery go on a twenty-four-hour shift. (   )

(b)

■ An example of *litotes* is (a) "The mackerel had a bad odor," (b) "The mackerel did not smell like Chanel No. 5." (   )

(b)

hyperbole

■ _____ The mosquitoes were rangy and enterprising, and they'd siphon a quart of blood before you noticed them.

hyperbole

■ _____ There's enough poetry on the boys' washroom walls to put Shakespeare out of business.

litotes

■ _____ Gangster Al Capone did not exactly win the Best Citizen award.

litotes

■ _____ Those cigarettes didn't do your lungs any good.

QUIZ

Write the letter that indicates the best example.

1. (c)
2. (e)
3. (f)
4. (d)
5. (b)
6. (a)

(   ) 1. alliteration   a. a hairdo like an unmade bed
(   ) 2. hyperbole   b. the *bar-r-room* of the trombones
(   ) 3. litotes   c. lively lads and lasses
(   ) 4. metaphor   d. Alice was sugar and cream.
(   ) 5. onomatopoeia   e. Lulu has an army of suitors.
(   ) 6. simile   f. Caruso was not a bad singer either.

7. **apostrophe** (ə-pos′trə-fē): addressing a personified object, or an absent person as though present. Example from Francis Thompson: "O world invisible, we view thee."

8. **metonymy** (mi-ton′ə-mē): a figure of speech in which the name of a thing is used for something else associated with it; virtually synonymous with *synecdoche.* Example: "The sailor was warned to stay away from the skirts."

■ In *apostrophe* the poet is emotionally involved with some absent person or some personified object and speaks directly

to it
_____ [to it / of it].

metonymy
(a)

■ "He was addicted to the bottle" is *met*_____ because "bottle" is associated with (a) liquor, (b) glassware. (   )

metonymy
metonymy
apostrophe

■ _____ Dinner is $2.95 a plate.
■ _____ Melvin has read Tennessee Williams.
■ _____ Robert Burns: "O Scotia! my dear, my native soil!"

metonymy

■ _____ The White House announces. . . .
■ Which line involves *apostrophe?* (a) William Wordsworth: "Milton! thou shouldst be living at this hour," (b) John Masefield:

(a)

"Oh London Town's a fine town." (   )

9. **oxymoron** (ok′si-mōr′on): a combination of two apparently contradictory words. Examples. "dazzling darkness," "devout atheism," "lively corpse."

10. **antithesis** (an-tith′i-sis): The strong contrast of expressions, clauses, sentences, or ideas within a balanced grammatical structure. Examples: "Life is short; art is long," "Give me liberty or give me death."

■ A seeming contradiction like "clever idiot" is an

oxymoron

*ox*_____.

■ "We must all hang together, or assuredly we shall all hang separately." This famous utterance by Franklin in 1776 illustrates

antithesis, does

*ant*_____, since it _____ [does / does not] present a contrast of ideas in a balanced pattern.

■ Which ending results in *antithesis?* "Johnny was in the church basement making taffy, and (a) wondering if Jimmy ever had so much fun," (b) "Jimmy was in the theater balcony making

(b)

love." (   )

oxymoron

■ "Militant pacifism" is an *ox*_____, and Sir Philip Sidney's reference to "living deaths, dear wounds, fair storms, and

oxymorons

freezing fires" includes four *ox*_____.

noisy
attractive

antithesis

(b)

(b)

personification

(a)

(a)

- An *oxymoron* might refer to a "_____ [strange / noisy] silence" or to an "_____ [attractive / unusual] repulsiveness."

- A contrast of ideas expressed as a balanced sentence is known as *ant*_____.

- An example of *antithesis* is (a) "You do not have to cut off your fingers to write shorthand," (b) "A cat has its claws at the end of the paws; a comma has its pause at the end of the clause." (   )

11. **personification** (pər-son′ə-fə-kā′shən): the giving of human qualities to something that is not human; for example, "sternfaced Duty" and "the murmuring pines." In *Modern Painters* (1856) John Ruskin objects to the *pathetic fallacy,* or falseness, in phrases like "the cruel crawling foam" or "weeping skies."

- *Personification,* like "the brow of the hill," gives human qualities to (a) people, (b) nonhuman things. (   )

- Endowing a nonhuman thing with the qualities of a person—as in "the happy dandelions" or "the gossipy bluejays"—is a figure of speech known as *p*_____.

- Which line involves *personification?* (a) Samuel Coleridge: "The one red leaf, the last of its clan, / That dances as often as dance it can," (b) Alfred Tennyson: "Comrades, leave me here a little, while as yet 'tis early morn." (   )

- Which line involves *personification?* (a) William Shakespeare: "Blow, winds, and crack your cheeks," (b) Christina Rossetti: "This Advent moon shines cold and clear." (   )

QUIZ

Write the letter that indicates the best example.

1. (e)
2. (d)
3. (c)
4. (a)
5. (b)

(   ) 1. personification   a. her bold shyness
(   ) 2. apostrophe   b. Man proposes; God disposes.
(   ) 3. metonymy   c. The farmer hired three hands.
(   ) 4. oxymoron   d. Here's to thee, oh Alma Mater!
(   ) 5. antithesis   e. the eye of the storm

12. **allusion** (ə-lo͞o′zhən): a passing reference to something; an indirect mention. Milton's poetry is peppered with classical *allusions,* that is, references to passages in world literature.

■ Mentioning Achilles or Sancho Panza or Blake's "The Tyger" would be a literary *al*_____.

■ A man makes a biblical *allusion* if he refers to his wife as his (a) "rib," (b) "ball and chain." (   )

■ "Everything that Tanya touches turns to gold." The writer has made a passing reference, or _____, to the story of King Midas.

■ "Well, I'll be a monkey's cousin!" This comment embodies an indirect reference, or _____, to (a) Darwinism, (b) Jeffersonian democracy. (   )

13. **irony** (i′rə-nē): saying the opposite of what is meant, by way of mockery: known as *verbal irony;* in general, the contrast between what is and what might reasonably be expected ("The Nudnick police station was burglarized").

■ When peace-loving Stephen Crane says, "War is kind," he is probably (a) serious, (b) ironic. (   )

■ "That's right," says your father, "have a good time, forget your homework, become a bum!" His advice is an example of *i*_____ because he really means (a) exactly what he says, (b) the opposite of what he says. (   )

■ In "A Modest Proposal" (1729) Jonathan Swift urges with tongue in cheek, or with *i*_____, that Englishmen should eat Irish infants.

■ *Verbal irony* is a form of (a) sarcasm, (b) eulogy. (   )

■ The baseball coach uses *irony* when he says, "You struck out five times—(a) such rotten luck!" (b) such a marvelous athlete!" (   )

14. **symbol** (sim′bəl): an object or a story element which has a basic meaning yet which also has another meaning; for example, a dove is a bird of the pigeon family yet it also stands for peace. In Hawthorne's *The Scarlet Letter,* the minister keeps putting his hand to his heart, a natural gesture but also a *symbol* of hidden guilt.

- A flag, a cross, or a handclasp may stand for something beside itself and thus each may be a *sy*_____.

- Appropriate *symbols* to suggest old age might be (a) withered leaves and dry ashes, (b) budding flowers and gushing waters. ( )

- *Symbolism* in fiction can exist (a) only in concrete objects such as an ivory leg, a livid scar, or a white whale, (b) in objects, characters, gestures, and situations. ( )

- As the Hemingway hero lies mortally wounded, he sees the buzzards circle closer and closer. The buzzards are a *s*_____ of (a) death, (b) hope. ( )

QUIZ

Write the letter that indicates the best definition.

(   ) 1. symbol   a. mockery by expressing opposites

(   ) 2. allusion   b. that which stands for something else

(   ) 3. irony   c. a casual reference to something

Supply the missing word in each sentence.

1. A gross exaggeration is a *hy*_____.
2. The repetition of initial letters in words is *al*_____.
3. Saying the opposite of what is really meant, in order to ridicule, is known as *ir*_____.
4. A comparison using "like" or "as" is a *si*_____.
5. Use of words that sound like what they mean is *on*_____.
6. Addressing the absent as though present is known as *ap*_____.
7. Naming of a thing to represent something closely associated with it is *me*_____.
8. "I was a stricken deer." Cowper's figure of speech is a *me*_____.
9. "The sun peered at me." This figure of speech is *pe*_____.
10. "Darkness visible." Milton's contradictory phrase is an *ox*_____.

Name the figure of speech in each example. The first letter of each answer is given.

11. Sam spends much; he earns little.   *a*_____
12. Respect the scepter, the sword, the flag.   *s*_____
13. Kay's wardrobe closet is about a mile long.   *h*_____
14. The pansies closed their little eyes.   *p*_____
15. Boom, crash, clang went the drum section.   *o*_____
16. lovely Lulu from Laredo   *a*_____
17. a head shaped like a Persian melon   *s*_____
18. Eat another plate.   *m*_____
19. a beach not without its beer cans and litter   *l*_____
20. O Eve, Eve, why did you eat the forbidden fruit?   *a*_____
21. He generously gave the church all of two cents.   *i*_____
22. Her brain is a storage vault.   *m*_____
23. The bitter sweetness of farewell.   *o*_____
24. We spoke of Plato, Chartres, Waterloo, Einstein's theory, and the art of Brando.   *a*_____
25. To err is human; to forgive, divine.   *a*_____

Check your test answers with the following key. Deduct 4% per error from a possible 100%.

1. hyperbole
2. alliteration
3. irony
4. simile
5. onomatopoeia
6. apostrophe
7. metonymy
8. metaphor
9. personification

10. oxymoron
11. antithesis
12. symbols
13. hyperbole
14. personification
15. onomatopoeia
16. alliteration
17. simile
18. metonymy

19. litotes
20. apostrophe
21. irony
22. metaphor
23. oxymoron
24. allusions
25. antithesis

Score: _____%

Characterization Words

bigot, **1**

braggart, **2**

buffoon, **3**

bungler, **4**

charlatan, **5**

colleague, **6**

connoisseur, **7**

culprit, **8**

dilettante, **9**

felon, **10**

feminist, **11**

glutton, **12**

gourmet, **13**

huckster, **14**

ingénue, **15**

luminary, **16**

magnate, **17**

martyr, **18**

nomad, **19**

oracle, **20**

pacifist, **21**

paragon, **22**

patriarch, **23**

prodigy, **24**

pundit, **25**

raconteur, **26**

recluse, **27**

ruffian, **28**

saboteur, **29**

schlemiel, **30**

skeptic, **31**

tippler, **32**

tycoon, **33**

urchin, **34**

virtuoso, **35**

zealot, **36**

The need to describe people arises constantly. You may write, for example, that Mr. More is a truck driver. That takes care of his occupation. But the reader may wish to know more about More. After all, truck drivers differ considerably in personality. One stops and changes a tire for you; another sideswipes your fender and jeers, "May I have the last dents?" The first is a *paragon;* the second is a *bungler,* a *ruffian,* or possibly—heaven forbid!—a *tippler.* Such characterization words can add a dimension to description.

This chapter is not about the names of jobs—architect, custodian, lion tamer—rather, it puts the spotlight on terms that characterize people.

A further challenge? Test your skill in the exercise at the end of this chapter involving an additional twenty-five characterization words.

EXERCISES

1. **bigot** (big′ət): a narrow-minded, prejudiced person.
2. **braggart** (brag′ərt): a very boastful person.
3. **buffoon** (bə-foon′): somebody who is always clowning around and trying to be funny.

bigot

- ■ "Nobody of that racial group should ever get voted into this high-minded country club," said the *bi*_____.

braggart

- ■ "I raised a hog so big that the snapshot of it weighs three pounds," said the *br*_____.

buffoon

- ■ In my coat pocket was a fat frog, placed there by the class *bu*_____.

braggart
bigot
buffoon

- ■ Every village has its conceited *br*_____, its intolerant *b*_____, and its life-of-the-party, lampshade-wearing *b*_____.

braggart
bigot
buffoon

- ■ The fishing trip? "I caught barrels of sea bass," said the _____. "I don't associate with common sailors," said the _____. "I nailed my shorts to the top of the mast," snickered the _____.

4. **bungler:** a clumsy, blundering fellow.
5. **charlatan** (shär′lə-tən): a quack; one who pretends to have expertise, as in medicine, that he doesn't have.
6. **colleague** (kol′ēg): a fellow worker in the same profession.

colleague

- ■ My professor was not in his office, so I spoke to his *co*_____.

bungler
charlatan

- ■ When the island "dentist" loosened the wrong tooth, I suspected he was a *bu*_____, but when he hit my skull with a coconut, I realized he was a *ch*_____.

colleague
colleague
charlatan, bungler

- ■ "Professional ethics prevent you from bad-mouthing a *co*_____," I said to the surgeon, "but I'm getting a heart transplant; and if your new *co*_____ is a diddling *ch*_____ or a clumsy *bu*_____, I'm coming back to haunt you."

colleague

bungler

charlatan

■ "Mr. Swindell is a former *co*_____ of mine," confided the lawyer, "and nobody is less qualified than that ignorant *bu*_____. His only expertise is to stage a car accident and sue for five million green ones. A first-class *ch*_____!"

7. **connoisseur** (kon′ə-sōōr′): an expert in a special field, generally in one of the fine arts or in matters of taste.
8. **culprit:** one who is guilty of a crime or fault.
9. **dilettante** (dil′i-tänt′): a dabbler in the arts and sciences; one who follows an art in a superficial way.

culprit

■ A one-fingered pickpocket stole a ring of keys from my pocket, but Detective Butts nabbed the *cu*_____.

connoisseur

■ Mr. Snorkel says our champagne is "frisky but somewhat unfocused." Only a *co*_____ of wine can talk like that.

dilettante

■ Hans poses as an expert in classical music, but his inane opinions show him to be a mere *di*_____.

connoisseur

■ A young girl, not at all an art *co*_____, saw a splash of ketchup on a Picasso—it had been unnoticed for several weeks— and we are now looking for the *cu*_____.

culprit

■ Whether this is a fake Rembrandt should be determined by (a) a dilettante, (b) a connoisseur. (   ) If we've been sold a forgery, we must go after the *cu*_____.

(b)

culprit

1. (g)	( ) 1. culprit	a. a fine arts expert
2. (e)	( ) 2. colleague	b. a clumsy fellow
3. (h)	( ) 3. braggart	c. a quack; a false "healer"
4. (f)	( ) 4. dilettante	d. a highly prejudiced person
5. (d)	( ) 5. bigot	e. a fellow worker; an associate
6. (a)	( ) 6. connoisseur	f. a dabbler in the arts
7. (i)	( ) 7. buffoon	g. one guilty of a prank or crime
8. (b)	( ) 8. bungler	h. a boaster
9. (c)	( ) 9. charlatan	i. a clown type

10. **felon** (fel′ən): a person who has committed a serious crime such as murder or burglary.
11. **feminist:** one who advocates economic, social, and political rights for women equal to those of men.
12. **glutton:** a person who greedily eats too much, or who has a great capacity for something. "I'm a *glutton* for soap operas."

glutton	■ "Tiny" Joe, a noted *gl*_____, ate six hot dogs.
feminist	■ Gloria, who despises male chauvinism, is an outspoken *fe*_____.
glutton felon	■ The robber whispered, "Hand it over, gal. I'm a *gl*_____ for cash." The bank clerk replied, "Straighten your tie. You're a *fe*_____ and you're on camera."
feminist felon glutton	■ Everybody has a dream. The *f*_____ dreams of equal pay for equal work; the *f*_____ dreams of a pardon from the governor; the *g*_____ dreams of roast pig.
glutton feminist felon	"When I eat, sparks fly from my knife and fork." _____ "Open those top jobs to women as well as men." _____ "Nineteen more years in the slammer. Wait for me, honey." _____

13. **gourmet** (goor′mā): a specialist in delicacies of the table; an excellent judge of fine foods and drink.
14. **huckster:** an aggressive salesperson, possibly of vegetables, fruit, and small articles.
15. **ingénue** (an′zhi-noō′): the role in a play of the sweet, innocent, inexperienced young woman.

ingénue	■ Flora is too sophisticated and matronly to be cast as the *in*_____.
gourmet	■ "Grape tarts and mulled wine," ordered the *g*_____.
huckster	■ "Fish! Nice fresh fish!" cried the *h*_____.
gourmet	■ Mr. Fresser loves exotic delicacies of the table. In fact, he's a dedicated *g*_____.
huckster gourmet	■ A stadium *h*_____ sold me a bag of eight stale peanuts, not exactly *g*_____ food.
ingénue	■ Donna looks young, pretty, and a bit stupid—the director says she'll be a perfect *in*_____.
huckster gourmet ingénue	"Buy your steel radials from Smiling Sam." _____ "Only a French chef understands frog legs." _____ "Just a li'l girl from Dingville, and—pure luck!—already I been invited to this city feller's apartment tonight to look at his picture albums." _____

16. **luminary:** a famous person inspirational to others.
17. **magnate** (mag′nāt): a powerful or influential person in business or industry.
18. **martyr** (mär′tər): one who suffers for a cause.

magnate

■ Andrew Carnegie was an early steel *m_____*.

martyr

■ Nathan Hale, hanged as a rebel, was a *m_____*.

luminary

■ Among film comedians, Chaplin was a *lu_____*.

magnate

luminary

martyr

■ Famous Americans of past years include Henry Ford, the automobile *m_____*, Ernest Hemingway, a *l_____* among prose writers, and Martin Luther King, a *m_____* to the cause of civil rights.

luminary

magnate

martyr

■ More American heroes: Thomas Edison was a *l_____* among inventors; James Hill was a railroad builder and *m_____*; and many a child has been a *m_____* to our sweat shops.

QUIZ

Write the letter that indicates the best definition.

1. (c)
2. (f)
3. (e)
4. (h)
5. (a)
6. (g)
7. (i)
8. (d)
9. (b)

(   ) 1. felon
(   ) 2. feminist
(   ) 3. glutton
(   ) 4. gourmet
(   ) 5. ingénue
(   ) 6. huckster
(   ) 7. luminary
(   ) 8. magnate
(   ) 9. martyr

a. a sweet, naive young woman
b. one who suffers for ideals
c. a criminal
d. a powerful industrial leader
e. a greedy eater
f. an advocate of women's rights
g. a pushy salesperson or peddler
h. a lover of fine foods
i. a famous person in some field

19. **nomad** (nō′mad′): a wanderer without a fixed home.
20. **oracle:** one who makes wise or prophetic statements.
21. **pacifist:** one who is opposed to war and violence or who, as a matter of conscience, resists the draft.

nomad

■ Hobo Hank travels everywhere. He's a *no_____*.

oracle

■ How prophetic! Linda is a true *or_____*.

pacifist	■ "In war, everybody loses," says the *pa*_____.
oracle	■ More rain? Let's consult the weather *o*_____.
nomad	■ Abou, a desert *n*_____, claims that a camel is really a horse put together by a committee.

nomad
pacifist

"My tribe will wander the Sahara forever." _____
"There never was a good war or a bad peace." _____
"I foresee a day when men and women will be judged only by their

oracle

merit." _____

22 **paragon** (par′ə-gon′): one who is a model of excellence.
23. **patriarch** (pā′trē-ärk′): the aging father or ruler of a family or tribe.
24. **prodigy** (prod′i-jē): a remarkably talented child or person; a marvel.

patriarch	■ The tribe was led by its white-haired *pat*_____.
prodigy	■ The five-year-old chess *pr*_____ blitzed me.
paragon	■ Jeeves, a *par*_____ among butlers, handled every detail.
prodigy	■ The Vesuvius eruption, burying Pompeii, was a tragic *pr*_____ of nature.
patriarch paragon	■ The priest eulogized the aged _____ of the clan, calling him a *par*_____ of virtue.

Little Wolfgang will play the five concertos by memory.

prodigy
_____

Sixty-two grandchildren danced at the picnic in his honor.

patriarch
paragon
_____

Helpful, talented, loving—the perfect spouse! _____

25. **pundit:** a very learned person.
26. **raconteur** (rak′on-tûr′): a skilled teller of anecdotes.
27. **recluse** (rek′lōos): one who lives alone; a hermit.

raconteur	■ Salty stories poured out of the *ra*_____ like sewage from a broken main.
pundit	■ We were dizzied by the philosophical lecture of the Harvard *pu*_____.
recluse	■ Fear of crime turned Fred into a lonely *r*_____.

■ Depth of learning is the mark of the (a) pundit, (b) recluse, (c) raconteur. (   )

(a)

■ The holy cave-dweller, a genuine *rec*_____, nearly fainted at the racy jokes of the *ra*_____.

recluse
raconteur

pundit
recluse

raconteur

"This is my third book on medieval culture." _____
"I like living alone. People turn me off." _____
"Did you hear the one about the old lady and the broccoli?"
_____

QUIZ

Write the letter that indicates the best definition.

1. (f)
2. (d)
3. (a)
4. (h)
5. (g)
6. (c)
7. (i)
8. (e)
9. (b)

( ) 1. nomad	a. one who is opposed to war
( ) 2. oracle	b. a hermit
( ) 3. pacifist	c. an extremely gifted child
( ) 4. paragon	d. one who is prophetic and wise
( ) 5. patriarch	e. one who tells anecdotes
( ) 6. prodigy	f. a wanderer
( ) 7. pundit	g. the old ruler of a tribe
( ) 8. raconteur	h. a model of excellence
( ) 9. recluse	i. a very scholarly person

28. **ruffian** (ruf′yən): a brutal, lawless person; a hoodlum.
29. **saboteur** (sab′ə-tûr′): one who deliberately damages machines or materials in time of war or labor disputes.
30. **schlemiel** (shlə-mēl′): *Slang.* an awkward unlucky person, easily victimized; a born loser.

saboteur

■ We caught the *sab*_____ just as he was pouring mucilage into the fludbunnies.

schlemiel

■ Tore his pants on the piano? What a *sc*_____!

■ The Good Humor man was brutally beaten by a bad-humored *ruf*_____.

ruffian

saboteur
schlemiel

■ The factory explosion was caused not by a *sa*_____, but by a *sc*_____ who stumbled and dropped a torpedo.

ruffian

■ In the alley I met a *ru*_____ who had knifed more people than a surgeon.

saboteur
ruffian
schlemiel

"I fixed the guns so they shoot backwards." _____

"Let's beat up on them little guys. . . ." _____

"I fell on my back and broke my nose." _____

31. **skeptic:** one with a doubting attitude toward matters that most people accept.
32. **tippler:** one who habitually drinks small quantities of alcoholic beverages.
33. **tycoon** (tī-kōōn′): a wealthy and powerful industrialist or businessperson.

skeptic

■ A flat earth? Columbus was a *sk*_____ about that.

tippler

■ My uncle, a chronic *ti*_____, drinks to calm himself. Sometimes he gets so calm he can't move.

skeptic

■ Oswald Spengler, in *The Decline of the West,* is a *sk*_____ about our future.

tycoon
tippler

■ Jason's career as an industrial *ty*_____ was ruined when he became a *ti*_____. "I took a snort only at odd hours—one, three, five. . . ."

skeptic
tycoon
tippler

"What good is space travel? It's for the birds." _____

"Our Cadillac franchises really paid off." _____

"I'm not so think as I drunk I am." _____

34. **urchin:** a small mischievous boy; any youngster.
35. **virtuoso** (vûr′chōō-ō′sō): a person with a dazzling technique in an art such as music.
36. **zealot** (zel′ət): one who is extremely devoted to a cause; a fanatic.

virtuoso

■ Paganini was a noted violin *vi*_____.

urchin

■ I chased the *ur*_____ who'd let the air out of our tires.

zealot

■ "Home run!" The Dodger *z*_____ behind me pounded my back.

virtuoso

■ Hoping to become a flute *v*_____, I asked the maestro about my execution. He favored it.

zealot
urchin

■ I'm an antiviolence *z*_____, but if I ever catch the *ur*_____ who dumped manure into my swimming pool, I'll kick him into orbit.

zealot

urchin

virtuoso

Velma is passionately involved in the antivivisection crusade.
_____

Please excuse Jimmy for being tardy yesterday. He was playing marbles. _____

The cellist gave a brilliant interpretation of Shnook's intricate "Sonata in Six Flats and a Basement." _____

QUIZ

Write the letter that indicates the best definition.

1. (b)
2. (e)
3. (f)
4. (h)
5. (g)
6. (d)
7. (i)
8. (a)
9. (c)

(   ) 1. ruffian
(   ) 2. saboteur
(   ) 3. schlemiel
(   ) 4. skeptic
(   ) 5. tippler
(   ) 6. tycoon
(   ) 7. virtuoso
(   ) 8. urchin
(   ) 9. zealot

a. a mischievous child
b. a hoodlum
c. a fanatic for a cause
d. a wealthy captain of industry
e. a war machine wrecker
f. a clumsy, unlucky person
g. one who hits the bottle
h. a doubter; a nonbeliever
i. a brilliant instrumentalist

Write the word studied in this chapter that will complete the sentence.

1. Only six and she studies calculus? A child *pr*_____!
2. Ingersoll doubted miracles and became a religious *sk*_____.
3. Joan of Arc died at the stake, a *ma*_____ to her faith.
4. To foresee the future, the Greeks consulted an *or*_____.
5. "Thou shalt not exploit women"—thus saith the *fem*_____.
6. Hank crowed that he would make four touchdowns, but the *br*_____ lost yardage.
7. "Popcorn! Buy your popcorn here," wheedled the *hu*_____.
8. In "My Sister Eileen" she starred as the innocent, lovable young woman—the *in*_____.
9. Should this mother of twelve bring yet another *ur*_____ into this inhospitable world?
10. Extremely knowledgeable, Samuel Johnson was the *pu*_____ of his era.
11. If he claims his medicine cures cancer, he's probably a *ch*_____.
12. The venerable *ra*_____ pelted us with a stream of baseball anecdotes.

Write True or False.

_____ 13. A business *tycoon* is a *magnate*.

_____ 14. A *pacifist* is a *ruffian*.

_____ 15. A *schlemiel* is a *bungler*.

_____ 16. A *gourmet* is a *connoisseur*.

_____ 17. A *dilettante* is a *virtuoso*.

_____ 18. A *recluse* is a *nomad*.

_____ 19. In time of war, a *saboteur* is a *felon*.

_____ 20. Both the *tippler* and the *glutton* consume too much.

Matching. Write the letter that indicates the best definition.

(   ) 21.   bigot
(   ) 22.   buffoon
(   ) 23.   culprit
(   ) 24.   paragon
(   ) 25.   zealot

a. a fanatic
b. a hunter of jungle animals
c. a big industrial leader
d. a prejudiced person
e. one guilty of a crime or offense
f. an insane person
g. one given to pranks and clowning
h. a flawless person; a role model

✚ KEY TO REVIEW TEST

Check your test answers with the following key. Deduct 4% per error from a possible 100%.

1. prodigy	10. pundit	19. True
2. skeptic	11. charlatan	20. True
3. martyr	12. raconteur	21. (d)
4. oracle	13. True	22. (g)
5. feminist	14. False	23. (e)
6. braggart	15. True	24. (h)
7. huckster	16. True	25. (a)
8. ingénue	17. False	
9. urchin	18. False	

Score: _____ %

Fill in the blanks at the left with the characterization words that fit the definitions. Although these words were not defined in this chapter, you should recognize most of them. Check your answers with the key at the end of the exercise. Use your dictionary to study any unknown words.

■ antagonist, apostate, aristocrat, avenger, cherub

1. _____ one who punishes to get even
2. _____ one who has deserted his or her faith
3. _____ an angelic child
4. _____ an opponent; an adversary
5. _____ a member of a proud, privileged class

■ clodhopper, confidant, conniver, disciple, dowager

6. _____ an elderly woman of dignity and wealth
7. _____ *Informal.* A country hick
8. _____ one who cooperates with evildoers
9. _____ a person entrusted with secrets
10. _____ a follower of a teacher or doctrine

■ factotum, jingoist, mendicant, orphan, pagan

11. _____ somebody hired to do all sorts of work
12. _____ a child without parents; a castoff
13. _____ one who favors a warlike foreign policy
14. _____ a heathen
15. _____ a beggar

■ paraplegic, parasite, parvenu, reactionary, scavenger

16. _____ an extreme conservative in politics
17. _____ one who searches through rubbish
18. _____ one who lives at the expense of another
19. _____ a paralyzed person
20. _____ one who is newly rich; an upstart

■ sycophant, tenant, thespian, truant, turncoat

21. _____ a traitor

22. _____ a student who skips school

23. _____ a self-serving flatterer

24. _____ one who occupies some property

25. _____ an actor or actress

KEY TO SUPPLEMENTARY EXERCISE

Check your test answers with the following key. Deduct 4% per error from a possible 100%.

1. avenger
2. apostate
3. cherub
4. antagonist
5. aristocrat
6. dowager
7. clodhopper
8. conniver
9. confidant

10. disciple
11. factotum
12. orphan
13. jingoist
14. pagan
15. mendicant
16. reactionary
17. scavenger
18. parasite

19. paraplegic
20. parvenu
21. turncoat
22. truant
23. sycophant
24. tenant
25. thespian

Score: _____ %

Computer Words

A few decades ago a marvelous device was born—the computer. Though simple enough in its infancy the computer has grown more sophisticated until it has now revolutionized science, industry, business, and publishing.

With computers, we can exchange messages in the form of e-mail in a twinkling with friends and businesspeople, whether they live in Atlanta or Zanzibar. Meanwhile, other computers work away quietly right under our noses. For instance, you (1) look at your digital watch, (2) withdraw cash at your bank, (3) buy fish at the supermarket, (4) bake the fish in a microwave oven—and computers have been involved every step of the way. And if that fish smells old enough to vote, you can use your personal computer to shoot a complaint to the store manager.

Since computers are sure to develop a thousand more uses, the ambitious student will not shun an acquaintance with computer vocabulary. . . . Incidentally, what's the word for that bunch of parallel lines on your box of granola?

This chapter presents twenty-five terms of "computerese" in programmed form, as well as a supplementary list of definitions.

EXERCISES

1. **computer:** electronic equipment that handles input/output information. It can (a) take in elements of information, known as data, (b) store data, (c) manipulate data, and (d) turn out meaningful results.
2. **microprocessor:** the computer's main thinking unit, all on a tiny silicon chip; its integrated circuits do the calculating and the carrying out of instructions.

does

■ A *computer* _____ [does / does not] include devices for input and output of information.

computer

■ Banks keep track of your deposits, withdrawals, dividends, and balance by means of a *com_____*.

microprocessor

■ The thinking and manipulation of data in a computer is done by the tiny *mic_____*.

microprocessor
computer
(c)

■ The highly intelligent *mic_____* which controls your *com_____* is about as big as (a) a golf ball, (b) a man's nose, (c) a fingernail. (   )

microprocessor

■ The integrated circuits for the *mi_____* are usually placed on (a) Swiss cheese, (b) a silicon chip, (c) a piece of paper. (   )

(b)

computer,
microprocessor
brain

■ Suppose you buy some impressive electronic equipment known as a *co_____*. Inside it is a small *mic_____* that acts like a _____ [brain / lung / liver].

3. **hardware:** the physical equipment of a computer system. *Hardware* includes such things as the keyboard, display screen, and printer.
4. **software:** computer programs. *Software* tells the computer how to respond to various commands.

software

■ A program of instructions to the computer may be stored on a floppy disk. The program is _____*ware*.

hardware	■ Electromechanical equipment such as your printer and keyboard are _____ *ware.*
hardware software	■ Your hi-fi set is, in some ways, like a computer. Your receiver, amplifier, and speakers are _____ *ware,* and your music and voice are _____ *ware.*
software hardware	■ Pencil-coded cards that can be fed into a computer for evaluation are known as _____ *ware;* whereas the disk drive, containing the motor, is _____ *ware.*
hardware software	■ The microprocessor, keyboard, and other _____ *re* are useless unless they are fed a program of instructions known as _____ *re.*

5. **RAM:** Random Access Memory. *RAM* stores up information in such a way that you can add to it or change it at any time.
6. **ROM:** Read Only Memory. *ROM* is stored information that you ordinarily cannot alter. [Remember: RAM cAn change; ROM cannOt.]

RAM ROM	■ Random Access Memory is referred to by its initials _____. Read Only Memory is referred to by its initials _____.
cAn	■ *RAM* is temporary storage, and you _____ [cAn / cannot] change the information in it.
cannOt	■ *ROM* is permanent storage, and you _____ [can / cannOt] change the information in it.
ROM	■ A program on a _____ [ROM / RAM] chip is like a phonograph record made by a manufacturer. You use it, but you cannot change it.
RAM	■ One advantage of _____ [ROM / RAM] is that you can easily make changes in it if you are composing a story or document.

Write the letter that indicates the best definition.

1. (c)
2. (d)

3. (f)

4. (e)

5. (a)

6. (b)

( ) 1. software	a. the "brains" of a computer
( ) 2. RAM	b. permanent, unerasable memory storage
( ) 3. hardware	c. a program of instructions to the computer
( ) 4. computer	d. temporary, changeable memory storage
( ) 5. microprocessor	e. components that handle input and output
( ) 6. ROM	f. physical equipment

7. **monitor:** the TV-like screen where you can see the text as it enters the system.
8. **terminal:** a work station consisting of a keyboard and monitor. Data can enter or leave a communication system from a *terminal*.

monitor

■ What you type on the keyboard you can read on the *mon*_____ .

monitor
terminal

■ A work station with a keyboard and a *mon*_____ is referred to as a *ter*_____ .

terminal

■ Each bank teller uses a *ter*_____ of the computer system.

monitor

■ The bank teller types data into the keyboard and then views the data on the *mon*_____ .

terminal

■ In businesses with a large computer system, the users may each sit at some distant *t*_____ and still share the same data.

9. **word processing:** an efficient system of preparing documents by computer. Corrections and changes in wording are easy to make.
10. **floppy disk:** an information storage device. You use a flexible magnetic plate, commonly 3.5" square, known as a *floppy disk,* or *diskette,* for storing information.

(a)

■ A floppy disk is (a) a device to store information, (b) a faulty backbone. ( )

- Processing of numerical data by computer is called data processing; processing of words is called w_____ p_____.

- Typed information can easily be revised and improved on a computer by the system of w_____ p_____. When editing is finished, you can store away the document for future use on a f_____ d_____.

- Corrections of mistakes in wording and layout of a term paper can be made most quickly and efficiently with (a) a portable typewriter, (b) a word processor. (   )

- The information storage device known as the fl_____ d_____ is used in wo_____ _____.

11. **cursor:** a blinking light or marker on the display screen that shows where the next keystroke will appear. It can be moved by special keys or by a device called a "mouse."

12. **merge:** combining a document with a list of variables. A word processor can "personalize" a standard letter by *merging* it with names on a mailing list.

- The term *cursor* refers to (a) a blinking marker, (b) an angry typist. (   )

- You can move the blinking marker, or *cu*_____, to the spot on the display screen where you want to type or make some kind of a change.

- To *merge,* on a word processor, is to _____ [combine / destroy] printed materials from different files.

- When a bill collector combines his standard threatening letter with listed names and amounts overdue, he uses _____ [merge / scotch tape].

- Looking at the screen, you know your next typing will appear where you see the blinking c_____.

- Advertisements in the mail that print your very own name in six places and say you've (almost) won a Cadillac are the result of (a) a miracle, (b) merge. (   )

Write the letter that indicates the best definition.

1. (d)
2. (c)
3. (f)
4. (a)
5. (b)
6. (e)

(   ) 1. cursor   a. writing documents by computer
(   ) 2. merge   b. where text can be read
(   ) 3. floppy disk   c. to blend sources of text
(   ) 4. word processing   d. a movable blinker
(   ) 5. monitor   e. a keyboard and screen
(   ) 6. terminal   f. a device to store information

---

13. **bar code:** machine-printed stripes that give information such as the product ID, size and model.
14. **binary:** belonging to a numbering system to the base 2. *Binary* numbers are expressed in the *binary* digits 0 and 1.

■ Numbers in the decimal system, such as 1776, are to the base 10; numbers in the *binary* system, such as 10110, are to the base

2

_____ [2 / 13].

■ Because electronic impulses can be either on or off, the digital

binary

computer uses the *b*_____ system to transmit numbers and letters (off = 0; on = 1).

■ The machine-printed stripes on a can of beans are a

bar code

_____ [symbol of purity / bar code].

■ You buy some chocolate googoos, and on the box is a bunch of

bar code
bar
code
(b)

parallel stripes known as a *b*_____ *c*_____.
The supermarket computer scans this *b*_____
*c*_____ and promptly (a) takes your picture, (b) prints the price of the googoos. (   )

binary

■ Although a digital computer operates on the *b*_____ mathematics system (base 2), it translates the results for us into the decimal system.

15. **byte:** the storage space needed to represent one letter or digit such as "g" or "6." A computer's memory is measured by the number of *bytes* it can hold.
16. **kilobyte:** approximately 1,000 bytes, referred to as "KB." A *megabyte* equals a million bytes and is referred to as "MB" and a *gigabyte* equals a billion bytes and is referred to as "GB."

(a)

■ A *byte* is (a) a unit of computer memory, (b) a canine's revenge. (   )

1,000

■ A *kilobyte* equals _____ [100 / 1,000] *bytes.*

(b)

■ A typewritten page, double-spaced, consists of about 2,000 letters and digits. This means that each typed page eats up storage of approximately (a) two bytes, (b) 2K, (c) 20K, (d) 2MK. (   )

kilobyte

bytes

■ The symbol *KB* stands for a *k*_____ of computer memory, which is equal to 1,000 *b*_____.

1,000, kilobytes

billion

■ The symbol *MB* stands for a *megabyte,* which is equal to a million *bytes,* or _____ [100 / 1,000] _____ [characters / kilobytes]. A *gigabyte* (GB) equals one _____ bytes.

kilobytes
(c)

■ A large disk storage (memory) is desirable in a computer. Thus, a floppy disk with a rated capacity of 1.4 MB (which is equal to 1,400 *k*_____) can remember approximately 700 (a) letters and digits, (b) words, (c) typewritten pages. (   )

17. **Internet:** a message and data forwarding system that links computer networks all around the world.
18. **database:** a large collection of data on a given subject that can be consulted by multiple users.

Internet

■ You can send a computer message to your cousin in New York or to Uncle Olaf in Copenhagen by means of the *In*_____.

(c)

■ The Internet is a communication system involving (a) six stations, (b) a small network of stations, (c) a worldwide network of networks. (   )

Internet
database

■ If the local library hasn't much information for your term paper on Daniel Boone, you should get on the *In*_____ and consult a *da*_____.

(c)

■ As salesperson, you want to find out if your department store chain has any Snazzy Swimsuits, size 9, on hand. You should consult (a) the custodian, (b) the president of the firm, (c) the inventory list database. (   )

Internet

database

■ Network linkage known as the *In*_____ benefits us in many ways. We chat with distant friends, keep an eye on Wall Street, or—feeling ill—consult a *d*_____ full of health facts.

QUIZ

Write the letter that indicates the best definition.

1. (g)
2. (b)
3. (e)
4. (f)
5. (c)
6. (h)

( ) 1. kilobyte   a. a million bytes
( ) 2. Internet   b. linked computer networks
( ) 3. byte   c. stripes on grocery product
( ) 4. database   d. numbering to base 10
( ) 5. bar code   e. storage space for one letter
( ) 6. binary   f. collection of information
    g. a thousand bytes
    h. numbering to base 2

---

19. **e-mail:** messages between computers. E-mail is short for electronic mail.
20. **fax:** the sending of graphic copies from one computer to another.

■ Most people refer to electronic mail as *e*_____.

■ A copy of your birth certificate could be scanned and sent over the phone lines by *f*_____.

■ *F*_____ is transmitted over telephone lines; but *e*_____ is transmitted by way of an Internet provider such as AOL or Earthlink. Thus, *RJones@aol.com* might be someone's _____ address; whereas 626-794-1313 might be his or her *f*_____ address.

■ To inform your rich Grandpa Jasper in Vienna most quickly about your new nine-pound baby—little Jasper—you should use (a) UPS, (b) e-mail, (c) priority mail. ( )

■ Rapid exchange of small talk by computer is usually carried on by (a) e-mail, (b) fax. ( ) Exact duplicates of documents are best transmitted by (a) fax, (b) floppy disk, (c) ROM. ( )

e-mail

fax

Fax
e-mail

e-mail
fax

(b)

(a)
(a)

21. **interface:** a link that permits different types of systems to work together. For example, an *interface* is needed between a computer and a printer.
22. **modem:** an interface between a computer or terminal and a telephone line. A *modem* is a MOdulator-DEModulator.

link

- An *interface* is a _____ [conflict / photo / link] between different kinds of equipment.

interface
modem

- Two computers can "communicate" over a long-distance telephone line if each uses a special *int*_____ called a *mo*_____.

telephone

- A *modem* links a computer or *terminal* to a _____ [telephone / clothes / bread] line.

modem

modem

- Computer signals are modulated into audible tones for telephone transmission by a *m*_____, then demodulated into computer signals at the receiving end by another *m*_____.

23. **format:** the layout of a document page. Format involves the predetermined arrangement of margin settings, tabs, print size, captions, lines, page numbers, and so on.
24. **justify:** to produce text with an even right-hand margin. Some printers can vary the space between words, and even between letters, so that lines are of equal length (*justified*).
25. **macro:** a few timesaving keystrokes that perform a sequence of frequently used tasks.

(b)

- When printers justify, they produce (a) a ragged right-hand margin (b) an even right-hand margin, (c) a legal document. (   )

- To avoid going again and again through the same series of computer procedures, you should make use of a *m*_____.

macro

- Indentations, double-spacing, number of lines to the page, margins—these are matters of _____ [cursors / megabytes / format].

format

- A boring sequence of computer tasks can be abbreviated by use of a *m*_____, which usually requires about _____ [3 / 38 /120] keystrokes.

macro
3

■ Format should be decided _____ [before / after] a document is printed.

■ Books and newspapers turn out neat, flush right-hand margins because their printers *j*_____ the copy.

■ Some word-processing printers can produce a handsome page arrangement, or *f*_____, because the printer has proportional spacing and can *j*_____ the lines.

■ A useful computer shortcut involving two or three keystrokes is called a _____ [macron, macro, matron].

QUIZ

Write the letter that indicates the best definition:

1. (a)
2. (d)
3. (c)
4. (b)
5. (e)
6. (g)
7. (f)

(   ) 1. justify   a. straighten the right-hand margin

(   ) 2. macro   b. any linking of two different systems

(   ) 3. modem   c. link of computer to telephone line

(   ) 4. interface   d. shortcut for series of tasks

(   ) 5. e-mail   e. messages by electronic mail

(   ) 6. fax   f. page layout

(   ) 7. format   g. sending pages by telephone line

Supply the missing words. Some letters are given.

1. The connected computer networks of the world are known as the *In*_____.
2. A large usable pool of data on a subject is called a *da*_____.
3. A *fl*_____ *d*_____ is a small plate that stores information.
4. A *mo*_____ is an interface between computer and telephone line.
5. In the *bi*_____ system, the numbering is to the base 2.
6. *For*_____ refers to page layout.
7. As text enters the system, we read it on the *mon*_____.
8. To produce an even right-hand margin, a printer must be able to *ju*_____.
9. *W*_____ *pr*_____ is a system for preparing documents.
10. The keyboard and printer are _____ *ware.*
11. The *cu*_____ blinks where typing will next appear.
12. A *ter*_____ consists of a keyboard and a display screen.

Write True or False.

_____ 13. Linking different computer systems requires an *interface.*

_____ 14. Computer programs are *software.*

_____ 15. *Merging* can help to "personalize" a master letter.

_____ 16. Parcels can be sent in a few seconds by *fax.*

_____ 17. An expensive *computer,* without input, can produce meaningful results.

_____ 18. A *byte* is a unit of computer memory.

_____ 19. A *bar code* is a list of ingredients on a candy wrapper.

_____ 20. A *megabyte* equals a million bytes.

Give the letter that indicates the best definition.

( ) 21. RAM   a. the brains of a computer

( ) 22. ROM   b. unchangeable stored information

( ) 23. microprocessor   c. a thousand bytes

( ) 24. e-mail   d. changeable stored information

( ) 25. kilobyte   e. electronic messages

Check your answers by the following key. Deduct 4% per error from a possible 100%.

1. Internet
2. database
3. floppy disk
4. modem
5. binary
6. format
7. monitor
8. justify
9. word processing

10. hardware
11. cursor
12. terminal
13. True
14. True
15. True
16. False
17. False
18. True

19. False
20. True
21. (d)
22. (b)
23. (a)
24. (e)
25. (c)

Score: _____ %

1. **acronym:** a word formed from the opening letters of a series of words, as COBOL from COmmon Business Oriented Language.
2. **algorithm:** the logical steps by computer that will solve a problem.
3. **boilerplate:** standard paragraphs or passages that can be inserted, for example, into contracts and "personalized" form letters.
4. **camera copy:** copy in shape to be photographed for offset printing.
5. **card readers:** devices that accept data from punched or marked cards.
6. **character:** a single letter, number, punctuation mark, or symbol.
7. **chip:** a tiny slice of silicon carrying integrated circuits.
8. **collate:** to place the pages of a document in proper order.
9. **data:** basic elements of information.
10. **delete:** to remove letters, words, or longer passages, after which the gap is automatically closed.
11. **disk drive:** a piece of hardware that spins the magnetic disks so that information can be added to them or read from them.
12. **file:** a collection of data in storage.
13. **file protection:** a method of making sure that a file is not accidentally erased.
14. **function keys:** keys that do special jobs: "delete," "move," "search," etc.
15. **input:** data put into the computer for processing.
16. **menu:** a list of choices offered on the screen to the computer user.
17. **microcomputer:** a small computer.
18. **microsecond:** one millionth of a second.
19. **Murphy's Law:** *Humorous.* If anything can go wrong, it will. Dropped bread lands with the peanut butter facing the rug.
20. **nanosecond:** one billionth of a second.
21. **output:** data put out by the computer, normally to the printer or screen.
22. **repagination:** renumbering the pages because of changes in the copy.
23. **scrolling:** moving the data on the screen up and down or sideways.
24. **search and replace:** the ability of a program to find specific words throughout a page or a document and replace them with certain other words.
25. **storage:** the part of the computer that holds information.

Psychology

A cynic has said that psychology "tells us what everybody knows, in language that nobody understands." His comment is more witty than accurate. Actually, psychology, which is the study of human behavior, tells us many things we don't know about ourselves and in language we can learn to understand quite well. In fact, the terms of psychology must be understood if we are to qualify in such diverse areas as social work, law, and medicine; or if we are to analyze the fiction of Faulkner, the poetry of Jeffers, the dramas of Hitchcock.

This chapter stresses twenty-five basic terms of psychology and presents fifty more definitions in a supplementary list. As you fill in the frames, try to relate the terms to people you have known or read about. Can you think of anyone with a *neurosis,* a *psychosomatic* illness, or a trace of *narcissism?* Have you yourself had a *traumatic* experience? Are you a *sibling* (or would you knock a person down for calling you that)? Words become more meaningful when you see how they apply to the life around you.

EXERCISES

1. **ambivalence** (am-biv′ə-ləns): conflicting feelings, such as love and hate, toward the same person or thing. You may have a deep affection for your parents and yet be angry because they interfere with your decisions; your attitude toward them, then, is one of *ambivalence.*

■ A child wants to pet a strange "doggie" but is fearful. The conflict of feelings is called *amb_____.*

ambivalence

■ Felix wants to order the giant hot fudge sundae, but he doesn't want to get fat. His attitude toward the sundae is one of *am_____.*

ambivalence

■ A star basketball player has *ambivalent* feelings toward his coach. This means that the athlete (a) can shoot with either hand, (b) has contradictory emotions. (   )

(b)

■ Wilmer wants to ask Alice for a date but worries that she will turn him down; Alice loves Jerry but has fits of jealousy when he talks to other girls; Jerry craves alcohol but realizes that it can ruin him. These conflicting attitudes illustrate *am_____.*

ambivalence

possible

■ It is _____ [possible / impossible] for a person to be both attracted and repelled by something. The condition is called *a_____.*

ambivalence

2. **aptitude** (ap′tə-to͞od′): the natural ability to acquire a skill or type of knowledge. A test of musical *aptitude,* for example, does not measure achievement but predicts future performance.

■ A high score in a mechanical-*aptitude* test means (a) that you have unusual ability as a mechanic, (b) that you could be trained to be a good mechanic. (   )

(b)

■ An achievement test measures what you can do now; an *apt_____* test predicts what you will be able to do with training.

aptitude

■ Glenna is extremely athletic, and although she has never played tennis she probably has an *ap_____* for it.

aptitude

does
aptitude

claustrophobia

(a)

claustrophobia

(a)

compensation

inferiority

compensation

success
compensation

kleptomania
dipsomania

■ Harvey is an excellent speller and scores high in a finger-dexterity test; apparently he _____ [does / doesn't] have an *a*_____ for typewriting.

3. **claustrophobia** (klô′strə-fō′bē-ə): morbid fear of being in enclosed or narrow places.

■ Linus feels stifled and fearful in an elevator or a closet. He has *cl*_____.

■ *Claustrophobia* manifests itself in an abnormal fear of (a) small rooms, (b) heights. (   )

■ A phobia involves excessive fear in the absence of real danger. The excessive fear and anxiety of a clerk who must work in a small, windowless office may be an indication of *cl*_____.

■ A person with *claustrophobia* would probably feel comfortable (a) in a meadow, (b) in a trunk. (   )

4. **compensation:** an attempt to make up for an undesirable trait by exaggerating a socially approved one.

■ A student who is weak in academic courses may try to excel in athletics—an example of *com*_____.

■ *Compensation* is an effort to excel in one activity in order to make up for a feeling of _____ [inferiority / accomplishment] in another.

■ Napoleon, Hitler, and Stalin were of short stature, and their drive for political power was possibly a form of *co*_____.

■ Igor was embarrassingly poor in athletics, so he tried doubly hard to become a _____ [success / failure] as a debater, an effort known as *c*_____.

5. **dipsomania:** an abnormal craving for alcoholic liquors.
6. **kleptomania:** an abnormal tendency to steal.

■ An irresistible impulse to steal is *klep*_____; an insatiable desire for alcohol is *di*_____.

drink
steal

dipsomania

kleptomania

(b)

(a)

- Emotional disturbances have been cited as a cause of *dipsomania,* or the tendency to _____ [steal / drink], and *kleptomania,* or the tendency to _____ [steal / drink].

- Alcoholics Anonymous is an excellent organization for those whose problem is *di*_____.

- "Stealing lingerie?" said the judge. "Looks like a case of *kl*_____. Ten days should be enough. After all, this is your first slip."

- *Kleptomania* is associated with (a) overeating, (b) shoplifting. (   )

- *Dipsomania* is associated with (a) boozing, (b) pocket picking. (   )

QUIZ

Write the letter that indicates the best definition.

1. (e)
2. (c)
3. (a)
4. (f)
5. (b)
6. (d)

(   ) 1. ambivalence   a. fear of small enclosures
(   ) 2. aptitude   b. alcoholism
(   ) 3. claustrophobia   c. capacity to learn
(   ) 4. compensation   d. irresistible stealing
(   ) 5. dipsomania   e. conflicting feelings
(   ) 6. kleptomania   f. making up for a shortcoming

7. **ego** (ē′gō): the conscious part of the personality, which has to deal with the id, the superego, and external reality, according to Freud. The *ego* does our logical thinking.
8. **id:** the primitive, instinctive, aggressive part of our personality. The pleasure-loving *id,* with which we are born, seeks immediate gratification regardless of consequences, but it is later held in check by the superego and ego, says Freud.
9. **superego:** the moralistic part of the personality which acts as a conscience to control the ego and the id. The *superego* is a product of parental and social training, and it sets up standards of right and wrong.

id

- A baby is like a little animal; it is swayed by the raw, instinctive part of its personality, the *i*_____.

- From its environment the child absorbs a sense of what is right and wrong. This developing conscience has been called the

superego

*su*_____.

The self-aware, thinking part of the mind is called the
*e*_____.

ego

The unconscious parts of the mind include the primitive drives, or
*i*_____, and the conscience, or *su*_____. The
conscious part of the mind, which does our thinking, is the
*e*_____.

id, superego

ego

The uncontrolled impulses of the *id* are likely to be
_____ [encouraged / condemned] by society. Such
uncontrolled impulses would probably produce (a) rapists,
burglars, gluttons, (b) priests, teachers, saints. (   )

condemned

(a)

Traditional values and ideals of society are represented by the
*su*_____. The *superego* strives for (a) pleasure,
(b) perfection. (   )

superego
(b)

The conscious, thinking part of you is called the *e*_____.
The *ego* operates according to the _____ [reality /
pleasure] principle.

ego
reality

Personalities can be distorted, says Freud, if either the animalistic
*i*_____ or the moralistic *s*_____ is too strong.
One's behavior should be controlled by the conscious aspect of the
mind, the *e*_____.

id, superego

ego

The concept of an *id, ego,* and *superego* was first developed by
(a) Sigmund Freud, (b) Charles Darwin. (   )

(a)

10. **extrasensory perception (ESP):** ability to gain knowledge
without use of the known senses. *ESP* refers to telepathy,
clairvoyance, or any other means of perceiving external events of
communicating by mental rather than physical means.

Extrasensory perception would be operative if you could send a
message by (a) brain waves, (b) Western Union. (   )

(a)

ESP is an acronym for *ex*_____ *per*_____.

extrasensory,
perception

You dream that your best friend is calling for help, and the next
day he falls down a well. Precognition, as illustrated here, is a type
of *ex*_____ *p*_____.

extrasensory,
perception

Most psychologists do not as yet believe in *extrasensory
perception* (usually abbreviated _____).

ESP

(d)

■ The term *ESP* does *not* refer to (a) clairvoyance, (b) precognition, (c) telepathy, (d) short-wave radio. (   )

11. **free association:** the free, unhampered, rambling talk by a patient by which his or her repressions are discovered.
12. **psychoanalysis** (sī′kō-ə-nal′ə-sis): a system of mental therapy, devised by Freud, whereby through free association and dream analysis certain conflictual material is released from the unconscious.

■ Freud's technique of treating mental illness is known as

psychoanalysis   *psy*_____ .

free   ■ Rambling from one topic to another is called *fr*_____
association   *as*_____ . This activity is common during sessions of
psychoanalysis   *psy*_____ .

■ The purpose of *psychoanalysis* is to help the patient overcome
(a)   problems that are basically (a) mental, (b) physical. (   )

■ A mental shock that occurred in infancy might be disclosed during
psychoanalysis,   a session of *ps*_____ by means of *fr*_____
free   *as*_____ .
association
■ Through *free association* one's unconscious wishes find
(b)   (a) concealment, (b) verbal expression. (   )

■ Psychologists do not accept all of Freud's theories, but he is
psychoanalysis   respected as the father of *p*_____*sis.*

■ QUIZ

Write the letter that indicates the best definition.

1. (f)   (   ) 1. ego   a. Freud's system of treatment
2. (d)   (   ) 2. id   b. conscience, or moral control
3. (b)   (   ) 3. superego   c. rambling monologue
4. (e)   (   ) 4. ESP   d. seat of animalistic impulses
5. (c)   (   ) 5. free association   e. thought transference
6. (a)   (   ) 6. psychoanalysis   f. thinking part of the mind

13. **hallucination** (hə-lōō′sə-nā′shən): the apparent witnessing of sights and sounds that do not exist.

hallucination

- "Yesterday upon a stair / I saw a man who wasn't there. . . ." The poet seems to have had a *hal*_____.

(a)

- The sights and sounds of a *hallucination* are (a) imaginary, (b) actual. (   )

hallucination

- Macbeth imagines that he sees the murdered Banquo sitting in front of him; Macbeth is experiencing a *ha*_____.

(b)

- *Hallucinative* drugs make one's sense impressions more (a) dependable, (b) undependable. (   )

14. **hypochondria** (hī′pə-kon′drē-ə): excessive worry about one's health; anxiety about minor or imaginary ailments.
15. **psychosomatic** (sī′kō-sō-mat′ik): referring to a physical disorder caused by emotional stress.

hypochondria

- Every morning Wilhelm gets up worried, looks at his tongue, and swallows thirty pills; his problem is *hyp*_____.

(a)

- A *hypochondriac* usually believes that his health is (a) failing, (b) perfect. (   )

psychosomatic

- Gus's ulcers act up when he works under pressure; his illness is probably *psy*_____.

psychosomatic
(a)

- Disorders such as asthma, dermatitis, and high blood pressure are sometimes *ps*_____, that is, caused by (a) emotional stress, (b) bacterial infection. (   )

hypochondria

- Julius with his imaginary illnesses suffers from *hy*_____; he caught his last disease from the *Reader's Digest.* His wife Lydia, overfearful of germs, boils dishes three times before using them; she also suffers from *h*_____.

hypochondria

psychosomatic

- Soldiers have sometimes developed a paralysis from fear of combat; such paralysis is _____*ic.*

16. **narcissism** (när′si-siz′əm): abnormal self-love; erotic pleasure obtained from admiration of one's own body or mind.
17. **Oedipus complex** (ed′ə-pəs): sexual attraction to the parent of the opposite sex and hostility toward the parent of the same sex.

narcissism

- *Narcissus* admired his own physical features; thus, Freud refers to such self-love as *nar*_____.

Oedipus
complex

- *Oedipus* loved his mother and hated his father; thus, Freud refers to a similar stage in child development as the *Oed*_____ *com*_____.

Oedipus
complex

- Little Jasper is competing with his father for the love of his mother; Jasper's feelings are referred to as the *O*_____ *c*_____.

narcissism

- The pretty people in TV commercials often say, "I love my hair—so soft and fragrant," "My skin is baby-smooth," "My breath is twenty-four-hours sweet and fresh, thanks to Putro"; such conceited lines suggest *nar*_____.

(b)

- The *Oedipus complex* involves rivalry for the love of the parent of (a) the same sex, (b) the opposite sex. (   )

narcissism

- A person who is obsessed with his or her own handsome appearance is exhibiting *na*_____.

QUIZ

Write the letter that indicates the best definition.

1. (c)
2. (b)
3. (d)
4. (a)
5. (e)

( ) 1. narcissism	a. love-mother, hate-father phase
( ) 2. psychosomatic	b. of illness caused by emotions
( ) 3. hypochondria	c. self-love
( ) 4. Oedipus complex	d. anxiety about one's health
( ) 5. hallucination	e. seeing what is nonexistent

18. **psychosis** (sī′kō′sis): a mental disorder such as paranoia or schizophrenia that involves very serious disorganization of the personality; insanity.
19. **paranoia** (par′ə-noi′ə): a mental disorder marked by delusions of persecution or of grandeur.
20. **schizophrenia** (skit′sə-frē′nē-ə): a mental disorder marked by splitting of the personality, a retreat from reality, and emotional deterioration.

(a)
(b)

- *Psychotic* people are (a) irrational, (b) rational. (   ) They tend to (a) cope with reality, (b) withdraw from reality. (   )

paranoia	■ The delusion that people are plotting behind your back and are "out to get you" is a symptom of *par*_____.
(a)	■ Another common symptom of *paranoia* is the delusion of (a) grandeur, (b) inferiority. ( )
(a)	■ A *schizophrenic* tends to be (a) withdrawn and mute, (b) the life of the party. ( )
paranoia	■ Delusions of grandeur ("I am Napoleon," "I am Jesus Christ") are symptoms of *pa*_____.
(b)	■ A major mental disorder is (a) neurosis, (b) a psychosis. ( )
psychosis	■ Hardening of blood vessels in the brain of an elderly person may result in a serious mental disorder, or *ps*_____.
schizophrenia

paranoia | ■ The *psychotic* who is rigid and unresponsive probably suffers from *sc*_____; the *psychotic* who shouts, "They conspire against me—I'll kill them—I'll rule the world!" probably suffers from *pa*_____. |

21. **rationalization** (rash′ən-ə-liz-ā′shən): justifying of unreasonable behavior by presenting false but plausible reasons to oneself or to others.

conceal	■ To *rationalize* one of our misdeeds is to _____ [reveal / conceal] the real motives behind it.
rationalization	■ Whenever Buster, who is overweight, orders another double banana split, he says, "I have to keep up my strength." Buster's excuse is an example of *rat*_____.
(b)	■ Big Country invades rich Little Country, saying, "We will restore better government." Big Country is probably indulging in (a) pure altruism, (b) rationalization. ( )
rationalization

(b) | ■ Self-justification, known as *ra*_____, is probably being used when a football coach explains a 79-6 loss this way: "We lost because (a) we were outplayed"; (b) them umpires was prejudiced." ( ) |

22. **regression:** going back to earlier, less mature behavior as an escape from a present conflict.

regression

■ Six-year-old Wilmer sees his new baby sister get all the attention, so he begins to wet his pants again. He is trying to solve his conflict by *reg*_____.

less

■ *Regression* involves a change to _____ [more / less] mature behavior.

regression

■ A young housewife keeps running back to the security of her parental home. This, too, is probably *reg*_____.

child

regression

■ A man loses his wife or his job and gets drunk. His escape to the irresponsible condition of a _____ [child / adult] is *r*_____.

23. **sibling:** a brother or sister.

siblings

■ The Grunches have three sons and two daughters, a total of five *sib*_____.

siblings

■ Suppose you have an older sister and a younger brother. This means that you have two *si*_____.

are not

■ Your cousins _____ [are / are not] your *siblings*.

is not

■ Wally, an only child, _____ [is / is not] a *sibling*.

sibling

■ Competition and jealousy between two brothers, between two sisters, or between a brother and a sister are aspects of *s*_____ rivalry.

24. **trauma** (trou′mə): an emotional shock which has a lasting effect.

major

■ A trauma is a _____ [minor / major] emotional shock.

(a)

■ Nellie has nightmares ever since her car accident. Its effect has been (a) traumatic, (b) salutary. (   )

trauma

■ Incest or other forms of sexual molestation can cause serious *tr*_____ in children.

trauma

(b)

■ The effects of an emotional shock, or *t*_____, are (a) temporary, (b) lasting. (   )

25. **voyeur** (vwä-yûr′): a Peeping Tom; one who obtains sexual gratification by looking at sexual objects or acts, especially secretively.

(a)

voyeur

(b)

(b)

an immature

■ A *voyeur* peeks into windows hoping to see (a) sexual acts, (b) television programs. (   )

■ A Peeping Tom, also known as a *vo*_____, derives particular pleasure from (a) exhibiting his body, (b) peeking in secret at the nakedness of others. (   )

■ Two men are using telescopes. The *voyeur* is the fellow peering (a) at Jupiter, (b) into bedrooms. (   )

■ Children go through a stage of intense curiosity about sex. Consequently, *voyeurism* is considered to be _____ [a mature / an immature] way of achieving sexual fulfillment.

QUIZ

Write the letter that indicates the best definition.

1. (e)
2. (c)
3. (h)

4. (b)
5. (g)

6. (d)
7. (a)
8. (f)

(   ) 1. psychosis   a. a lasting emotional shock
(   ) 2. paranoia   b. justifying with false reasons
(   ) 3. schizophrenia   c. delusions of grandeur and persecution
(   ) 4. rationalization   d. a brother or sister
(   ) 5. regression   e. serious mental disorder (general term)
(   ) 6. sibling   f. a Peeping Tom
(   ) 7. trauma   g. escape via less mature behavior
(   ) 8. voyeur   h. splitting of personality

Write the word studied in this chapter that will complete the sentence.

1. Abnormal self-love is *na*_____.
2. Morbid fear of small, enclosed places is *cl*_____.
3. That part of the unconscious mind that acts as a conscience is the *su*_____.
4. A brother or sister is a *si*_____.
5. A splitting of the personality and withdrawal from reality is *sc*_____.
6. Conflicting feelings, like love and hate, for the same person are known as *amb*_____.
7. A son's desire for his mother and rivalry with his father is the *Oed*_____ *c*_____.
8. Physical illness caused by emotional stress is *ps*_____.
9. Reverting to less mature behavior as an escape is *reg*_____.
10. Excessive desire for alcohol is *di*_____.
11. Abnormal anxiety about one's imagined illnesses is *hy*_____.
12. A compulsion to do shoplifting is *kl*_____.
13. A lasting emotional shock is a *tr*_____.
14. One who peeks into windows to see sex acts is a *vo*_____.
15. Uncle Fritz claims he is General Grant and that the neighbors are plotting to poison him. Fritz has symptoms of *pa*_____.

Write True or False.

_____ 16. The purpose of an *aptitude* test is to measure achievement.

_____ 17. The *ego* is the conscious part of the personality.

_____ 18. *Hallucinations* can be caused by drugs.

_____ 19. *Free association* is a technique used in psychoanalysis.

_____ 20. A *psychosis* is a fairly common, minor nervous ailment.

_____ 21. Unusually keen vision and hearing are referred to as *extrasensory perception* (*ESP*).

_____ 22. The *id,* which is powerful during one's infancy, passes out of existence when one reaches maturity.

_____ 23. A certain blind girl tries doubly hard to master the piano; her efforts are a form of *compensation.*

_____ 24. *Rationalization* means logical reasoning, the avoidance of fallacy.

_____ 25. *Psychoanalysis* is a method of treating mental illness.

KEY TO REVIEW TEST

Check your test answers with the following key. Deduct 4% per error from a possible 100%.

1. narcissism	10. dipsomania	19. True
2. claustrophobia	11. hypochondria	20. False
3. superego	12. kleptomania	21. False
4. sibling	13. trauma	22. False
5. schizophrenia	14. voyeur	23. True
6. ambivalence	15. paranoia	24. False
7. Oedipus complex	16. False	25. True
8. psychosomatic	17. True	
9. regression	18. True	

Score: _____ %

1. **abnormal psychology:** the study of abnormal behavior, including neurosis, psychosis, and other mental disorders.
2. **acrophobia** (ak′rə-fō′bē-ə): a fear of high places.
3. **aggression:** behavior that aims to hurt someone or what he or she stands for.
4. **amnesia** (am-nē′zhə): partial or total loss of memory; specifically, forgetting one's own identity.
5. **atavism** (at′ə-viz′əm): reversion to an earlier ancestral characteristic.
6. **behaviorism:** the doctrine that humans react automatically, like a machine, to stimuli.
7. **clairvoyance** (klâr-voi′əns): the alleged ability to see objects or to know things beyond the range of the senses.
8. **compulsion:** an irresistible impulse to perform an irrational act.
9. **conditioned reflex:** a response set off by a second stimulus associated with the primary stimulus; for example, secretion of saliva set off in Pavlov's dog by a dinner bell.
10. **defense mechanism** (mek′ə-niz′əm): an unconscious adjustment to block out unpleasant memories, feelings, or knowledge.
11. **dementia praecox** (di-men′shə prē′koks): former term for schizophrenia.
12. **dissociation** (di-sō′sē-ā′shən): a splitting apart of mental elements, involving loss of control over memory and motor processes.
13. **dualism:** the state of being twofold; the theory that a person consists of two entities—body and mind.
14. **Electra complex:** a daughter's unconscious sexual attachment to her father and hostility to her mother.
15. **empathy:** one's participating in the feelings and spirit of another person or thing.
16. **exhibitionism:** a tendency to behave so as to attract attention; self-exposure.
17. **extrovert** (eks′trō-vûrt): a person actively interested in his or her environment and other people rather than in himself or herself.
18. **fixation:** an abnormal attachment to some person, object, or idea.
19. **Freudian** (froi′dē-ən): pertaining to Sigmund Freud's methods of psychoanalysis, which emphasize the techniques of free association and transference and try to give the patient an insight into his unconscious conflicts and motives.
20. **gustatory** (gus′tə-tôr′ē): relating to the sense of taste.
21. **hysteria** (hi-ster′ē-ə): emotional frenzy marked by sensory and motor disturbances.
22. **identification**: the putting of oneself in the place of someone else and unconsciously sharing his admirable qualities.
23. **infantilism** (in-fan′tə-liz′əm): extreme immaturity of mind and body in an adult.
24. **inhibition** (in′i-bish′ən): the blocking of one impulse by another.
25. **intelligence quotient (I.Q.):** the mental age multiplied by 100 and then divided by the actual age.
26. **introspection:** analysis of one's own mental and emotional states.
27. **intuition** (in′too-ish′ən): awareness of something without conscious reasoning.
28. **kinesthetic** (kin′is-thet′ik): pertaining to muscle sense or the sensation of position, movement, and tension in the body.
29. **libido** (li-bē′dō): the drive for sex gratification.
30. **masochism** (mas′ə-kiz′əm): the deriving of sexual pleasure from being hurt or humiliated.
31. **maturation** (mach′oo-rā′shən): completion of growth process in the body and the accompanying behavioral changes.

32. **megalomania** (meg′ə-lō-mā′nē-ə): delusions of wealth, power, and self-importance.
33. **melancholia** (mel′ən-kō′lē-ə): a mental disorder characterized by extreme gloominess and depression of spirits.
34. **neurasthenic** (nūr′əs-then′ik): afflicted with fatigue, worry, pains, and so on, because of emotional conflicts.
35. **neurosis** (nū-rō′sis): an emotional disorder, less severe than a psychosis, characterized by anxieties, obsessions, compulsions, and physical complaints.
36. **obsession:** an idea or desire that haunts the mind.
37. **parapsychology** (par′ə): the study of clairvoyance, telepathy, and other apparently supernatural phenomena.
38. **phobia** (fō′bē-ə): any irrational or morbid fear.
39. **pleasure principle:** automatic adjustment of one's thoughts to secure pleasure and to avoid pain.
40. **projection:** ascribing one's own motives to someone else, thus relieving one's ego of guilt feelings.
41. **psychedelic** (sī′ki-del′ik): of a mental state, usually drug-induced, marked by entrancement and blissful aesthetic perceptiveness.
42. **psychodrama:** the acting out of situations related to one's problem, as a form of cathartic therapy.
43. **Rorschach test** (rôr′shäk): the analysis of personality by means of responses to inkblot designs.
44. **sadism** (sad′iz-əm): the deriving of sexual pleasure from hurting one's partner.
45. **stimulus** (stim′yoo-ləs): anything that excites an organism, organ, or part into activity.
46. **subjective:** reflecting a person's feelings and thinking rather than objective reality.
47. **sublimation:** the channeling of psychic energy into socially acceptable activities.
48. **subliminal** (sub-lim′ə-nəl): below the level of consciousness but perceptible by the subconscious.
49. **synapse** (si-naps′): the point where a nerve impulse passes from one neuron to the next.
50. **xenophobia** (zen′ə-fō′bē-ə): fear or hatred of strangers and foreigners.

Business and Law

actuary, **1**
affidavit, **2**
collateral, **4**
foreclosure, **6**
franchise, **8**
indictment, **9**
injunction, **10**

larceny, **7**
libel, **11**
lien, **13**
negotiable, **5**
notarize, **3**
perjury, **15**
precedent, **16**

prospectus, **17**
realty, **14**
solvent, **19**
speculation, **18**
subpoena, **12**
voucher, **20**

This chapter is recommended to only two groups of students:

1. Those going into business or law
2. Those not going into business or law

All citizens, in short, must wet their feet in commercial law. In the words of the jurist Sir William Blackstone, good citizens "cannot, in any scene of life, discharge properly their duty either to the public or to themselves, without some degree of knowledge in the laws" (1753).

Pick up a newspaper and you read of *indictments, injunctions, libel suits,* and *felonies.* Buy a house and you must talk of *realty, collateral, mortgages,* and *easements.* Open a pizza parlor and you bandy words like *franchise, prospectus, solvent,* and *vouchers.* Inescapably, you live in a world of business law.

First, master the twenty programmed words, then become acquainted with the fifty terms in the supplementary list. You will meet these words again—possibly during life's crises—and you will be grateful that you recognize them.

EXERCISES

1. **actuary** (ak′choo-er′ē): a person who calculates risks, premiums, and the like, for insurance purposes.

actuary

■ The insurance company mathematician who uses statistical records to figure out what rates to charge is called an *ac_____.*

(a)

■ If you wanted to insure your outdoor music festival against rain, the *actuary* would first consult (a) the probabilities of rain on that date, (b) an astrology book. (   )

actuary

(b)

■ The statistical expert of an insurance company, who is known as an _____, must be especially qualified in (a) poetry, (b) mathematics. (   )

(b)

■ If an insurance company keeps charging too low a premium for the company to make a profit (an unlikely situation), the fault is probably that of (a) the filing clerks, (b) the actuaries. (   )

2. **affidavit** (af-i-dā′vit): a sworn, written statement witnessed by an authorized person.
3. **notarize** (nō′tə-rīz′): to authenticate or certify a document through a notary public.

notarize

■ A public official known as a notary public will put his or her seal and signature on your wedding certificate, in other words, *n_____* it.

(b)

■ An *affidavit* is a sworn legal statement (a) spoken in court, (b) written and witnessed. (   )

affidavit
notarize

■ A hit-and-run motorist has smashed your parked VW. If your star witness is too ill to testify in court for you, his testimony should be submitted in the form of an *af_____*, that is, a sworn statement that a notary public would *n_____.*

(b)

■ It is necessary to *notarize* (a) your English composition, (b) a birth certificate. (   )

affidavit

■ To avoid having to pay out-of-state tuition, a college student sometimes needs a sworn, written statement, or *af*_____, testifying that he or she has been a resident of the state for a full year. This *affidavit* must be by (a) a member of congress,

(b) — (b) somebody who has known the student for the past year. (   )

notarize
affidavit
(a)

■ An important function of a notary public is to certify, or *n*_____, a sworn statement known as an *a*_____, which deals as a rule with (a) legal matters, (b) doctors' prescriptions. (   )

    4. **collateral** (kə-lat′ər-əl): any security, such as stocks and bonds, that guarantees the payment of a loan.
    5. **negotiable** (ni-gō′shē-ə-bəl): legally transferable to a third party: said of checks, promissory notes, and securities.

(a)

■ *Collateral* is (a) security that guaranteees payment of a debt, (b) a tricky football maneuver. (   )

can

■ A *negotiable* instrument, such as most personal checks, _____ [can / cannot] be made payable to a third party.

negotiable

■ If a bill of exchange or a promissory note uses a phrase such as "pay to bearer" or "pay to the order of," that financial instrument is *n*_____.

collateral

■ Most people who buy a house must borrow money from a bank and must guarantee repayment of that bank loan with some sort of *c*_____, usually a mortgage on the house.

negotiable,
collateral

■ If transferable, your shares of stock are said to be *n*_____ and may be used as *c*_____ to secure a loan.

collateral

■ A farmer might use his crop or his farm equipment as security for a loan, in other words, as *c*_____.

Write the letter that indicates the best definition.

1. (c)
2. (a)
3. (e)
4. (d)
5. (b)

(   ) 1. actuary   a. a written statement made on oath
(   ) 2. affidavit   b. transferable to a third party
(   ) 3. notarize   c. an expert on insurance risks
(   ) 4. collateral   d. security for a loan
(   ) 5. negotiable   e. to certify a document officially

---

6. **foreclosure** (for-klō′zhər): legal action resulting in the forced sale of property, such as a house, on which regular mortgage payments have not been kept up.
7. **larceny** (lar′sə-nē): theft. Stealing property valued above a certain amount, possibly five hundred dollars or as fixed by state law, is *grand larceny;* stealing a lesser amount is *petit* (or *petty*) *larceny.*

(a)

■ During dry, unproductive years, many wheat farms met *foreclosure* because of (a) non-payment of mortgages, (b) the high price of wheat. (   )

(a)

■ *Larceny* refers to (a) theft, (b) wife-beating. (   )

foreclosure

■ Failure to make mortgage payments can result in *fo*_____.

larceny

■ The plant manager who misappropriates (steals) several thousand dollars in company funds is guilty of a serious crime, specifically, grand *l*_____.

foreclosure

■ Sneaky Sam ignores the "easy $399.99 monthly payments" he owes on his Chevy and loses the car by *fo*_____, after which he steals a new Thunderbird and is convicted of grand

larceny

*la*_____.

(b)

■ You lend Shlepp fifty thousand green ones to buy a restaurant. Instead of making mortgage payments to you, he gambles away his income playing poker. You should reward him with (a) a charge of larceny, (b) foreclosure. (   )

8. **franchise** (fran′chīz): the right to vote; also, a special privilege granted by the government or by a corporation: for example, a *franchise* to operate a bus line, a *franchise* to operate a McDonald's Restaurant.

(b)

■ To exercise one's *franchise* means (a) to jog, (b) to vote. (   )

■ The root *franc,* from Old French, means "free." Thus, the *franchise* granted by the city council to the telephone company or to the waterworks is (a) a special, exclusive privilege, (b) a heavy tax. (   )

(a)

■ The competition of two or three gas companies in the same town would result in excessive digging and inefficiency; therefore, one company is usually granted the exclusive right to operate, known as a *f*_____.

franchise

■ Since a *franchise* restrains others from entering the same business or trade, it tends to establish (a) a legal monopoly, (b) open competition. (   )

(a)

■ Suppose you want to be the only distributor of Wingding Waterbeds in Snorkelville; you might apply for the local *f*_____.

franchise

■ In 1920 the Nineteenth Amendment to the Constitution gave women the *f*_____, also known as suffrage, which means (a) the right to suffer in the kitchen, (b) the right to vote. (   )

franchise

(b)

9. **indictment** (in-dīt′mənt): a formal accusation by a grand jury.
10. **injunction** (in-jungk′shən): a legal order requiring that certain people do, or refrain from doing, certain things.

■ Amanda's fickle boyfriend is found shot to death. The grand jury prepares an *indictment* against Amanda. This means that she (a) is guilty, (b) must face trial. (   )

(b)

indictment

■ The formal accusation by a grand jury is an *in*_____.

injunction

■ To prevent a neighbor from erecting a "spite" fence that would shade your yard, you would file an *in*_____.

(b)

- An *injunction* is (a) a word like *and, but, or, for,* and *nor,* (b) a court order to prevent or to enforce action. (   )

indictment

- The grand jury has reason to believe that the city manager accepted "payola" (bribes); therefore, the jury brings him to trial by means of an _____.

injunction

- The Dingle Duo signed a contract to play exclusively for your night club, yet they intend to play for your competitor next week. You can stop them by means of a court order known as an

  _____.

injunction

indictment

- Each night a certain insecticide factory pours lethal wastes into the air; this unneighborly practice is stopped by a court order known as an _____. Later the manager apparently sets fire to the factory for insurance purposes. To bring him to trial, the grand jury issues an _____.

✚ QUIZ

Write the letter that indicates the best definition.

1. (d)
2. (c)
3. (a)
4. (b)
5. (e)

(   ) 1. foreclosure   a. a special privilege
(   ) 2. larceny   b. accusation by a grand jury
(   ) 3. franchise   c. theft
(   ) 4. indictment   d. forced sale for non-payment
(   ) 5. injunction   e. a legal restraining order

---

11. **libel** (līʹbəl): the writing or printing of something false or damaging about someone.
12. **subpoena** (sə-pēʹnə): a legal order directing a person to appear in court to testify.

(a)

- You would be guilty of *libel* if you spread lies about a person (a) in your writing, (b) in your speeches. (   )

libel

- Defaming your sheriff by word of mouth would be slander; defaming him in a magazine article would be *l*_____.

(b)

- A *subpoena* is a legal order that requires a person (a) to go back to work, (b) to testify in court. (   )

subpoena	■ You are accused of a felony, but the witness who could clear you says he is too busy to come to your trial. You may have to *s*_____ him.
libel, wrote	■ You might be sued for *l*_____ if you _____ [said / wrote] that the new scoutmaster was (a) "a remarkable shaper of boys' character," (b) "a drunken pervert who sells dope
(b)	to the boys." ( )
libel	■ In a so-called letter of recommendation to Mr. Shoat, your boss refers to you as "a paranoiac pickpocket and a stinking swindler." You instigate a *l*_____ suit against your boss and— since Shoat is somewhat reluctant to testify—you request the court
subpoena	to issue a *s*_____ for Shoat. If Shoat ignores the *subpoena* he is in *contempt of court.*

13. **lien** (lēn): a claim on a property as security against payment of a debt.
14. **realty** (rē′əl-tē): real estate; land and buildings.

(b)	■ Real estate is known as (a) reality, (b) realty. ( )
realty	■ A realtor deals in *r*_____; that is, he helps you buy or
(a)	sell (a) house and land, (b) stocks and bonds. ( )
(b)	■ A *lien* on a property is (a) a building or fence that leans against it, (b) a claim against it. ( )
lien	■ The right of a creditor to control another person's property in order to satisfy a debt is a *l*_____.
realty	■ When you buy a home or other *r*_____, you should be
lien	aware of any claim, or *l*_____, of creditors against that property.
lien	■ Suppose you build a garage for Mr. Grob and he refuses to pay for your labor. You can protect your claim by taking out a *l*_____ on Grob's property.

15. **perjury** (pûr′jə-rē): the telling of a lie by a witness under oath; false testimony in court, considered a felony.

(a)	■ *Perjury* is (a) lying, (b) stealing. ( )

perjury

■ Sonya testifies falsely in court that Bill was playing checkers with her at her apartment at the time of the bank robbery. She has committed *p*_____.

(b)

■ *Perjury* refers to (a) ordinary fibbing, (b) lying about a vital matter in court while under oath to tell the truth. (   )

perjury

(a)

■ Suppose you see your friend Fleegle speed through a red light and cause a three-car smashup, yet you swear in court that the light was green. You are guilty of *p*_____, an offense regarded by the court as (a) a felony, (b) fairly trivial. (   )

QUIZ

Write the letter that indicates the best definition.

1. (c)
2. (a)
3. (b)
4. (e)
5. (d)

(   ) 1. libel
(   ) 2. subpoena
(   ) 3. lien
(   ) 4. realty
(   ) 5. perjury

a. legal order to appear in court
b. a claim on property
c. written defamation of character
d. the telling of lies at a trial
e. real estate

16. **precedent** (pres'ə-dənt): a legal decision that may serve as an example for a later one.

(a)

■ A *precedent* is an earlier law case that is (a) similar to the present one, (b) different from the present one. (   )

precedent

■ Lawyers like to cite prior legal decisions that can serve as a *p*_____ for the present case.

precedent

■ Sometimes the divorced father is given custody of the children—let us consider the case of *Spatz v. Spatz* as a *p*_____.

(b)

■ The lawyer said that Ringo's lawsuit was without *precedent*. This means that (a) Ringo would lose the case, (b) no case like it had ever been tried in court. (   )

17. **prospectus** (prə-spec'təs): a statement outlining a proposed business undertaking or literary work.

18. **speculation:** making risky business investments in the hope of big profits.

■ A *prospectus* for a business venture is a review of (a) past achievements, (b) future possibilities. (   )

(b)

■ Before offering a contract, a publishing company will expect to see at least an outline, or *p*_____, of your proposed book.

prospectus

■ *Speculation* refers to a kind of (a) ornamenting of garments with specks, (b) business gambling. (   )

(b)

■ Much frantic *speculation* has taken place (a) in Wall Street, (b) in the Grand Canyon. (   )

(a)

■ Buying and selling for quick profit is known as *s*_____. *Speculation* very commonly involves investing in (a) astronomy, (b) real estate. (   )

speculation

(b)

■ The new Low-Cal Pizza Company has painted a rosy picture of its prospects in its initial *p*_____. Better buy shares of its stock if you are interested in *s*_____.

prospectus
speculation

19. **solvent** (sol′vənt): able to pay all one's debts.
20. **voucher:** a receipt showing payment of a debt.

■ A business firm is *solvent* (a) if it has some money in the bank, (b) if it can pay all of its bills. (   )

(b)

■ A firm may go bankrupt when it is no longer *s*_____.

solvent

■ A *voucher* is (a) a receipt showing that a debt has been paid, (b) a stinging insect. (   )

(a)

■ When you take an all-expenses-paid trip, you had better hang on to every *v*_____.

voucher

■ The Clumpy Cleaners haven't been able to pay salaries for two weeks. "We're almost clean out of funds," says Mr. Clumpy. "Our company isn't *s*_____.

solvent

■ If the Internal Revenue agent doubts any expense in your income tax statement, show him a *v*_____.

voucher

■ The accountant for our Mucilage Manufacturing Company has gone over every bill, asset, and *v*_____. She says that our future is sticky but that we are still *s*_____.

voucher
solvent

Write the letter that indicates the best definition.

1. (d)

2. (b)

3. (e)

4. (c)

5. (a)

(   ) 1. precedent   a. evidence of payment

(   ) 2. prospectus   b. an outline of a future undertaking

(   ) 3. speculation   c. able to meet financial responsibilities

(   ) 4. solvent   d. an earlier, similar law case

(   ) 5. voucher   e. risky investment for fat profit

Supply the missing word in each sentence. The first letter of the answers are given.

1. To tell a lie in court while sworn to tell the truth is *p*_____.
2. A firm that can pay all its debts is *s*_____.
3. A receipt showing that a payment has been made is a *v*_____.
4. A judicial decision that furnishes a model for deciding a later, similar case is a *pr*_____.
5. Legal action to sell property for lack of mortgage payments is *f*_____.
6. In most towns an electric company is given an exclusive privilege to operate, known as a *f*_____.
7. A claim on a property, such as a mortgage or a bill for unpaid taxes, is a *l*_____.
8. You can make a reluctant witness attend a trial by serving him a court order called a *s*_____.
9. The insurance expert who calculates risks and premiums is an *a*_____.
10. The grand jury brings a possible criminal to trial by issuing a formal accusation known as an *i*_____.

Write True or False.

_____ 11. An *affidavit* requires the signature of an authorized witness.

_____ 12. *Negotiable* bonds can be cashed only by the original purchaser.

_____ 13. If you make false accusations in a radio speech, defaming another person, you are guilty of *libel*.

_____ 14. To secure a loan a person could use his house as *collateral*.

_____ 15. Buying farmland and buildings in the hope of selling at a profit is a form of *speculation*.

_____ 16. *Larceny* is a sexual offense.

_____ 17. *Realty* means "not imaginary."

_____ 18. A *prospectus* might describe a proposed business venture or a proposed literary production.

_____ 19. A notary public is able to *notarize* an affidavit.

_____ 20. An *injunction* is a highway intersection.

Check your answers by the following key. Deduct 5% per error from a possible 100%.

1. perjury	8. subpoena	15. True
2. solvent	9. actuary	16. False
3. voucher	10. indictment	17. False
4. precedent	11. True	18. True
5. foreclosure	12. False	19. True
6. franchise	13. False	20. False
7. lien	14. True	

Score: _____ %

1. **ad valorem** (ad və-lōr′əm): in proportion to the value: said of a duty on imports.
2. **amortization** (am′ər-ti-zā′shən): gradual settling of a debt by installment payments.
3. **annuity** (ə-noo′i-tē): a sum of money paid yearly to a person during his lifetime.
4. **beneficiary** (ben′ə-fish′ə-rē): a person who is to receive funds or other property under a trust, will, or insurance policy.
5. **broker:** a person who buys and sells securities for his customers.
6. **cartel** (kär-tel′): an international syndicate that aims at monopoly and price-fixing.
7. **cashier's check:** a check backed by the bank's own funds and signed by the cashier.
8. **caveat emptor** (kā′vē-at emp′tôr): *L.,* let the buyer beware, implying that one buys at his or her own risk.
9. **codicil** (kod′ə-sil): an addition or supplement to a will.
10. **copyright:** the exclusive right for a limited period to print and dispose of a literary or artistic work.
11. **covenant:** a solemn agreement; a formal, sealed contract.
12. **de facto** (dē fak′tō): *L.,* in fact; actually existing, whether legal or not; distinguished from *de jure* (dē joor′i), according to law.
13. **deflationary:** characterized by a decline in prices caused by a decrease in spending.
14. **easement:** the right or privilege of making a special, limited use of someone else's property: as, a right of way.
15. **eminent domain:** the right of a governmental body to take private property for public use upon giving just compensation to the owner.
16. **encumbrance:** a claim or lien upon a property.
17. **ex post facto** (eks pōst fak′tō): *L.,* having retroactive effect: as an *ex post facto* law.
18. **foreclosure:** public sale by court order of property on which the mortgage has not been paid.
19. **habeas corpus** (hā′bē-əs kôr′pəs): *L.,* a writ that would free a prisoner who is held without legal charges; literally, "Have the body."
20. **intestate** (in-tes′tāt): having made no will before death.
21. **ipso facto** (ip′sō fac′tō): *L.,* by that very fact.
22. **jurisprudence:** a system or philosophy of law.
23. **kangaroo court:** *colloq.* an unauthorized and irregular court which ignores or perverts normal legal procedure.
24. **lame duck:** a lawmaker or officeholder who continues in office for a time after his or her defeat for reelection.
25. **legal tender:** money which may be lawfully used in payment of debts.
26. **litigation** (lit′ə-gā′shən): legal action; a lawsuit.
27. **misdemeanor** (mis′di-mē′nər): a minor offense; a crime less serious than a felony.
28. **moratorium** (mor′ə-tor′ē-əm): legal authorization to delay the payment of debts, as in an emergency.
29. **mortgage** (mor′gij): the pledging of property as security for payment of a debt.
30. **negligence** (neg′li-jəns): the failure to exercise such care as one would ordinarily expect of a reasonable, prudent person.
31. **plenary** (plē′nə-rē): full; attended by all members: as, a *plenary* session.
32. **pocket veto:** veto of a congressional bill, at the end of a session, for lack of presidential action.

33. **preferred stock:** shares which receive dividends or distributed assets first, before common stock gets any.
34. **probate** (prō′bāt): the process by which a will is proved to be authentic or valid.
35. **proviso** (prə-vī′zō): a stipulation or condition that is attached to a contract or a statute.
36. **quitclaim:** a deed giving up one's claim to some property or right of action.
37. **ratification:** approval; confirmation.
38. **requisition:** a formal written order or request, as for certain equipment.
39. **respondent:** the defendant.
40. **restitution:** reimbursement for loss or damage.
41. **scrip:** a temporary paper to be redeemed later for money or other benefits.
42. **statute** (stach′oot): an established law or rule.
43. **stipend** (stī′pend): a salary, pension, or allowance.
44. **submarginal:** unprofitable; unproductive; not worth cultivating.
45. **syndicate** (sin′də-kit): an association of individuals formed to conduct a business enterprise requiring much capital.
46. **tort:** any injury or damage for which a civil suit can be brought.
47. **usury** (yōō′zhə-rē): lending money at an unlawfully high rate of interest.
48. **venue** (ven′yōō): the locality where a legal case is tried.
49. **waiver:** the voluntary giving up of a right.
50. **working capital:** the excess of current assets over debts and obligations.

Social Science

You are sitting, ambitious to learn and free of sin, in your history classroom. The professor begins to sprinkle unfamiliar terms into the lecture: *Monroe Doctrine, protocol, sanctions, mercantilism*. What's he saying?—has your teacher lost a few shingles? You are tempted to blame the scholarly professor for the communication gap, but—more wisely—you decide to close the gap yourself by getting acquainted with some basic terms of social science.

Study carefully the words and definitions at the beginning of each frame. For fuller explanations, consult a dictionary or an encyclopedia. Then fill in the blanks.

✚ EXERCISES

1. **agrarian** (ə-grer′ē-ən): relating to farmlands and their ownership.
2. **bourgeois** (boor-zhwä′): middle-class; commonplace, conventional, respectable and smug; a member of the middle class, known as the *bourgeoisie*.

(a)

■ An *agrarian* area produces (a) crops, (b) fish. (   )

(b)

■ *Bourgeois* culture is (a) aristocratic, (b) run of the mill. (   )

bourgeois

■ Football, hot dogs, tabloids, and soap operas are especially popular in *bo*_____ society.

agrarian

■ California grows rice, cotton, and fruit; in fact, it has a thriving *ag*_____ industry.

agrarian
bourgeois

■ Russian communists seized the beets, cabbages, and potatoes raised in the *a*_____ areas, as well as the shops and possessions of the *b*_____ class.

3. **capitalism:** an economic system in which the means of production and of distribution are privately owned.
4. **communism:** a totalitarian system of government in which the state owns all means of production and commonly suppresses individual liberties.

(a)

■ A citizen is allowed to manufacture bicycles or frisbees and grow rich under (a) capitalism, (b) communism. (   )

communism

■ Your rights to speak freely, travel, or leave the country are restricted by *c*_____.

capitalism

■ Farmers, bankers, and barbers can be in business for themselves under our system of *c*_____.

communism

communism

■ A Russian recalls, "During Stalin's era of _____, free speech wasn't dead—only the speakers were." He continues: "A dog bragged he was well fed under Russian *c*_____. 'Then why did you leave that country?' he was asked.—'Well, sometimes I like to bark.' "

5. **nepotism** (nep′ə-tiz-əm): favoritism to relatives, especially in public appointments.
6. **spoils system:** the practice of distributing appointive public offices to party workers after a victory.

■ Our mayor awarded a fat painting contract to Winky, his brother-in-law. We smell *nep_____.*

nepotism

■ Andrew Jackson, on becoming president, rewarded his backers and cronies by giving them public offices. This was the *sp_____ sy_____.*

spoils system

■ City Manager Trueheart gave cushy public jobs to his brother, his son-in-law, and his cousin. An alert citizen accused him of *n_____.*

nepotism

■ Public appointments by President U. S. Grant to his backers resulted in scandals. Civil service reform soon ended the *s_____ s_____.*

spoils system

■ Mayor Schmaltz appointed his wife to be his private secretary at $86,000 a year. She usually dropped in to work at his city office on Tuesday afternoons, unless she had a hair appointment. The mayor was charged with _____.

nepotism

QUIZ

Write the letter that indicates the best definition.

1. (e)
2. (f)
3. (a)
4. (d)
5. (c)
6. (b)

( ) 1. communism   a. jobs for party backers
( ) 2. nepotism   b. private ownership system
( ) 3. spoils system   c. middle-class
( ) 4. agrarian   d. of farmlands
( ) 5. bourgeois   e. totalitarianism
( ) 6. capitalism   f. favoritism to kin

7. **gubernatorial** (go͞o′bər-nə-tôr′ē-əl): pertaining to a governor or the office of governor.
8. **lame duck:** a public official who is completing a term in office after failing to get reelected.

■ A *gubernatorial* candidate is one who runs for (a) governor, (b) congress. ( )

(a)

lame duck	■ Senator Jaime Buck was defeated in the November election. For the next two months Jaime Buck is a *l*_____ *d*_____.
gubernatorial	■ Governor Mary Smith served as mayor and as congresswoman before she won her *gu*_____ seat.
(b)	■ A congressman who loses his bid for reelection is referred to as (a) a gubernatorial fish, (b) a lame duck. ( )
lame duck gubernatorial	■ Governor Kelly, outvoted last week by a female candidate, is now a *l*_____ *d*_____ and has already lost some of his *g*_____ effectiveness.

9. **bureaucracy** (byoo-rok′rə-sē): government by numerous bureaus and officials, marked by inflexible routine and red tape.
10. **lobby:** a special interest group that tries to get legislators to vote for or against a bill.

(c)	■ A *lobby* is (a) a government bureau, (b) a tennis volley, (c) a pressure group. ( )
bureaucracy	■ Petty officials, a pile of forms to fill out, and red tape are marks of a governmental *bu*_____.
bureaucracy	■ Ivan liked quick action—not the endless lines, delays, certificate requirements, and insolent officials of Russian *bu*_____.
lobby lobby, lobby	■ To influence members of Congress, the tobacco industry has a *l*_____, the National Rifle Association has a *l*_____, and teachers have a *l*_____.
bureaucracy	■ To open a little coffee shop, I needed the approval of nine different city offices—what a *b*_____!

11. **Gresham's law** (gresh′əmz): the principle that bad money tends to drive good money out of circulation.
12. **monetary** (mon′i-ter′ē): pertaining to money or coinage.

monetary	■ The penny may some day be eliminated from our American *mo*_____ system.
(b) Gresham's	■ Fearing inflation, people prefer to stash away (a) paper money, (b) gold and silver coins. ( ) This is in accordance with *Gr*_____ law.

monetary

■ Americans were often puzzled by the farthings, shillings, and crowns of England's *m*_____ system.

(b)
Gresham's law

■ The dimes and quarters that circulate nowadays are the ones that contain (a) all silver, (b) some copper. (   ) For this we can blame *Gr*_____ *l*_____.

monetary,
Gresham's

■ Grinding out tons of paper money won't solve a nation's *m*_____ problems, according to _____ law.

QUIZ

Write the letter that indicates the best definition.

1. (b)
2. (a)
3. (e)
4. (f)
5. (c)
6. (d)

(   ) 1. lame duck   a. special interest group
(   ) 2. lobby   b. reelection loser
(   ) 3. monetary   c. "Good money hides."
(   ) 4. bureaucracy   d. regarding the governor
(   ) 5. Gresham's law   e. of money and coinage
(   ) 6. gubernatorial   f. petty officials and red tape

13. **bloc** (blok): a coalition of nations or factions for a common cause.
14. **sanctions:** a measure, such as a boycott or blockade, taken by one or more nations against another nation to enforce demands.

bloc

■ The League of Nations acted as a *b*_____ in 1933 to cut off all trade with Italy because of its invasion of Ethopia. Their

sanctions

action was known as *sa*_____.

(c)

■ *Sanctions* against a nation usually take the form of (a) invasion, (b) bombing, (c) boycott. (   )

bloc
bloc

■ In World War II, Great Britain, France, and the United States fought as a *b*_____ against the Germany-Japan *b*_____.

sanctions

■ If human rights are violated in a foreign country, our nation may threaten _____ against that country. To be most effective, though, we should act as part of an international

bloc

_____.

15. **felony** (fel′-ə-nē): a major crime such as murder, rape, or burglary, usually punished in the United States by more than a year of imprisonment.
16. **genocide** (jen′ə-sīd′): the systematic killing of an entire people or nation.

genocide
- ■ In Africa a powerful tribe completely wiped out a weaker one—an act of *ge*_____.

felony
- ■ Jones will spend two years in the "slammer" because forging checks is a *fe*_____.

(c)
- ■ Putting to death an entire racial group is called (a) fratricide, (b) matricide, (c) genocide, (d) regicide. (   )

felony
- ■ Theft of a six-pack of beer is a misdemeanor; theft of an automobile is a *f*_____.

(b)
- ■ You murder your gossipy neighbor. You are guilty of (a) a misdemeanor, (b) a felony, (c) genocide. (   )

17. **mediation** (mē′dē-ā′shən): deliberation to settle a dispute between nations or persons.
18. **symposium** (sim-pō′zē-əm): a conference on a given topic in which various opinions are expressed.

symposium
- ■ Contrasting viewpoints were presented by experts in a *sym*_____ on bilingual education.

mediation
- ■ Our tragic Civil War might have been prevented by *me*_____ between North and South.

symposium
- ■ Five papers on how to lose weight were read in a *s*_____ held yesterday at the Fatburger restaurant.

mediation

mediation
- ■ The United Nations tries to stop wars by promoting *m*_____. Unfortunately, a strong nation that is knocking the stuffing out of a weaker nation usually feels it has little to gain by *m*_____.

symposium
- ■ Several football players were invited to present their views in a *s*_____ on "The Battering of Wives."

Write the letter that indicates the best definition.

( ) 1. mediation	a. a crime such as burglary
( ) 2. sanctions	b. a presentation of viewpoints
( ) 3. symposium	c. an alliance of nations
( ) 4. bloc	d. arbitration
( ) 5. felony	e. killing a race
( ) 6. genocide	f. pressure by boycott

---

19. **Malthusian theory** (mal-th$\overline{oo}$′zē-ən): If world population is unchecked, it will outrun means of support and inevitably lead to war, famine, and disease.

20. **Monroe Doctrine:** Any attempt by a European power to interfere in the affairs of Spanish-American countries would be regarded by the United States as a hostile act.

■ President Monroe issued his famous doctrine in 1823, warning European countries to (a) fight communism, (b) keep hands off America, (c) stop shooting lame ducks. (   )

■ Populations increase faster than food supply, causing famine, wars, and other disasters, according to the *Mal*_____ theory.

■ The Monroe Doctrine issued by our young nation may be regarded as an assertion of (a) power, (b) neutrality, (c) weakness. (   )

■ If people propagate like rabbits, the world is headed for tragedies—such is the message of the *M*_____ *t*_____.

■ When Russia began arming Cuba with nuclear warheads, President John Kennedy called attention to the *M*_____ *D*_____.

21. **pacifism** (pas′ə-fiz′əm): opposition to war and violence of any kind.

22. **prohibition** (pro′hi-bish′ən): the forbidding by law of the sale or use of alcoholic beverages (1920–1933).

■ Refusal on religious or moral grounds to serve in the army is known as (a) prohibition, (b) extradition, (c) pacifism. (   )

prohibition	■ Beer, wine, and whiskey were illegal during the Roaring Twenties, the era of national *pro*_____.
pacifism	■ Quakers, morally opposed to war, are dedicated to *pa*_____.
prohibition	■ Private clubs, called *speakeasies,* dispensed "moonshine" in spite of *p*_____.
(c)	■ *Pacifism* is opposition to (a) slavery, (b) welfare, (c) violence. ( )
(b)	■ *Prohibition* opposed (a) cigarettes, (b) alcohol, (c) fat meat. ( )

23. **apartheid** (ə-pärt′hīt′): discrimination and segregation enforced against nonwhites, as was practiced in the Republic of South Africa.
24. **naturalization:** the process of becoming a citizen.
25. **suffrage** (suf′rij): the right to vote.

suffrage	■ Feminists fought for the right to vote, and finally in 1920 the Nineteenth Amendment granted *suf*_____ to women.
naturalization	■ An immigrant can become an American citizen by a process called *nat*_____.
(c)	■ *Suffrage* refers to a citizen's (a) pain and agony, (b) taxes, (c) right to vote. ( )
apartheid	■ The blacks of South Africa suffered from a policy of discrimination known as *ap*_____.
naturalization	■ Children under eighteen become a citizen automatically when the head of the family undergoes *n*_____.
(b)	■ *Apartheid* denied the basic rights of citizenship to (a) Catholics, (b) nonwhites, (c) the unemployed. ( )
suffrage naturalization	■ If you are born in the United States, you are granted the privilege of *s*_____ without your going through the process of *n*_____.
apartheid	■ Many white people in Johannesburg, sympathetic to the blacks, opposed the unjust policy of *a*_____.

Write the letter that indicates the meaning.

1. (e)
2. (a)
3. (d)
4. (b)
5. (c)
6. (g)
7. (f)

( ) 1. naturalization
( ) 2. pacifism
( ) 3. prohibition
( ) 4. suffrage
( ) 5. apartheid
( ) 6. Malthusian theory
( ) 7. Monroe Doctrine

a. antiviolence
b. right to vote
c. enforced segregation
d. antialcohol
e. becoming a citizen
f. "Hands off, Europeans!"
g. "Overpopulation is bad."

Write the word studied in this chapter that will complete the sentence.

1. A city manager awarded "gravy-train" contracts to his brothers—this was *ne*_____.

2. Ben won't take part in war or violence. He believes in *pa*_____.

3. Labor and management should resolve disputes by *me*_____.

4. The government owns all shops and factories in a system of *c*_____.

5. A Greek can become an American voter by means of *na*_____.

6. The slaying of an entire Indian tribe was an act of *ge*_____.

7. England, France, and the United States fought as a *b*_____ in World War I.

8. The Volstead Act, banning liquor, ushered in the era of *pr*_____.

9. "Don't mess with American nations," warns the *M*_____ *D*_____.

10. Men could vote, but not until 1920 did we have woman *s*_____.

11. One powerful special interest group in Congress is the gun *l*_____.

12. Congressman Dingle wasn't reelected? Then he's a *l*_____ *d*_____!

13. "Jailbird" Joe now realizes that forgery is a *fe*_____.

14. Appointing friends to public office after a political victory was the *s*_____ *s*_____.

15. Separation of blacks from whites in South Africa was called *ap*_____.

Write True or False.

_____ 16. The *bourgeois* class are aristocratic, with refined tastes.

_____ 17. *Capitalism* permits private ownership of farms.

_____ 18. People distrust gold and silver coins, according to Gresham's law.

_____ 19. Overpopulation may cause famine and war, according to the *Malthusian theory.*

_____ 20. A *bureaucracy* usually produces simplified, efficient, streamlined action.

Write the letter that indicates what the word at the left is associated with.

(　　) 21. monetary   a. orchestral music
(　　) 22. sanctions   b. money
(　　) 23. agrarian   c. farming
(　　) 24. gubernatorial   d. presenting of viewpoints
(　　) 25. symposium   e. dancing
                              f. economic pressure; boycott
                              g. governor

KEY TO REVIEW TEST

Check your test answers with the following key. Deduct 4% per error from a possible 100%.

1. nepotism	10. suffrage	19. True
2. pacifism	11. lobby	20. False
3. mediation	12. lame duck	21. (b)
4. communism	13. felony	22. (f)
5. naturalization	14. spoils system	23. (c)
6. genocide	15. apartheid	24. (g)
7. bloc	16. False	25. (d)
8. prohibition	17. True	
9. Monroe Doctrine	18. False	

Score: _____ %

1. **Abolitionist:** one who favored wiping out Negro slavery in the United States.
2. **amnesty** (am'ni-stē): a general pardon, as to political offenders, extended by a government.
3. **blitzkrieg** (blits'krēg): a lightning-speed military offensive.
4. **civil disobedience:** refusal to comply with government policy as a matter of conscience; passive resistance.
5. **conjugal** (kon'jə-gəl): pertaining to marriage, or the relationship of husband and wife.
6. **egalitarian** (i-gal'i-târ'ē-ən): equalitarian; believing that all men should have equal political and social rights.
7. **espionage** (es'pi-ə-nij): spying to secure military and political secrets.
8. **ethnocentrism** (eth'nō-sen'triz-əm): the belief that one's own race, country, or culture is superior to all others.
9. **Gandhiism** (gän'dē-iz'əm): passive resistance to achieve reform, as advocated by Mahatma Gandhi.
10. **ghetto** (get'ō): a section of the city in which many members of a minority group, such as Jews or Negroes, find it necessary to live.
11. **humanitarian:** a philanthropist; one devoted to human welfare.
12. **Jim Crow:** *colloq.* discrimination against blacks.
13. **junta** (jun'tə): a group of political schemers; a faction; a cabal.
14. **manifesto:** a public declaration of views and intentions.
15. **miscegenation** (mis'i-jə-nā'shən): marriage between members of different races.
16. **Montessori method** (mon'ti-sôr'ē): a system aiming at self-education of a child through guidance rather than enforced discipline.
17. **nihilism** (nī'ə-liz'əm): rejection of customary beliefs in religion, government, morality, etc.
18. **oligarchy** (ol'ə-gär'kē): government by a few persons.
19. **protocol** (prō'tə-kôl'): the proper courtesies to be observed in diplomatic affairs.
20. **schism** (siz'əm): a split in a church or other organized group caused by differences of opinion.
21. **secession** (si-sesh'ən): formal withdrawal, as of a state from the union.
22. **sedition:** stirring up of rebellion against the government.
23. **tory** (tôr'ē): an extreme political conservative; reactionary.
24. **yellow journalism:** the featuring of cheap, sensational news to increase newspaper sales.
25. **Zionism** (zī'ə-niz'əm): a movement originally to reestablish a Jewish nation, now to aid Israel.

Natural Science

An atomic scientist once said, "Some day we'll be able to heat huge apartment buildings with one little piece of coal." His friend responded, "My landlord does that already."

Progress in natural science is accelerating on many fronts: atomics, communications, genetics, medicine, television, meteorology, and outer space. Unbelievable changes will yet be made during our lifetime. To keep pace, we must understand the vocabulary of science. Yet students have made astonishing errors: "Taxidermy is driving a cab"; "Humus is what makes you laugh"; "Genes are blue pants"; "A woofer is a big dog"; "Torques live in eastern Europe."

This chapter emphasizes thirty basic terms of natural science. Absorb those definitions. Also assimilate the supplementary list of fifty terms at the end of this chapter—they'll add muscle to your grip on science.

EXERCISES

1. **acoustics** (ə-kō͞os′tiks): the laws of sound; the sound-transmitting qualities of a room or hall.
2. **decibel** (des′ə-bel): a measure of the volume of a sound; one tenth of a bel.
3. **resonance** (rez′ə-nəns): reinforced vibration resulting from the vibration, at the same frequency, of another body.

decibel

■ Gene loved to turn up his boombox to a *d*_____ rating of 90—that was before he went deaf.

resonance

■ Alice's Stradivarius violin has lovely *re*_____. Unfortunately, those who built this hall knew nothing about

acoustics

*ac*_____.

(c)

■ A *decibel* is a measure of (a) resonance, (b) sweetness, (c) loudness. (   )

resonance

■ Pavarotti hit a high note and the *r*_____ shattered his favorite wine goblet.

acoustics

■ The *a*_____ of Hollywood Bowl are so splendid that a croaking frog sounds like an opera star.

4. **alchemy** (al′kə-mē): medieval chemistry which sought mainly to change lead into gold and to find the elixir of perpetual youth.
5. **fission** (fish′ən): the splitting of an atom, with release of energy.
6. **mutation** (myō͞o-tā′shən): variation from the parent type.

fission

(c)

■ Splitting the nucleus of a heavy atom into nuclei of lighter atoms is called nuclear *f*_____, a process that releases (a) small fish, (b) honey, (c) atomic energy. (   )

alchemy

(b)

■ Chemistry was once known as *al*_____, and the goal of most alchemists was to turn lead into (a) energy, (b) gold, (c) plastics. (   )

mutation

alchemy

■ Suppose that among your thousand rose bushes you found one without thorns, and you were able with cuttings to produce a new, thornless variety of rose—a true *mu*_____. You'd really get gold, unlike those early fumbling chemists who practiced *a*_____.

■ The tremendous power of a hydrogen bomb is the result of (a) dynamite, (b) fishin', (c) fission. (   )

■ Smith's dog Sheila has two tails, both of which she likes to wag, but all her puppies have one tail. Her freakish condition is, apparently, not a genuine *m*_____.

QUIZ

Write the letter that indicates the best definition.

(   ) 1. acoustics   a. reinforced vibration
(   ) 2. alchemy   b. a measure of loudness
(   ) 3. decibel   c. atom splitting
(   ) 4. fission   d. variation from ancestry
(   ) 5. mutation   e. medieval chemistry
(   ) 6. resonance   f. quality of sound in a hall

7. **ampere** (am′pēr): the standard unit of electric current, equal to the current sent by one volt through a resistance of one ohm.
8. **megaton** (meg′ə-tun): the explosive power of one million tons of TNT.
9. **seismic** (sīz′mik): pertaining to earthquakes.

■ Electric current is measured in (a) volts, (b) amperes, (c) megatons. (   )

■ A *megaton* is as destructive as how much TNT? (a) one million tons, (b) one thousands tons, (c) one million pounds. (   )

■ When the house began to shake, Gwen knew it was a *sei*_____ disturbance; so she ran dripping out of the bathtub and into the street.

■ Megan studies under a hundred-watt lamp. The bulb takes an electric current of approximately one *a*_____.

■ Joe kidded that the *se*_____ earth movement was so great that his house now has a new zip code.

seismic
megaton

ampere

■ What a shaker! It registered *s*_____ power of 6.3 on the Richter scale, far greater than a *meg*_____. Benny followed his usual ritual—he stood in the doorway and screamed. Our house was left without any electric current, not a single *a*_____.

10. **carcinogen** (kär-sin′ə-jən): any substance that causes cancer.
11. **cardiac** (kär′dē-ak′): referring to the heart area or to heart disease.
12. **therapy** (ther′ə-pē): the treatment of disease.

cardiac

■ Jason had a fast heartbeat. An electrocardiogram (EKG) indicated he had no *ca*_____ abnormalities. He'd merely fallen in love.

carcinogen

■ Don't smoke! Tobacco is a *c*_____.

carcinogen

therapy

■ Melvin's job exposed him to lead dust, a *c*_____. He developed a lung ailment for which he is receiving *th*_____.

cardiac
therapy

■ Ole had a *c*_____ bypass, and now takes mild exercise as *t*_____.

therapy
cardiac
carcinogen

■ Medical experts are driving Sam crazy. One day they'll recommend buffalo milk as *t*_____ for his *c*_____ problem, and a week later they'll find that buffalo milk contains a dangerous *c*_____.

QUIZ

Write the letter that indicates the best definition.

1. (c)
2. (a)
3. (f)
4. (e)
5. (b)
6. (d)

( ) 1. ampere
( ) 2. carcinogen
( ) 3. cardiac
( ) 4. megaton
( ) 5. seismic
( ) 6. therapy

a. cancer-causing substance
b. relating to an earthquake
c. unit of electric current
d. treatment for disease
e. measure of explosiveness
f. pertaining to the heart

13. **catalyst** (kat′ə-list): a substance that speeds up a chemical reaction but itself undergoes practically no change.

14. **osmosis** (oz-mō′sis): the passing of a fluid through a membrane to equalize pressures.
15. **viscera** (vis′ər-ə): the internal organs such as the intestines and liver.

osmosis

- Water molecules will pass through a membrane toward a sugar or mineral solution. This process, called *os*_____, is vital to plants and animals.

(c)

- The *viscera* include (a) the throat, (b) the kneecaps, (c) the intestines. (   )

catalyst

- Platinum particles serve as a *cat*_____ to speed the production of sulphuric acid. Like other *catalytic* agents the platinum (a) disappears, (b) is unchanged, (c) turns to sodium ash. (   )

(b)

osmosis

- Roots of plants absorb water by the process of *os*_____.

viscera

- Jack the Ripper slashed viciously across the abdomen and into his victim's *vi*_____.

catalyst

- The alumni reunion was dull and listless until peppy Pattie arrived. What a social *ca*_____!

osmosis
viscera

- Dissolved food materials pass by *o*_____ through the walls of the *v*_____ and are absorbed into the bloodstream.

16. **centrifugal force** (sen-trif′yə-gəl): the force tending to push a thing *outward* from the center of rotation. (Opposed to *centripetal force* which tends to draw a thing *inward* toward the center of rotation.)
17. **inertia** (in-ûr′shə): the tendency of matter to remain at rest or to move at uniform velocity in a straight line unless acted upon by an external force.
18. **torque** (tôrk): a force tending to produce rotation.

inertia

- The boulder resting in the park tends to stay at rest because of its *in*_____

(a)

- Whirl a rock on a string above your head and the rock tends to break away from you because of (a) centrifugal force, (b) centripetal force, (c) torque. (   )

torque

■ When you use a screwdriver to rotate the head of a screw, you are applying *t*_____.

inertia

■ Unless acted on by other forces, a satellite in outer space tends to move at constant speed in a straight line. This property of matter is called *i*_____.

(c)

■ At the county fair you ride a speedy Loop-the-Loop in which you briefly ride upside down. Luckily, you are held up safely at the ceiling against gravity by an outward thrust known as (a) inertia, (b) centripetal force, (c) centrifugal force. ( )

(c)

■ The merry-go-round is kept rotating by a force known as (a) a troika, (b) a truck, (c) torque. ( )

QUIZ

Write the letter that indicates the best definition.

1. (f)
2. (a)
3. (e)
4. (b)
5. (c)
6. (d)

( ) 1. catalyst   a. outward push
( ) 2. centrifugal force   b. seeping through membranes
( ) 3. inertia   c. rotation producer
( ) 4. osmosis   d. intestines
( ) 5. torque   e. resistance to change
( ) 6. viscera   f. chemical reaction spur

---

19. **congenital** (kən-jen′ə-təl): existing from birth.
20. **gene** (jēn): an element in the chromosomes that transmits hereditary characteristics.
21. **viable** (vī′ə-bəl): physically fitted to live, said of a fetus or a seed.

viable
congenital

■ Dr. Shlepp says Mia's five-month fetus is *v*_____. The poet Byron was born lame—his was a *con*_____ deformity.

gene

■ My big ears, like the ears of an alert jackass, are attributable to a *g*_____ from my big-eared daddy, his only gift to me.

congenital

■ Our school principal must think I was born stupid because he called me a *c*_____ idiot.

gene

■ Bob's height, his hazel eyes, his ski-slope nose—each trait was determined by some *g*_____ from his parents.

viable

congenital
gene

- ■ We planted the seeds of corn that we found in the ancient Egyptian tomb, but they were no longer *vi*_____.

- ■ Color blindness is a *c*_____ condition which is hereditary in families with a defective *g*_____.

22. **humus** (hū′məs): organic matter in soils, produced by decay of vegetable and animal stuff.
23. **hybrid** (hī′brid): the offspring of two plants or animals of different varieties.
24. **maturation** (mach′ə-rā′shən): attainment of maturity; completion of growth.

hybrid

- ■ The mule is a *hy*_____ animal, the offspring of a mare and a jackass.

humus

- ■ Lucy uses a compost pile of decayed grass and food wastes, called *hu*_____, to enrich her garden soil.

maturation
maturation

- ■ These oranges are green, and Junior shouldn't have picked them until they reached *ma*_____. Junior's brains haven't reached *m*_____ either.

hybrid

- ■ If you cross-pollinate tall and short garden peas, the first generation of the *h*_____ peas will be tall, according to Gregor Mendel's laws of heredity.

maturation
humus

- ■ Your cabbages will achieve *m*_____ more quickly if you apply organic _____ to the soil.

hybrid, hybrid

- ■ Greater vigor usually results from the crossing of varieties, as is true of *h*_____ corn and *h*_____ barley.

QUIZ

Write the letter that indicates the best definition.

1. (c)
2. (e)
3. (b)
4. (f)
5. (a)
6. (d)

( ) 1. congenital
( ) 2. gene
( ) 3. humus
( ) 4. hybrid
( ) 5. maturation
( ) 6. viable

a. full growth
b. organic soil
c. existing at birth
d. able to survive
e. transmitter of traits
f. product of cross-breeding

25. **solar** (sō′lər): pertaining to the sun.
26. **solstice** (sol′stis): the time when the sun is farthest from the equator, at about June 21 and December 22.
27. **zenith** (zē′nith): the point in the sky directly over an observer: opposed to *nadir* (nā′dər), the lowest possible point.

solar

■ The earth is part of the *s*＿＿＿＿＿＿ system.

■ *Zenith* is located (a) on the horizon, (b) below you, (c) above you. (　)

(c)

■ Our summer *solstice* occurs at about (a) June 21, (b) March 21, (c) September 22, (　), at which time the sun with respect to the equator will be (a) overhead, (b) farthest north, (c) farthest south. (　)

(a)

(b)

solar

■ A ＿＿＿＿＿＿ eclipse is an eclipse of the sun.

■ Freddie was born at the time of our winter *solstice.* His birthday occurs in (a) December, (b) June, (c) September. (　)

(a)

■ In the tropics, only mad dogs and Englishmen are outside at noon while the sun is at its *z*＿＿＿＿＿＿.

zenith

28. **supersonic:** greater than the speed of sound; faster than 738 miles per hour.
29. **trajectory** (trə-jek′tə-rē): the path described by something hurtling through space, especially the path of a projectile.
30. **troposphere** (trop′ə-sfēr′): the atmospheric zone next to the earth that contains clouds and winds, below the stratosphere.

troposphere,
supersonic

■ The blazing comet, descending from the stratosphere and dipping into our *tr*＿＿＿＿＿＿, was traveling with *su*＿＿＿＿＿＿ velocity.

trajectory

■ Longfellow shot an arrow into the air and it fell to earth he knew not where, because he didn't keep an eye on its *tr*＿＿＿＿＿＿.

trajectory
supersonic

■ Our military enemy misjudged the *tr*＿＿＿＿＿＿ of their rocket, so that it hurtled with almost *s*＿＿＿＿＿＿ speed into our donkey.

(a)

■ Clouds and rain occur in the (a) troposphere, (b) bathysphere, (c) stratosphere. (　)

(b)

■ When your pilot says, "We've just reached supersonic speed," you are moving at about (a) 350 mph, (b) 750 mph, (c) 7500 mph. (   )

QUIZ

Write the letter that indicates the best definition.

1. (d)
2. (f)
3. (a)
4. (c)
5. (e)
6. (b)

(   ) 1. solar   a. faster than sound
(   ) 2. solstice   b. the highest point
(   ) 3. supersonic   c. path of a missile
(   ) 4. trajectory   d. pertaining to the sun
(   ) 5. troposphere   e. zone of air and clouds
(   ) 6. zenith   f. beginning of summer or winter

Write the word studied in this chapter that will complete the sentence.

1. The unit of electrical current—don't be shocked!—is the *a*_____.

2. The unit of volume of sound—you hear me!—is the *de*_____.

3. The explosive power of a million tons of TNT equals—barroom!—a *me*_____.

4. This zone of clouds and wind in which we breathe the smog—sniff, sniff!—is the *tr*_____.

5. A jet plane that flies faster than sound has—whee!—*su*_____ speed.

6. Heart stoppage—farewell!—is *ca*_____ arrest.

7. A seventh-month fetus is—wah!—*vi*_____.

8. At noon the summer sun is—phew!—at its *ze*_____.

9. A convulsive earth movement is—rumble, rumble!—a *s*_____ disturbance.

10. Early chemistry sought mainly to transmute metals—aha, gold!—and was known as *al*_____.

11. June 22 was the date of our summer *so*_____.

12. The mating of a male lion and a female tiger produces a *hy*_____ animal called a liger.

13. Bananas are picked green, but they turn yellow when they reach *ma*_____.

14. A grindstone, to keep rotating, requires a force called *t*_____.

15. My piano teacher was born with six fingers on her left hand—a *con*_____ condition. But what great bass chords!

Write True or False.

_____ 16. A *carcinogen* is a *therapy* to prevent cancer.

_____ 17. A *catalyst* is a feline disease.

_____ 18. The *trajectory* is the path of a missile.

_____ 19. *Osmosis* often occurs in the *viscera.*

_____ 20. *Centrifugal force* pushes outward from the center of rotation.

Write the letter that indicates the best definition.

(   ) 21. acoustics   a. unit of heredity
(   ) 22. fission   b. comic talk
(   ) 23. gene   c. qualities of sound
(   ) 24. humus   d. relating to the sun
(   ) 25. solar   e. catching trout
     f. organic matter in soil
     g. splitting atoms

KEY TO REVIEW TEST

Check your test answers with the following key. Deduct 4% per error from a possible 100%.

1. ampere	10. alchemy	19. True
2. decibel	11. solstice	20. True
3. megaton	12. hybrid	21. c
4. troposphere	13. maturation	22. g
5. supersonic	14. torque	23. a
6. cardiac	15. congenital	24. f
7. viable	16. False	25. d
8. zenith	17. False	
9. seismic	18. True	

Score: _____ %

1. **absolute zero:** the lowest possible temperature, theoretically -273.18 degrees C., at which molecular motion ceases.
2. **acceleration:** the increased rate of change in velocity.
3. **adaptation** (ad′əp-tā′shən): a change in structure or function by which an organism adjusts better to its environment.
4. **aerodynamics** (âr′ō-dī-nam′iks): the branch of physics that studies gases in motion, including their mechanical effects and other properties.
5. **aneroid barometer** (an′ə-roid′): an instrument which measures atmospheric pressure by its effect on the flexible top of a metal box containing a partial vacuum.
6. **anticyclone:** a high pressure area in which the spiral currents flow clockwise in the Northern Hemisphere.
7. **asexual** (ā-sek′shoo-əl): without sex; reproducing itself without sexual union.
8. **ballistics** (bə-lis′tiks): the science dealing with the flight behavior and impact of projectiles.
9. **Bessemer process** (bes′ə-mər): making steel by forcing a blast of air through molten pig iron to remove impurities.
10. **Bohr theory** (bōr): the theory of Niels Bohr that electrons absorb or radiate energy when changing orbits.
11. **Brownian movement:** the zigzag movement of microscopic particles suspended in fluids, caused by collisions with molecules.
12. **centripetal force** (sen-trip′ə-təl): the force tending to draw a thing inward toward the center of rotation.
13. **cretinism** (krē′tən-iz′əm): idiocy and deformity resulting from a congenital thyroid deficiency.
14. **cybernetics** (sī-bər-net′iks): a comparative study of computers and the human nervous system to help explain brain processes.
15. **cyclotron** (sī′klə-tron′): an apparatus that gives high velocity and energy to protons and deuterons so they can smash nuclear targets.
16. **dominant:** *genetics.* designating a hereditary character which prevails over and masks a *recessive* character.
17. **electrolysis** (i-lek′trol′ə-sis): the decomposition of a chemical solution by means of an electric current.
18. **electrostatics:** a branch of physics that deals with electricity at rest known as static electricity.
19. **foot-pound:** a unit of work, enough to raise a one-pound mass a distance of one foot.
20. **fulcrum** (ful′krəm): the support on which a lever turns.
21. **galvanic** (gal-van′ik): of electricity from a battery; convulsive; startling.
22. **generic** (jə-ner′ik): pertaining to a genus or class; having a broad general application.
23. **geocentric** (jē′ō-sen′trik): regarding the earth as center of the universe.
24. **geophysics** (jē′ō-fiz′iks): the physics of the earth, dealing with tides, winds, earthquakes, magnetic fields, etc.
25. **gynecology** (gī′nə-kol′ə-jē): the branch of medicine dealing with women's diseases.
26. **gyroscope** (jī′rə-skōp′): a rotating device used to stabilize ships and planes.
27. **hermetic** (hûr-met′ik): airtight; completely sealed to keep air and liquids from getting in or out.
28. **histology** (hi-stol′ə-jē): the microscopic study of tissue structure.

29. **horticulture:** the cultivation of garden plants.
30. **hydraulic:** using water or other liquid, as a *hydraulic* brake.
31. **hygrometer** (hī-grom′ə-tər): an instrument for measuring humidity.
32. **immunology:** the branch of medicine which deals with immunity to disease.
33. **isobar** (ī′sə-bär′): a line on a weather map connecting points having the same barometric pressure.
34. **isotope** (ī′sə-tōp′): any of two or more forms of a chemical element, each with its individual mass number and radioactive behavior.
35. **kinetic energy** (ki-net′ik): energy resulting from the motion of a body: opposed to *potential* energy.
36. **Lamarckism** (lə-mär′kiz-əm): Lamarck's evolutionary theory that acquired characteristics can be inherited.
37. **malleable** (mal′ē-ə-bəl): pliable; capable of being hammered and shaped without breaking: said of metals.
38. **materia medica** (mə-tēr′ē-ə med′ə-kə): drugs and other remedial substances.
39. **Mendelism** (men′də-liz′əm): Gregor Mendel's principles of heredity, which predict characteristics of the offspring in cross-breeding.
40. **metabolism** (mə-tab′ə-liz′əm): the sum of physical and chemical processes which supply energy to the body.
41. **metallurgy** (met′ə-lûr′jē): the science of separating metals from ores and refining them for use.
42. **natural selection:** the adaptation of a species to its environment through survival of the fittest.
43. **oscillation** (os′ə-lā′shən): the fluctuation between maximum and minimum values, as of an alternating current.
44. **periodic table:** an arrangement of chemical elements by atomic number to exhibit groups and families.
45. **pituitary** (pi-too′ə-ter′ē): a gland at the base of the brain that secretes hormones affecting growth and metabolism.
46. **qualitative analysis:** the determining of the ingredients in a substance.
47. **quantum theory** (kwon′təm): the theory that radiant energy is not smooth flowing but discontinuous and emitted in definite units called *quanta.*
48. **rectifier:** any device, such as a vacuum tube, which converts alternating current into direct current.
49. **simian** (sim′ē-ən): pertaining to monkeys or anthropoid apes.
50. **spectrum:** a band of colors observed when a beam of white light passes through a prism.

Poetry

It is not enough to say of a verse, "How pretty that is" or "That's a remarkable phrase." To analyze a poem we must be familiar with certain basic technical terms. It is important to know the various figures of speech **(see Chapter 14).** We must also recognize such aspects of versification as hexameter, anapest, and inversion, and such types of poems as sonnet, quatrain, and dramatic monologue. Nor should we turn blank at the mention of blank verse, confusing it, perhaps, with free verse.

Analysis cannot hope to explain completely the mysterious nature of poetry, "untwisting all the chains that tie / The hidden soul of harmony"; yet a knowledge of poetic terms can be a real step toward a richer appreciation of poetry.

■ **EXERCISES**

1. **scansion** (skan′shən): the analysis of verse to show its meter and rhyme scheme. *Scansion* marks include ˘ for an unaccented syllable, ′ for an accented syllable, and | for a foot division.

2. **foot:** the basic unit of verse meter, consisting usually of two or three syllables of which ordinarily one is stressed. The number of feet to the line determines the meter.

scansion
feet

■ Metrical analysis, or *sc*_____, tells you the number and type of _____ [feet / figures of speech] in each line of verse.

scansion
(b)

■ The process of poetic *sc*_____ is (a) emotional, (b) analytical. (   )

feet
scansion

■ The number of metric units, or _____ [bars / feet], in a line of verse is calculated by *sc*_____.

three

■ The number of *feet* in Robert Burns' verse "Your locks were like the raven" is _____ [three / seven].

3. **iamb** (ī′amb): an unstressed syllable followed by a stressed syllable; for example, "tŏníght," "dĕný," "ănd nów," "mў lóve."

4. **trochee** (trō′kē): a stressed syllable followed by an unstressed syllable; for example, "fástĕr," "dámsĕl," "dýĭng," "flíng ĭt."

iamb
second

■ The *iambic* foot, or *ia*_____, consists of two syllables with the stress on the _____ [first / second] syllable.

trochee
first

■ The *trochaic* foot, or *tr*_____, consists of two syllables with the stress on the _____ [first / second] syllable.

Before each example of a metrical foot write *iamb* or *trochee*.

trochee
iamb
iamb
trochee
trochee

■ _____ hanging
■ _____ the sky
■ _____ to dream
■ _____ drink it
■ _____ Edith

Before each example of verse write *iambic* or *trochaic*.

iambic
trochaic
iambic

■ _____ To be or not to be . . .
■ _____ Come and trip it as ye go.
■ _____ I struck the board and cried . . .

Chapter Twenty-one   273

5. **anapest** (an′ə-pest′): two unstressed syllables followed by a stressed syllable; for example, "ŏf thĕ mén"; "tŏ rĕjóice"; "ĭntĕrfére."
6. **dactyl** (dak′til): a stressed syllable followed by two unstressed syllables; for example, "síńg tŏ thĕ"; "fléeĭng frŏm"; "rápĭdlў."

anapest
third

■ The *anapestic* foot, or *an*_____, consists of three syllables with the stress on the _____ [first / third] syllable.

dactyl
first

■ The *dactylic* foot, or *da*_____, consists of three syllables with the stress on the _____ [first / third] syllable.

Before each sample metrical foot write *anapest* or *dactyl*.

anapest
dactyl
dactyl
anapest
anapest

■ _____ of the king
■ _____ laughing with
■ _____ fade in the
■ _____ with Elaine
■ _____ in despair

Before each verse sample write *anapestic* or *dactylic*.

dactylic
anapestic

■ _____ Maiden most beautiful, mother most bountiful . . .
■ _____ And the sheen of their spears was like stars on the sea

7. **caesura** (si-zhoor′ə): a pause within the line of verse, indicated in scansion by two vertical lines, thus ‖. The *caesura* usually coincides with a pause in the thought, as at a major mark of punctuation.

caesura
(b)

■ In scansion the pause known as the *ca*_____ is indicated by (a) a snaky line, (b) two vertical lines. (   )

caesura
(b)

■ Alexander Pope wrote, "One truth is clear, Whatever is, is right." A pause known as a *c*_____ belongs after (a) "truth," (b) "clear." (   )

caesura, (a)

■ "Beowulf spake, bairn of Ecgtheow." The pause, or _____, belongs after (a) "spake," (b) "bairn." (   )

Write the letter that indicates the best definition or example.

1. (e)
2. (d)
3. (c)
4. (a)
5. (g)
6. (f)
7. (b)

(   ) 1. anapest
(   ) 2. trochee
(   ) 3. iamb
(   ) 4. foot
(   ) 5. scansion
(   ) 6. caesura
(   ) 7. dactyl

a. the basic unit of verse meter
b. a foot like "tenderly"
c. a foot like "the stars"
d. a foot like "kissing"
e. a foot like "in her home"
f. a pause within the verse
g. metrical analysis

8. **tetrameter** (te-tram′i-tər): a line of poetry containing four feet; example from Lord Tennyson of iambic *tetrameter:* "I come from haunts of coot and hern." Shorter lines are the *trimeter,* three feet; the *dimeter,* two feet; and the *monometer,* one foot.

9. **pentameter** (pen-tam′i-tər): a line of poetry containing five feet; example from John Keats of iambic *pentameter:* "When I have fears that I may cease to be."

10. **hexameter** (hek-sam′i-tər): a line of poetry containing six feet. Longer and less common than the *hexameter* line are the *heptameter,* seven feet, and the *octameter,* eight feet.

tetrameter

■ A verse containing four metrical feet is a *tet*_____.

pentameter

■ A verse containing five metrical feet is a *pen*_____.

hexameter

■ A verse containing six metrical feet is a *hex*_____.

three

two

■ The *trimeter* line has _____ [three / four] feet, and the *dimeter* has _____ [two / five] feet.

(b)

■ A *tetrameter* is to a pentameter as (a) six is to five, (b) four is to five, (c) five is to six. (   )

tetrameter

hexameter

■ A *pentameter* has one more foot than a _____, and it has one less foot than a _____.

four

■ The final foot of a line is sometimes shortened, or "truncated"; how many feet are there in William Blake's line, "Tyger! Tyger! burning bright"—not counting the feet on the tiger? _____ [three / four]

(a)

■ In other words, Blake's line is (a) trochaic tetrameter, (b) iambic trimeter. (   )

iambic pentameter
trochaic
tetrameter

iambic hexameter

anapestic
pentameter
dactylic hexameter

- Thomas Gray's "The curfew tolls the knell of parting day."
  *i*_____ *p*_____.
- Thomas Carew's "He that loves a rosy cheek." _____
  _____.
- Edmund Spenser's "God helpe the man so wrapt in Errours endless traine!" _____ _____.
- Robert Browning's "And I paused, held my breath in such silence, and listened apart." _____ _____.
- The Bible's "How art thou fallen from heaven, O Lucifer, son of the morning!" _____ _____.

11. **poetic license:** a writer's assumption that one may deviate from accepted standards of correctness for artistic effect. *Poetic license* has been cited to excuse violations of grammar, diction, rhythm, rhyme, and historical facts.

(b)

- *Poetic license* is sometimes mentioned to excuse (a) lack of productivity, (b) departures from correctness. (   )

poetic
(b)

- "The owl, for all his feathers, was a-cold." Here Keats has exercised *p*_____ *license* (a) to alter a fact, (b) to patch his iambic rhythm. (   )

(a)

- Shakespeare's tampering with facts and dates in his historical dramas is usually attributed to (a) poetic license, (b) dishonesty. (   )

QUIZ

Write the letter that indicates the best definition.

1. (d)
2. (a)
3. (c)
4. (b)

(   ) 1. hexameter   a. a verse with five feet
(   ) 2. pentameter   b. a verse with four feet
(   ) 3. poetic license   c. an author's right to break rules
(   ) 4. tetrameter   d. a verse with six feet

12. **masculine rhyme:** a rhyme limited to the stressed last syllable; single rhyme. Examples: "kiss" and "miss," "late" and "fate," "repent" and "consent."
13. **feminine rhyme:** a rhyme of two or three syllables, with the stress on the first syllable; also called double-rhyme or triple-rhyme. Examples: "stranger" and "danger," "sleeping" and "creeping," "saddening" and "maddening."

- In *masculine rhyme* the similarity of sounds appears in (a) the one stressed last syllable, (b) two or more syllables. (   )

  (a)

- Two-syllable rhyme, or double-rhyme, is called *fem_____ rhyme.*

  feminine

- _____ "hate" and "fate" — *masculine*
- _____ "sheep" and "sleep" — *masculine*
- _____ "flicker" and "sicker" — *feminine*
- _____ "complain" and "refrain" — *masculine*
- _____ "glory" and "story" — *feminine*

14. **internal rhyme:** rhyming within the line; for example, "And nations rush faster toward disaster."
15. **inversion:** a reversal in the natural word order to help out the rhyme or rhythm. *Inversions* are now usually considered undesirable: "And them behold no more shall I."

- A rhyme between two words in the same line is called *in_____ rhyme.*

  internal

- A turning about of the normal word order is called *in_____.*

  inversion

- "And oh what bliss if her I could kiss"—this verse _____ [does / does not] have *internal* _____ and _____ [does / does not] contain *inversion.*

  does, rhyme
  does

- _____ We were the first who ever burst — *internal*
- _____ In her attic window the staff she set — *inversion*
- _____ The invited neighbors to the husking come — *inversion*
- _____ For the moon never beams without bringing me dreams — *internal*

16. **heroic couplet:** two rhyming lines in iambic pentameter, usually expressing a complete, epigrammatic thought, a verse form favored by Alexander Pope. Examples: "A little learning is a dangerous thing; / Drink deep, or taste not the Pierian spring."
17. **quatrain** (kwo′trān): a four-line stanza, variously rhymed. Example: "I never saw a moor, / I never saw the sea; / Yet know I how the heather looks, / And what a wave must be."

- The *heroic couplet* consists of _____ [two / four] lines that _____ [rhyme / do not rhyme] and which usually express (a) a complete thought, (b) part of a run-on thought. (   )

  two
  rhyme
  (a)

quatrain

(b)

quatrain

third

couplet
Pope
complete

- A four-line stanza of poetry is called a *q*_____.

- The rhyming pattern of *quatrains* is (a) always *abab,* (b) variable. (   )

- Folk ballads make common use of the four-line stanza, or _____.

- The rhyming pattern of the *quatrain* in Edward FitzGerald's *The Rubaiyat* (1859) is *aaba,* which means that its _____ [first / third] line is unrhymed.

- The two-line rhyme known as the *heroic c*_____ was a favorite of _____ [Pope / T. S. Eliot], and it usually expresses a _____ [complete / incomplete] thought.

18. **sonnet:** a fourteen-line poem in iambic pentameter with a prescribed rhyming and structural pattern. The *English,* or *Shakespearean, sonnet* consists of three quatrains and a couplet, rhyming *abab cdcd efef gg;* the *Italian,* or *Petrarchan, sonnet* consists of an octave (having eight lines) followed by a sestet (having six lines) and rhymes *abba abba cde cde* (the rhyme scheme of the sestet may vary).

fourteen

(a)

sonnet, (a)

sonnet, (b)

- The *sonnet* is _____ [twelve / fourteen] lines long and is in iambic (a) pentameter, (b) hexameter. (   )

- If its fourteen lines consist of three quatrains and a couplet, the *s*_____ is (a) English, (b) Italian. (   )

- If its fourteen lines consist of an octave and a sestet, the _____ is (a) English, (b) Italian. (   )

19. **blank verse:** unrhymed iambic pentameter. *Blank verse* is used in the dramas of Shakespeare and Marlowe and in other serious English poetry such as Milton's *Paradise Lost.*

20. **free verse:** rhythmical lines of irregular length without fixed metrical pattern and usually without rhyme; also called *vers libre. Free verse* has the rhythms and cadences of natural speech.

(b)

- The magnificent *blank verse* of *Macbeth* and *Julius Caesar* is (a) rhymed, (b) unrhymed. (   )

(a)

- *Blank verse* consists of lines that are unrhymed and (a) in iambic pentameter, (b) of various lengths and stresses. (   )

■ On the other hand, unrhymed lines of irregular length are
f_____ *verse.*

■ A line of *vers libre,* or *f*_____ *verse,* has (a) five
stresses, (b) no fixed metrical pattern. (   )

■ Walt Whitman, Amy Lowell, and Carl Sandburg often use lines of
irregular length and rhythm, known as _____ *verse.*

■ "For who would bear the whips and scorns of time"—this
representative line from *Hamlet* _____ [is / is not] in
iambic pentameter; and so this unrhymed drama is in
_____ *verse.*

QUIZ

Write the letter that indicates the best definition.

(   ) 1. sonnet
(   ) 2. blank verse
(   ) 3. quatrain
(   ) 4. free verse
(   ) 5. heroic couplet

a. a four-line stanza
b. two rhymed lines in iambic
   pentameter
c. a patterned fourteen-line poem
d. unrhymed iambic pentameter
e. unrhymed verses of irregular length

Supply the missing word in each sentence.

1. The basic unit of verse measure is the *f*_____.
2. The analysis of rhythm and meter is known as *sc*_____.
3. A four-line stanza is a *q*_____.
4. Rhyming within a line of poetry is *i*_____ *rhyme*.
5. A pause within a line of verse is a *ca*_____.
6. A metrical line of four feet is a *t*_____.
7. A metrical line of six feet is a *h*_____.
8. A metrical foot consisting of a stressed syllable followed by an unstressed syllable is a *tr*_____.
9. Twisting poetic words into unnatural order is called *in*_____.

Write True or False.

_____ 10. The *anapest* consists of two unstressed syllables followed by a stressed syllable.

_____ 11. *Blank verse* uses an irregular number of metrical feet to the line.

_____ 12. The Shakespearean *sonnet* rhyme pattern is *abab cdcd efef gg*.

_____ 13. The *heroic couplet* is unrhymed.

_____ 14. A *poetic license* costs a small fee and entitles a qualified person to write verse.

_____ 15. A *pentameter* line consists of seven feet.

_____ 16. Examples of *feminine rhyme* are "writing" and "biting," "fashion" and "passion."

Write the letter that indicates the best completion.

(   ) 17. An example of a *dactylic* foot is (a) "dancing," (b) "in the town," (c) "the farmer," (d) "tenderly."

(   ) 18. An example of an *iambic* foot is (a) "favor," (b) "depend," (c) "of a cloud," (d) "faltering."

(   ) 19. An example of *masculine rhyme* is (a) "cringe" and "lunge," (b) "measure" and "treasure," (c) "ships" and "lips," (d) "dine" and "time."

(   ) 20. *Free verse* has (a) regular meter, (b) speech rhythms, (c) rhyming restrictions, (d) stanzaic pattern.

 KEY TO REVIEW TEST

Check your test answers with the following key. Deduct 5% per error from 100%.

1. foot	8. trochee	15. False
2. scansion	9. inversion	16. True
3. quatrain	10. True	17. (d)
4. internal	11. False	18. (b)
5. caesura	12. True	19. (c)
6. tetrameter	13. False	20. (b)
7. hexameter	14. False	

Score: _____ %

1. **Alexandrine** (al-ig-zan′drin): a line composed of six iambic feet; an *iambic hexameter.* The Alexandrine is popular in French poetry.
2. **ambiguity** (am′bə-gyoo′i-tē): an expression having two or more possibly contradictory meanings; also refers to multiple suggestiveness which enriches poetry. William Empson's *Seven Types of Ambiguity* (1931) explores the nature of such hinted suggestions.
3. **ars poetica** (ärz pō-et′i-kə): the art of poetry.
4. **carpe diem** (kär′pi dī′em): "seize the day," a Latin phrase implying that one must enjoy the present moment, for tomorrow may be too late. The *carpe diem* theme appeared in *Ecclesiastes'* "Eat, drink, and be merry" and has run through literature like a scarlet thread.
5. **Cavalier poetry:** graceful, sophisticated, witty verses written during the reign of Charles I (1625–1649) by lyric poets Thomas Carew, Sir John Suckling, Richard Lovelace, and others. *Cavalier poetry* deals typically with beloved maidens and constancy and the importance of enjoying the present moment.
6. **dramatic monologue:** a narrative poem in which a single speaker gives his or her version of a dramatic situation, meanwhile exposing his or her own personality quirks; for example, Robert Browning's "My Last Duchess" (1842), which tells a story and incidentally reveals the viciousness of the narrator himself.
7. **elegy** (el′i-jē): a formal, melancholy poem, often a lament for the dead. Notable *elegies* include Gray's "Elegy Written in a Country Churchyard" (1750) and Whitman's "When Lilacs Last in the Dooryard Bloom'd" (1866).
8. **enjambment** (en-jam′mənt): the running on of a sentence from one line of verse into the next without a pause at the end of the line. Such a run-on line is in contrast to the more customary end-stopped line.
9. **haiku** (hī′koo): a delicate Japanese poem of three unrhymed lines consisting of five, seven, and five syllables, respectively. The *haiku* usually alludes in some way to a season.
10. **in medias res** (in mē′di-əs rēz): in the midst of things, that is, in the middle of the narrative. Homer begins an epic *in medias res,* then describes in flashbacks those incidents which led to this crisis.
11. **invocation:** an appeal for inspiration and guidance from a deity or Muse, at the beginning of an epic. Homer's *Iliad* begins with an *invocation* to Calliope, the Muse of epic poetry.
12. **kenning:** a metaphorical compound name for something in Anglo-Saxon poetry. *Kennings* in Beowulf include "whale-road" for "sea" and "foamy floater" for "ship."
13. **laureate** (lôr′ē-it): a poet recognized as the most eminent in a country. Poets *laureate* of England have included Wordsworth, Tennyson, and Masefield.
14. **light verse:** short, light-hearted poems. Witty, sophisticated *light verse* has been written by Dorothy Parker, Ogden Nash, Phyllis McGinley, and others.
15. **metaphysical conceit:** an ingenious, sustained comparison between things apparently highly dissimilar. In "A Valediction: Forbidding Mourning" (1633) John Donne compares the souls of two lovers to the two legs of a compass.
16. **metaphysical poetry:** highly intellectual, philosophical poetry marked by clashing emotions, jarring versification, and startling conceits, as written by John Donne, George Herbert, and other seventeenth-century writers. *Metaphysical poets* were often intensely analytical of human emotions.

Foreign Expressions

a cappella, **1**	faux pas, **10**	sine qua non, **19**
ad nauseum, **2**	hoi polloi, **11**	status quo, **20**
aficionado, **3**	Homo sapiens, **12**	sub rosa, **21**
à la carte, **4**	laissez faire, **13**	tour de force, **22**
avant-garde, **5**	magnum opus, **14**	tout de suite, **23**
bête noir, **6**	par excellence, **15**	vox populi, **24**
c'est la vie, **7**	persona non grata, **16**	Wunderkind, **25**
con amore, **8**	potpourri, **17**	
déjà vu, **9**	savoir-faire, **18**	

English has become a *smörgäsbord* (Swedish: "a buffet of assorted foods") of terms taken from at least fifty languages.

Many imported words have been used so much that they are now completely absorbed into the English language. Here are a few examples:

American Indian: moccasin, moose	Hebrew: amen, kosher
Arabic: algebra, magazine	Irish: slogan, whiskey
Chinese: tea, typhoon	Italian: ballot, piano
Dutch: cole slaw, sleigh	Latin: cereal, report
French: buffet, chauffeur	Persian: pajamas, sugar
German: kindergarten, waltz	Russian: samovar, vodka
Greek: acrobat, alphabet	Spanish: alligator, cigar

A second group of foreign expressions are often used but are not yet generally regarded as adopted. Such terms are written in italics until our language assimilates them. Meanwhile the status and popular pronunciation of these words keep changing. When in doubt, consult a good dictionary for current practice as to how best to pronounce a foreign expression and whether to italicize it.

Abbreviations used in this chapter include *Fr.* (French), *G.* (German), *Gk.* (Greek), *It.* (Italian), *L.* (Latin), *Sp.* (Spanish).

Master the twenty-five foreign expressions that are programmed in this chapter. Then warm your acquaintanceship with the forty terms in the supplementary list.

1. **a cappella** (ä′kə-pel′ə): *It.* singing without instrumental accompaniment. "The church choir sang *a cappella.*"
2. **ad nauseum** (ad′nô′ zē-əm): *L.* to a disgusting degree. "One tourist complained about food and plumbing and prices *ad nauseum.*"

■ The chorus will now sing *a cappella,* so the orchestra will be (a) silent, (b) sawing away. (   )

■ My pianist was in jail that evening. Consequently, I sang my solo *a cap*_____.

■ Our football captain kept referring *ad nauseum* to his own heroic achievements. He should probably have been more (a) modest, (b) detailed. (   )

■ The biology assistant, who hated snakes, had to handle them day after day *a*_____ *na*_____.

■ When the sergeant took a shower, he sang *a ca*_____; and, ignorant of sharps and flats, he bellowed "Sorrento" tunelessly and endlessly *a*_____ *n*_____.

3. **aficionado** (ə-fish′yə-nä′də): *Sp.* a devoted follower of some sport or art. "José was an *aficionado* of bullfighting until he got trampled."
4. **à la carte** (ä lə kärt′): *Fr.* with a separate price for each dish on the menu; lit., according to the card. "Our guests, with an eye for expensive items, order *à la carte.*"

■ An *aficionado* of soccer _____ [hates / loves] the game.

■ The baseball sailed into the bleachers, where it was gloved by a young *af*_____.

■ It's wise to order *à la carte* if you want (a) the standard full meal, (b) two or three special items. (   )

■ Bill has a barrel of allergies and had to select his dishes *à la c*_____.

COVER THIS STRIP

(a)

a cappella

(a)

ad nauseum

a cappella

ad nauseum

loves

aficionado

(b)

à la carte

■ No, Joey, I won't push the fat worms onto your fishhooks. Better ask that *af*_____ of fishing to help you.

aficionado

■ My plump friend, with a tear in his eye, selected a spinach salad *à* _____ _____.

à la carte

5. **avant-garde** (a-vänt gärd′): *Fr.* the leaders in new artistic movements. "Walt Whitman was among the *avant-garde* to throw off the shackles of rhyme."

6. **bête noir** (bāt nwär′): *Fr.* a person or thing that one fears and dislikes; lit., black beast. "Algebra had always been his *bête noir.*"

■ Rudy sometimes chased me home from school. He was my _____ [*avant-garde* / *bête noir*].

bête noir

■ No fashions are too bizarre, if only they are created by the *av*_____ *-ga*_____ among Parisian designers.

avant-garde

■ If not the first, Schonberg was among the *av*_____- *ga*_____ to compose in the twelve-tone technique.

*avant-
garde*

■ Speak softly and carry a big stick, especially if the neighborhood dogs are your *b*_____ *no*_____.

bête noir

■ By the time my ancestor Gaspar started fooling around with impressionism, the *av*_____-*g*_____ was already into cubism. Gaspar might have painted ceilings, but he was deathly afraid of ladders. They were his *b*_____ *n*_____.

avant-garde

*bête
noir*

QUIZ

Write the letter that indicates the best definition.

1. (f)
2. (e)
3. (c)
4. (a)
5. (b)
6. (d)

( ) 1. *avant-garde*   a. each dish priced separately
( ) 2. *bête noir*   b. without accompaniment
( ) 3. *aficionado*   c. an ardent fan
( ) 4. *à la carte*   d. to a sickening degree
( ) 5. *a cappella*   e. something one fears
( ) 6. *ad nauseum*   f. the leaders in art

7. **c'est la vie** (sā la vē′): *Fr.* Such is life. "The prisoner had been making big money—a half-inch too big. *C'est la vie.*"
8. **con amore** (kän ä-mō′rā): *It.* with love; tenderly (used as a direction to musicians). "The lullaby is to be sung *con amore.*"

■ The musical instruction *con amore* is usually seen in sheet music involving (a) military marches, (b) love songs. (   )

■ Sophia kissed the gift box of chocolates where Giuseppe had written "c_____ am_____."

■ The sheepherder gambled his life savings on one throw of the dice—and lost. "C_____ l_____ v_____," he shrugged. "Too ba-a-a-ad."

■ "Yesterday Giuseppe nibbled my ear c_____ am_____," muttered Sophia. "Today he eloped with my best friend. Well, c_____ _____ v_____."

9. **déjà vu** (dā-zha vü′): *Fr.* the feeling that a new situation has happened before. "He first saw Lisa with a sense of *déjà vu,* as though he was reliving a dream."
10. **faux pas** (fō pä′): *Fr.* a social blunder; lit., a false step. "Asking the hostess how much she weighed was a *faux pas,* Clarence."

■ We entered Pokeville, and *déjà vu!* It was as though I had (a) been here before, (b) never seen such a lousy town. (   )

■ Kay had seen so many pictures of Mt. Fujiyama that her first sighting of it filled her with d_____ v_____.

■ A *faux pas* is (a) a pathway for forest beasts, (b) an error in etiquette such as sneezing into the punch bowl. (   )

■ Spilling soup on his necktie was bad enough, but wiping his tie on the linen tablecloth was a definite f_____ p_____.

■ With a terrible sense of d_____ v_____, I was sure that Uncle Louie was now going to tell Father Clancy the one about the priest and the rabbi—what a f_____ p_____!

(margin answers)

(b)

con amore

C'est la vie

con amore c'est la vie

(a)

déjà vu

(b)

faux pas

déjà vu

faux pas

11. **hoi polloi** (hoi pə-loi′): *Gk.* the common people: a somewhat contemptuous term. "The king sneered at the ignorance and sweat of the *hoi polloi.*"

12. **Homo sapiens** (hō′mō sā′pē-enz): *L.* modern man; human being; lit., wise man. "Of all creatures, *Homo sapiens* is the only one who writes symphonies."

■ The scientific term *Homo sapiens* suggest that human beings have (a) wisdom, (b) a drinking problem. (   )

■ No animals had enough brains and ability to pollute the air, water, and earth except *Ho_____ sap_____.*

■ The masses, known as *hoi polloi,* were held in _____ [high regard / contempt] by royalty.

■ A truly democratic country has neither lofty aristocrats nor lowly *h_____ po_____.*

■ Ignorant *ho_____ po_____* are, nevertheless, members of *Ho_____ sa_____,* and with education they can reach the stars.

![] **QUIZ**

Write the letter that indicates the best definition.

(   ) 1. *faux pas*   a. lovingly
(   ) 2. *hoi polloi*   b. thinking man
(   ) 3. *Homo sapiens*   c. That's life.
(   ) 4. *c'est la vie*   d. the masses
(   ) 5. *con amore*   e. a breach of etiquette
(   ) 6. *déjà vu*   f. the illusion of a replay

1. (e)
2. (d)
3. (b)
4. (c)
5. (a)
6. (f)

13. **laissez faire** (les′ā fâr′): *Fr.* the policy of noninterference in business or in individual conduct; lit., let do. "Government should try to keep its nose out of industrial or private affairs, according to the doctrine of *laissez faire.*"

14. **magnum opus** (mag′nəm ō′pəs): *L.* the masterpiece of a writer or artist; lit., a great work.

■ Under *laissez faire* our industries would operate with _____ [very few / numerous] government controls.

■ Some parents lay down rigid rules; others, more permissive, tend to practice *la_____ fa_____.*

■ A *magnum opus* is (a) a huge wine bottle, (b) an artist's masterpiece. ( )

■ John Roebling and his son built several suspension bridges, but Brooklyn Bridge (1883) was certainly their *mag_____ op_____.*

■ Adam Smith wrote on economic theory, and in *Wealth of Nations,* his *m_____ op_____,* he developed the "let alone" doctrine of *la_____ fa_____.*

15. **par excellence** (pär ek′sə-läns′): *Fr.* excellent beyond comparison. "Benjamin Franklin and the others framed a constitution *par excellence.*"

16. **persona non grata** (pər-sō′nə nän grät′ə): *L.* an unwelcome person; esp., a diplomat unacceptable to another government. "His cigar smoking made him *persona non grata* at the theater."

■ To be *persona non grata* means that one is (a) a popular person, (b) not welcome. ( )

■ Anna Pavlova was a ballet dancer *par excellence.* This means her dancing was (a) up to par, (b) exceptionally good. ( )

■ If a diplomatic representative from Slobbovia is found to be operating a spy ring in Washington, D.C., our State Department would call him *per_____ n_____ gr_____.*

■ Jeff went to the men's room whenever a restaurant bill arrived, and soon he was *per_____ n_____ gr_____* at the dinner parties.

■ My barber is a mediocre stylist, but he is a conversationalist *p_____ exc_____.*

■ Show me a freshman who reads one library book a week, and I'll show you a student *p_____ ex_____.*

17. **potpourri** (pō-po͞o-rē′): *Fr.* a miscellany or mixture of unrelated things. "Buster's pockets held a *potpourri* of his treasures."

18. **savoir-faire** (sav′wär fâr′): *Fr.* a ready knowledge of what to say or do in any situation; lit., knowing how to do. "Always smooth, always at ease, my friend was not lacking in *savoir-faire.*"

■ "Our junior high band will now perform a musical *potpourri.*" This announcement means we'll have the doubtful pleasure of hearing (a) a medley of tunes, (b) a symphony. (   )

■ At noon Times Square was crowded with clerks, shoppers, laborers, bankers, and pickpockets—a regular *pot*_____.

■ A person with *savoir-faire* tends to be (a) tactful, skillful, and adaptable; (b) flustered, awkward, and naive. (   )

■ I was a country boy in Manhattan. I didn't have *sav*_____-*f*_____. In fact, I didn't have bus fare.

■ Pierre stepped into the room where a woman was taking a bubble bath. "Sorry, sir," he said, retreating. Pierre had *s*_____-*f*_____.

■ The *Reader's Digest* mixes short articles, anecdotes, quips, quotes, and quizzes; it presents a *po*_____.

QUIZ

Write the letter that indicates the best definition.

(   ) 1. *laissez faire*   a. an undesirable person
(   ) 2. *magnum opus*   b. knowing always how to act
(   ) 3. *par excellence*   c. one's masterpiece
(   ) 4. *persona non grata*   d. supremely good
(   ) 5. *potpourri*   e. noninterference
(   ) 6. *savoir-faire*   f. a miscellany

19. **sine qua non** (sī′nē quā non′): *L.* something absolutely essential; lit., without which not. "The telephone has become a *sine qua non* of teenage romance."
20. **status quo** (stā′təs quō′): *L.* the existing condition; lit., state in which. "An ambitious executive will try to do more than maintain the *status quo.*"

■ Defenders of the *status quo* in a society are likely to be (a) the underprivileged, (b) the wealthier class. (   )

status quo

■ Women were kitchen slaves until they decided to rebel against the
sta_____ q_____.

sine qua non

■ A well-stocked library is the very _____ [*laissez faire /
sine qua non*] of a college.

sine qua non

■ "Idiot!" bawled bakery foreman Schultz, a slow man with a
compliment. "You forgot caraway seeds! They're the
sin_____ q_____ n_____ of a
pumpernickel."

sine qua non
status
quo

■ Our labor union says that a paid vacation on Ground Hog's Day is
a *si*_____ q_____ n_____ of a new
contract; but company officials support the *st*_____
q_____.

21. **sub rosa** (sub rō′zə): *L.* secretly; confidentially; lit., under the
rose, which was a symbol of secrecy. "The delicatessens agreed
sub rosa to raise the price of salami."
22. **tour de force** (to͞or də fors′): *Fr.* a remarkable achievement; a
stroke of genius; lit., a feat of skill. "Lindbergh's flight was a *tour
de force* that won him instant admiration."

(b)

■ The phrase *tour de force* describes an accomplishment that is
(a) rather boring, (b) sensational. (   )

tour de force

■ To ride a unicycle on a high wire and juggle five oranges—what a
t_____ d_____ f_____!

(a)

■ A *sub rosa* transaction is one that takes place (a) in secret, (b) on a
TV network. (   )

sub rosa

■ Clym pops his cork when he learns that his wife Eustacia has been
meeting *s*_____ ro_____ with her old flame
Wildeve.

sub rosa
tour
de force

■ "That's George Koltanowski," said an onlooker to me
s_____ ro_____. "He once played thirty-four
simultaneous games of chess blindfolded, a real *t*_____
d_____ f_____."

23. **tout de suite** (to͞ot swēt′): *Fr.* immediately; right away; lit., all in
succession. "I'm neck-deep in quicksand! Help me *tout de suite!*"
24. **vox populi** (voks pop′yə-lī′): *L.* public opinion; lit., the voice of the
people; abbrev., *vox pop.* "Congress must not ignore *vox populi.*"

(c)

■ *Vox populi* refers to (a) a popular song, (b) our growing population, (c) public sentiment. (   )

(c)

■ "The sergeant returned *tout de suite*." This means he came back (a) with his sweetheart, (b) to the sound of bugles, (c) right away. (   )

vox populi

■ Letters written to the editors of American newspapers are fairly representative of *vo_____ po_____.*

tout
de suite

■ Coach Cardiac was fuming: "We're trailing 14 to 13 with a minute to go. Let's try that trick play *to_____ d_____ s_____.*"

vox populi
tout de suite

■ Governor Goofov expresses contempt for our state laws and for *v_____ pop_____.* He should be impeached *t_____ d_____ s_____.*

25. **Wunderkind** (voon′dər kint′): *G.* a child prodigy; lit., a wonder child. "This baby reads? She's a *Wunderkind!*"

(a)

■ A *Wunderkind* is (a) a brilliant youngster, (b) a thunderstorm along the Rhine. (   )

Wunderkind

■ Wolfgang Amadeus Mozart was composing music at age four and giving piano concerts at seven. Austria hailed him as a *Wun_____.*

Wunderkind

■ She sang, she danced, she acted; and tiny Shirley Temple quickly became Hollywood's *W_____.*

QUIZ

Write the letter that indicates the best definition.

1. (c)
2. (f)
3. (a)
4. (d)
5. (g)
6. (b)
7. (e)

( )	1. *sine qua non*	a.	secretly
( )	2. *status quo*	b.	the voice of the people
( )	3. *sub rosa*	c.	an indispensable thing
( )	4. *tour de force*	d.	a remarkable accomplishment
( )	5. *tout de suite*	e.	a wonder child
( )	6. *vox populi*	f.	the current condition
( )	7. *Wunderkind*	g.	immediately

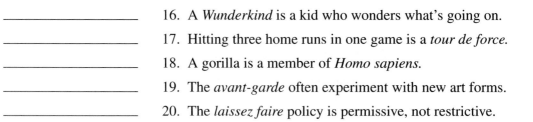

Supply the missing words. The opening letters are given.

1. The Greek aristocrats sneered at the lowly *h*_____ *pol*_____.

2. Saying "Hi, babe!" to the mayor's wife was a horrible *f*_____
   *p*_____.

3. The rich get richer and the poor get babies. *C*_____ *la v*_____.

4. A country's leaders must listen to *v*_____ *pop*_____.

5. Nothing rattles Ronald. He has *sav*_____-*f*_____.

6. This wedding song must be sung sweetly and *c*_____ *am*_____.

7. I don't know soccer rules. Better ask an *afi*_____.

8. One official met *s*_____ *ro*_____ with members of the Mafia.

9. *War and Peace* was Leo Tolstoi's *mag*_____ *o*_____.

10. I don't want the full meal. I'll order *à l*_____ *c*_____.

11. Your accompanist has passed out. Just sing *a ca*_____.

12. *High Noon* was a western movie *p*_____ *exc*_____.

13. The closet held a *pot*_____ of shoes, tools, wigs, and apples.

14. Some old people resist change. They prefer the *st*_____ *q*_____.

15. I asked the boss for a raise and was turned down *to*_____ *de*
    *s*_____.

Write True or False.

_____ 16. A *Wunderkind* is a kid who wonders what's going on.

_____ 17. Hitting three home runs in one game is a *tour de force.*

_____ 18. A gorilla is a member of *Homo sapiens.*

_____ 19. The *avant-garde* often experiment with new art forms.

_____ 20. The *laissez faire* policy is permissive, not restrictive.

Write the foreign expression for each definition. The opening letters are given.

Definitions

21. *ad n*_____   to a disgusting degree

22. *b*_____ *no*_____   something feared

23. *d*_____ *v*_____   the feeling of reliving a scene

24. *p*_____ *n*_____ *g*_____   an unwelcome individual

25. *s*_____ *qua n*_____   an indispensable thing

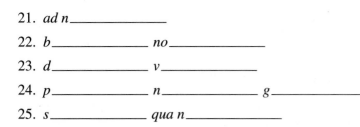

KEY TO REVIEW TEST

Check your test answers with the following key. Deduct 4% per error from a possible 100%.

1. *hoi polloi*	10. *à la carte*	19. True
2. *faux pas*	11. *a cappella*	20. True
3. *C'est la vie*	12. *par excellence*	21. *ad nauseum*
4. *vox populi*	13. *potpourri*	22. *bête noir*
5. *savoir-faire*	14. *status quo*	23. *déjà vu*
6. *con amore*	15. *tout de suite*	24. *persona non grata*
7. *aficionado*	16. False	25. *sine qua non*
8. *sub rosa*	17. True	
9. *magnum opus*	18. False	

Score: _____ %

1. **ad hoc** (ad hok′): *L.* for this purpose only. "She appointed an *ad hoc* committee which later made its report and was dissolved."

2. **ad infinitum** (ad in-fə-nī′təm): *L.* to infinity. "Every creature has smaller creatures inside 'im, and so on and so on *ad infinitum*."

3. **au courant** (ō kōō-rän′): *Fr.* well informed on current matters; up to date. "The old man read news magazines and so kept *au courant*."

4. **bona fide** (bō′nə fīd′): *L.* in good faith; genuine. "Two park benches for ten dollars? Was this nice man making me a *bona fide* offer?"

5. **bon vivant** (bôṅ vē-väṅ′): *Fr.* a person who enjoys good food, drink, and luxury. "I have all the requirements of a *bon vivant* except money."

6. **carte blanche** (kärt′ bläṅsh′): *Fr.* full authority to do as one thinks best. "The governor of the island gave us *carte blanche* to shoot film anywhere."

7. **cause célèbre** (kôz′ sə-leb′r): *Fr.* a famous legal case or controversy. "The O. J. Simpson affair was a *cause célèbre* during the mid-nineties."

8. **caveat emptor** (kā′vē-at emp′tôr): *L.* Let the buyer beware; buy at your own risk. "Flea market sales are final, so it's *caveat emptor*."

9. **coup de grâce** (kōō də gräs′): *Fr.* death blow; lit., stroke of mercy. "Our shop was losing money, and the workers' strike was the *coup de grâce*."

10. **coup d'état** (kōō dā-ta′): *Fr.* a sudden, powerful political stroke, esp. the forcible overthrow of government. "In a bloody *coup d'état* the army leaders seized command of the young republic."

11. **cul-de-sac** (kul′də-sak′): *Fr.* a passage closed at one end; a blind alley. "Trapped in a *cul-de-sac!* They'd put all their Basques in one exit."

12. **de facto** (dē fak′tō): *L.* actually existing though possibly without legal sanction. "Their *de facto* government is ruled by a tyrant and two lunatics."

13. **de jure** (dē joor′ē): *L.* legally so. "Democratic processes have set up a *de jure* government."

14. **dernier cri** (der-nyä krē′): *Fr.* the latest fashion; the newest thing. "Olga's gown is the *dernier cri* from Paris—from Paris, Texas, that is."

15. **e.g.** (abbrev. of *exempli gratia*): *L.* for example. "Grandpa collects various items, *e.g.,* beer bottle caps."

16. **entre nous** (äṅ-trə nōō′): *Fr.* between us; confidentially. "Let's settle this fender-scratching accident *entre nous*."

17. **esprit de corps** (es-prē′ də kôr′): *Fr.* enthusiastic spirit and loyalty of a group. "Football games contributed to the *esprit de corps* at Acne Junior High."

18. **ex officio** (eks ə-fish′ē-ō): *L.* because of one's office or position. "The vice president is the *ex officio* president of the Senate."

19. **ex post facto** (eks pōst fak′tō): *L.* having retroactive effect. "Congress is not allowed to pass *ex post facto* laws."

20. **fait accompli** (fe-ta-koṅ-plē′): *Fr.* an accomplished fact, a thing already done, so that opposition is useless. "Mother hated the colors, but our paint job was a *fait accompli*."

21. **gemütlich** (gə-müt′lish): *G.* cheerful; agreeable. "The tavern was cozy and the atmosphere *gemütlich*."

22. **hic jacet** (hik jā′sit): *L.* here lies. "*Hic jacet* Hy Fee, dentist, filling his last cavity."

23. **hors de combat** (ôr də koṅ-ba′): *Fr.* put out of the fight; disabled. "In six minutes our 'indestructible' fullback was *hors de combat*."

24. **hors d'oeuvre** (ôr dûrv′): *Fr.* an appetizer. "I nibbled an *hors d'oeuvre* with my little finger extended."

25. **in absentia** (in ab-sen′shē-ə): *L.* in absence; although not present. "The philanthropist was awarded his honorary degree *in absentia.*"

26. **ipso facto** (ip′sō fak′tō): *L.* by that very fact. "A driver with high alcoholic blood level is *ipso facto* a lawbreaker."

27. **modus operandi** (mō′dəs op′ə-ran′dē): *L.* method of operating. "Zelda studied the new computer to figure out its *modus operandi.*"

28. **nom de plume** (nom də ploom′): *Fr.* a pen name; pseudonym. "George Sand is the *nom de plume* of a Frenchwoman who wrote novels."

29. **nouveau riche** (noo-vō rēsh′): *Fr.* a newly rich person, possibly lacking in taste and culture. "One of the *nouveau riche* nailed up a Picasso in the bathroom."

30. **op. cit.** (abbrev. of *opere citato*): *L.* in the work cited. "The footnote reads 'Dingle, *op. cit.,* p. 99.' "

31. **pièce de résistance** (pyes də rā-zē-stäns′): *Fr.* the main dish of a meal; the principal work of a group. "The *pièce de résistance* of the program was 'Concerto for Tuba in Six Flats and a Garage.' "

32. **prima facie** (prī′mə fā′shē): *L.* at first sight before investigation. "Fudd's possession of the stolen jewels is *prima facie* evidence of his guilt."

33. **pro bono publico** (prō bō′nō pub′li-kō): *L.* for the public good. "Gumbo Center has dedicated its town hall *pro bono publico.*"

34. **pro tem** (abbrev. of *pro tempore*): *L.* for the time being. "Harpo will be chairman *pro tem,* until we get organized."

35. **quid pro quo** (kwid prō kwō′): *L.* one thing in exchange for another. "The oil companies got you elected and now they want their *quid pro quo.*"

36. **raison d'être** (rā′zōṅ det′rə): *Fr.* reason for existing. "The exploration of nature was John Muir's *raison d'être.*"

37. **rara avis** (rer′ə ā′vis): *L.* a very unusual person; lit., a rare bird. "Our new plumber is a *rara avis.* He brought all the necessary tools."

38. **sotto voce** (sot′ ō vō′chē): *It.* in an undertone. "Moosehead explained his escape plan *sotto voce* to his cellmate."

39. **table d'hôte** (tab′əl dōt′): *Fr.* a complete meal as detailed on the menu. Cf., *à la carte.* "Vegetarian Vivian ordered *à la carte;* Hungry Harry, *table d'hôte.*"

40. **tête-à-tête** (tāt′ə tāt′): *Fr.* a private chat between two persons. "Ben and Agatha enjoyed their *tête-à-tête* at the Greasy Platter."